Current Chinese Economic Report Series

The Current Chinese Economic Reports series provides insights into the economic development of one of the largest and fastest growing economies in the world; though widely discussed internationally, many facets of its current development remain unknown to the English speaking world. All reports contain new data, which was previously unknown or unavailable outside of China. The series covers regional development, industry reports, as well as special topics like environmental or demographical issues.

More information about this series at http://www.springer.com/series/11028

Ben Shenglin · Jiefang Yu
Yue Gu · Jiamin Lv · Lijun Zhang
Huichao Gong · Hanting Gu
Qi Shuai

In Pursuit of Presence or Prominence?

The Prospect of Chinese Banks' Global Expansion and Their Benchmarks

Ben Shenglin
School of Management
Zhejiang University
Hangzhou, Zhejiang
China

Jiefang Yu
School of Economics
Zhejiang University
Hangzhou, Zhejiang
China

Yue Gu
Zhejiang University
Hangzhou, Zhejiang
China

Jiamin Lv
School of Economics
Zhejiang University
Hangzhou, Zhejiang
China

Lijun Zhang
PricewaterhouseCoppers China
Beijing
China

Huichao Gong
School of Economics
Zhejiang University
Hangzhou, Zhejiang
China

Hanting Gu
School of Economics
Zhejiang University
Hanghzou, Zhejiang
China

Qi Shuai
School of Economics
Zhejiang University
Hangzhou, Zhejiang
China

ISSN 2194-7937   ISSN 2194-7945   (electronic)
Current Chinese Economic Report Series
ISBN 978-981-10-7729-6   ISBN 978-981-10-7730-2   (eBook)
https://doi.org/10.1007/978-981-10-7730-2

Jointly published with Zhejiang University Press

The print edition is not for sale in China Mainland. Customers from China Mainland please order the print book from: Zhejiang University Press.

Library of Congress Control Number: 2018931476

Printed on acid-free paper

This Springer imprint is published by Springer Nature
The registered company is Springer Nature Singapore Pte Ltd.
The registered company address is: 152 Beach Road, #21-01/04 Gateway East, Singapore 189721, Singapore

Preface

In Pursuit of Presence or Prominence?—The Prospect of Chinese Banks' Global Expansion and Their Benchmarks has been released as scheduled last year. Compared with last year, there are some gratifying changes this year.

This year, we carried out a detailed analysis of selected 16 representative international banks among the global systemically important banks, and the 16 selected banks were evaluated under the same "Bank Internationalization Index" system. The 16 banks are all from developed countries with rich international experience, long history, and different roadmaps. Their international development has high reference significance for Chinese banks struggling on the journey of internationalization.

The subtitle *"The Prospect of Chinese Banks' Global Expansion and Their Benchmarks"* of this year is an extension. Considering that these banks basically represented the highest level of internationalization in the world today, by benchmarking the "advanced", we could assist Chinese banks to find the gap, identify developing opportunities, and improve the aspect of internationalization.

This year, we have borrowed relevant theories in enterprise internationalization to analyze the main factors influencing bank internationalization. Although it is still at the entry level, it shows our effort to trace the root causes. In the future, the report will further extract relevant theories.

We have specifically included a single chapter of risk cases this year. Not only because the risk prevention is the mainstream this year and the risk management is the basis of banking industry but also internationalization would increase the diversity of risk sources and complexity of risk management which need pay attention to. Many cases showed that the lessons are profound, the consequences are serious, and the damages are difficult to recover and even deadly.

We have successfully launched the English version this year, thanks to one of our members James and his team from Pricewaterhouse Coopers, whose professionalism and globalization complement our original team. The publication of the English version will bring more opportunities for international communication, and also bring more focus on our young team. We are looking forward to transforming the public attention to our future motivation.

It is gratifying that the effort of the team has not changed, so does their beginner's mind and blossoming youth. In the completion of the report, it was the eve of RMB officially being included in the SDR basket, and coincided with the good news that China ranked second in terms of foreign direct investment in 2015 with net export of capital. In my opinion, Chinese banks' internationalization will usher the accelerated developing opportunities, and we look forward to being resonant with the thriving era.

Pudong, China   Ben Shenglin
September 2016   China Executive Leadership Academy

The Project Team

Project Leaders

Dr. Ben Shenglin, Dean, Academy of Internet Finance, Zhejiang University, Professor of Banking & Finance, School of Management, Zhejiang University, Executive Director, International Monetary Institute, Renmin University of China
   Yu Jiefang, Deputy Director, Finance Department, School of Economics, Zhejiang University, Associate Professor

Members

Yue Gu, Zhejiang University
Jiamin Lv, Zhejiang University
Lijun Zhang, PwC China
Huichao Gong, Zhejiang University
Hanting Gu, Zhejiang University
Qi Shuai, Zhejiang University

Expert Advisory Committee (Alphabetical Order of Last Name Pinyin)

Tong Cao, Chairman, XFinTech
Weidong Chen, Director General, International Financial Research Institute, Bank of China
Zhihuan E, Chief Economist, Bank of China (Hong Kong)
Jinpu Jiao, Chairman, Shanghai Gold Exchange
Yu Jin, Chairman, Bank of Shanghai
Jun Liu, Deputy CEO, China Everbright Group
Wei'an Wang, Director, Institute of Financial Research, Zhejiang University

Yongli Wang, CEO, LeFinance
Songzuo Xiang, Deputy Director, International Monetary Institute, Renmin University of China
Zaiping Yang, Vice-Chairman, China Banking Association
Lijun Zhang (James Chang), PwC China Financial Services Management Consulting Leader
Xiaopu Zhao, Deputy Director-general, Central Leadership Group-Finance & Economy
Changwen Zhao, Director-general, Development Research Center of the State Council (DRC)
Haiying Zhao, Chief Risk Officer, China Investment Corporation
Xijun Zhao, Associate Dean, School of Finance, Renmin University of China

Expert Committee Secretary-General

Jiefang Yu, Associate Director, School of Economics Finance Department, Zhejiang University
Ke Song, Associate Director, International Monetary Institute, Renmin University of China

Sponsoring Institutions

Center for Internet and Financial Innovation (CIFI), Zhejiang University
Institute of Financial Research (IFR), Zhejiang University
International Monetary Institute (IMI), Renmin University of China

Contents

List of Figures

List of Tables

Abstract

Based on the result of CBII (Chinese Bank Internationalization Index) which was first released in 2015, the *In Pursuit of Presence or Prominence?—The Prospect of Chinese Banks' Global Expansion and Their Benchmarks* introduced Banks Internationalization Index ("BII"). We expanded our Banks Internationalization Index (BII) by choosing two groups of data including bank's number of overseas branches, overseas assets and revenue, etc. In addition to analyzing representative Chinese banks' internationalization, 16 of the Global Systemically Important Banks (G-SIBs) were selected as benchmarks. Thus, in this report, we not only summarized Chinese banks' achievements in global markets but also compared the differences between Chinese and foreign banks. We also explored the future roadmap of internationalization and risks during the process, in order to provide a good reference for Chinese banks. Based on the results of our BII output and other relevant data on bank's internationalization, this report has reached conclusions as below:

Growth rate of Chinese banks' BII has declined and the gaps between China's Big 5 Banks and listed banks have narrowed. On one hand, the consolidated BII of China's Big 5 Banks was 8.90 in 2015 with a growth rate of 4.1% compared to 8.54 in 2014, lower than the growth rate in 2014 was 12.0%. Among them, Bank of China still achieved the highest BII of 21.57, then successively followed by Industrial and Commercial Bank of China (8.94), Bank of Communications (7.15), China Construction Bank (4.33), and Agricultural Bank of China (3.41). Meanwhile, the consolidated BII of China's five listed banks was only 2.7 with a growth rate of 10.1% in 2015, which was much lower compared to 2014 (20.7%). China CITIC Bank and Shanghai Pudong Development Bank ranked 20 and 22 with their BII of 4.36 and 3.66, respectively, which was closely followed by China Construction Bank (ranked 21st) and Agricultural Bank of China (ranked 23rd). The overall progress of internationalization is still outstanding.

Chinese banks' global network has covered most countries with the focus on "the Belt and Road" Initiatives. Chinese banks continued to follow their strategies as "from near to far; from the developed countries to developing countries" when expanding their global networks in overseas countries. China's Big 5 Banks have established branches in 57 countries, among which the number of branches in Asia accounted for 44.4%. The Belt and Road countries have become first-priority target destination for Chinese banks' overseas investment. In 2015, Bank of China opened five branches in Southeast Asia along the Silk Road and successfully issued the world's first "Belt and Road" bond of 4 billion dollars. China Construction Bank also established five new branches in Europe in 2015, located in the United Kingdom, France, Spain, Italy, and the Netherlands.

Chinese banks' international influence has been recognized but their BII were still well behind foreign banks. In 2015, China had four banks qualified as G-SIBs, which were Industrial and Commercial Bank of China, Agricultural Bank of China, Bank of Communications, and China Construction Bank. We now have the same number of G-SIBs as France and United Kingdom (13.3% of the whole list), however, we were still behind US who had 8 G-SIBs in total. In our BII system, the average BII of 16 foreign banks was 53.65, which was six times higher than consolidated BII of China's Big 5 banks and 19.9 times higher than consolidated BII of Chinese listed banks. Bank of China, the bank with the highest BII in China, only ranked 16th among the 26 banks and its BII was only 1/4 of Standard Chartered Bank (88.84) who came first. The breadth and depth of Chinese banks' business activities in overseas markets were still not competitive compared to foreign banks. In 2015, the number of countries where HSBC's branches were operating was 2.4 times higher than China's Big 5 Banks consolidated. Moreover, the number of HSBC's overseas branches was 43.7 times higher than China's Big 5 Banks consolidated. However, among all operational indicators, the gap between Chinese and foreign banks in overseas loans was the smallest. It implied that the profit model for most Chinese banks was still limited to interest spread income even though they were enhancing their presence in overseas intermediary business.

Chinese banks' total overseas assets kept growing while foreign banks were already at mature stage. By the end of 2015, the total amount of China's Big 5 Banks' overseas assets amounted to 9.87277 trillion RMB with a significant growth rate of 14.2%. Their overseas assets accounted for 11.8% of their total assets and remained same as 2014. In contrast, signs of foreign banks reaching the mature stage for their globalization were more prominent. For the selected 16 foreign banks, although the growth rate of their foreign assets, deposits, loans, and employment in the past 10 years was near to zero, their business scale in domestic and overseas markets were almost the same. The proportion of among the top 5 foreign banks' overseas assets was all above 60%.

Chinese banks' overseas business had yielded promising outcomes, but there still lied a long road ahead of them for internationalization. In 2015, total amount of China's Big 5 Banks' overseas revenue reached 200 billion RMB with overseas profit exceeding 100 billion RMB for the first time, of which the growth rate was 17.0% and 6.7%, respectively, compared to 2014. Their profitability in overseas markets is improving rapidly. However, except for the Bank of China, the overall overseas operating revenue and profits of Chinese banks only accounted for less than 10%, significantly dropped behind foreign banks. In 2015, the average overseas operating revenue to the total operating revenue ratio for China's Big 5 banks

(8.0%) was only 1/7 of the average level of the selected foreign banks (59.4%). The average overseas profits to the total profits ratio for China's Big 5 Banks (8.3%) were only 1/8 of the average level of the selected foreign banks (68.7%). We could see there still lied a long way ahead for Chinese banks to continuously develop their overseas business in the future.

The country size and its economy scale, internationalization of its currency, its positioning of banking business, etc., were the factors affecting Chinese banks' progression in internationalization. Based on our case study, we noticed that these factors will benefit banks in that country to develop their business internationally. And their universal banks and wholesale banks were more active in foreign countries compared to retail banks. Nevertheless, the born-international pattern of banks' internationalization required banks to be equipped with multiple features, which made it more difficult for other banks to replicate. That explained the reasons that most banks were more inclined to adopt traditional international pattern for their overseas expansion.

Risk incidents emerged continuously, which showed that robust risk management was still critical for banks' success in internationalization. It was frequently reported in the media that financial institutions suffered great loss, lawsuit, or penalties due to various types of risks incidents. According to the statistics, number of litigations against JPMorgan Chase, Citigroup, Goldman Sachs, Bank of America, and Wells Fargo reached 150 and $95 billion in economic loss from 2008 to 2014. Compared to foreign banks, Chinese banks were more easily exposed to potential risks during their international expansion, given their lack of operational experience and resources in foreign countries. Since 2000, Chinese banks were reported to have more than 10 risk incidents, mainly caused by their reckless business expansion, weak risk control, and limited legal knowledge. Therefore, Chinese banks shall attach greater importance to risk prevention and control in their international operation as well as actively learn experience from foreign banks.

Prologue

During 2015, with the complexity of international economy kept growing, the significance of new normal state of Chinese economy increasing, the achievement of RMB internationalization and the strategy of "the Belt and Road" Initiatives deepening, Chinese banks' footprints in internationalization continued to expand. Chinese banks' influence on international market was enhanced with their growing business presence and maturing branch networks in foreign countries.

From their first attempt in Hong Kong during the early stage of overseas expansion to their presence in global network, Chinese banks were paired with Chinese enterprises expanding overseas, and transformed themselves from placing a strong emphasis on interest rate spread to attracting MNC clients and enhancing cross-border services. While Chinese banks have been well known for their unparalleled assets under management, they have become increasingly active to have their voice heard and focus on primary target on the world stage. By the end of 2015, the total overseas assets, revenues, and EBT (Earnings before tax) for Chinese banks amounted to 9.8 trillion, 200 billion, and 100 billion, respectively, in RMB, increasing by 14.2%, 17%, and 6.7% compared to 2014. Among all listed commercial banks, China CITIC Bank and China Merchants Bank (CMB) achieved remarkable overseas revenue as 2 Billion yuan in 2015.

In correspondence with their progress, Chinese banks' international influence was well recognized on the international stage. Although China had four banks qualified as G-SIBs in 2015, the gap between Chinese banks and global top banks remained in respect of business scale and exploitation degree of new markets. It was an obvious challenge encountered by Chinese banks as well as a great opportunity in terms of harnessing the implications from others' expansion experience, and strategically positioning themselves toward the chosen direction. With financial protectionism and anti-globalization movement on the rise, the internationalization of Chinese banks required risk management to be implemented effectively with the commitment to prevent potential crisis through the course of their future expansion in global markets.

In the context of increasingly complex and diversified economic environment, Chinese banks must be fully aware of their current standing, actively seize market opportunities, constantly learn from their lessons and experiences on the track of internationalization, reasonably plan their blueprints on overseas expansion, and enhance their development strategies. This year, *In Pursuit of Presence or Prominence?—The Prospect of Chinese Banks' Global Expansion and Their Benchmarks* introduced the concept of Banks Internationalization Index (BII) based on the 2015 assumptions and we expanded the coverage of BII by embracing a series of determinants which included but not limited to bank's number of overseas branches, revenues, profitability, talent pool, and geographic distribution through most current data and analysis to enrich the thinking and enable the understanding of their status quo.

Chapter 1
Changes in the Domestic and International Economy

Compared with 2014, the global economic conditions grew more complicated in 2015. Volatility of world economy presented a rising trend in general, whereas China maintained a steady growth. "Address overcapacity, reduce inventory and de-leverage" has become the reform direction. Interest rate marketization, RMB internationalization, internet finance, and "the Belt and Road" Initiatives led and shaped the overseas development of Chinese companies.

1.1 Growing Complexity in Global Economy

International layout and order were under accelerating adjustment, thus becoming more complicated. Firstly, the global economy gradually recovered under profound adjustment with evident divergence. Secondly, market risks increased with rising volatility in the global financial market. Thirdly, with the deepening intertwine with global political diplomacy, unstable factors and uncertainties of economy increased. Therefore, the global economy was expected to maintain a slow growth for a long time until the global governance mechanism fundamentally changed.

Specifically, it can be seen from the major developed economies (see Table 1.1) that economy of the United States and the United Kingdom regained stability with a relatively fast recovery. Secondary and tertiary industries of US kept expanding. Under this circumstance, on December 17th, 2015, the Federal Reserve raised the federal funds rate by 25 basis points, officially setting off its plan of raising interest rate. The Eurozone started to stabilize its economy with lower unemployment rate. However, the internal economic growth diverged. Except for core countries like Germany, France, and some emerging Eastern European market, other Eurozone countries still struggled with sovereign debt and trapped at the bottom of the

© Zhejiang University Press and Springer Nature Singapore Pte Ltd. 2018
B. Shenglin et al., *In Pursuit of Presence or Prominence?* Current Chinese
Economic Report Series, https://doi.org/10.1007/978-981-10-7730-2_1

economic cycle. Moreover, refugee issues and terrorist attacks increased uncertainties of Eurozone development. As for Japan, its economy fluctuated greatly along with sharp plunge in consumption level in 2015. In spite of the relatively stable unemployment rate, Japan presented a slow economic recovery with intensified economic downward pressure, the prospect of which remained to be seen.

Compared to developed economies, the majority of emerging economies (see Table 1.2) showed an accelerated pace in economic development, but with increasingly intensified internal discrepancies in recent years. Affected by the global financial crisis, the growth of Asia Pacific slowed down, whereas countries such as R.O. Korea, India, and Vietnam were making stable recovery. Particularly, India replaced China as the fastest-growing economy. China, Indonesia, and Malaysia showed slower pace in development and growth. Russia and Brazil, these two resource-based countries, were greatly affected by the global environment, experiencing negative growth in the first two quarters of 2015.

Furthermore, the economic divergence and imbalance of different countries has led to violent fluctuations in the global economic recovery. Especially, the United States launched its Quantitative Easing Monetary Policy in order to bail out and stimulate its economic recovery after the international financial crisis. The policy caused US Dollars continuously to depreciate, and outflow of US Dollars to increase. This consequently brought up commodity prices and currency appreciation of emerging economies, along with inflated asset price bubbles. In recent years, the US economy took the lead in recovery, along with the exit from the quantitative easing and the entry into the interest rate hike cycle gradually. Thereby, this triggered a slump in commodity prices, depreciation of currencies other than US Dollars and high volatility in global stock markets. Figures 1.1 and 1.2 showed separately the global crude oil price and exchange rate fluctuations of major countries. Figure 1.1 showed that the global crude oil price had risen slightly since the beginning of 2015, then fell substantially afterwards. By the end of 2015, the prices of Brent and WTI oil were 37.28 and 37.04 US dollars per barrel respectively with a decline of about 30% all the year round.

As seen in Fig. 1.2, the US Dollar was gradually stepping into the interest rate hike cycle leading to US Dollar continually strengthening, whereas other currencies presented a depreciation in value with different magnitudes. In 2015, Pound was depreciated by 5.1%, while in Asia-Pacific region, depreciation in RMB, Singapore Dollar, and Thai Baht, reached the level between 5 and 10%. Euro and Polish Zloty were depreciated at about 10%, and the depreciation rate of Malaysian Ringgit and Turkish Lira hit a record as 20%. The only currency with relatively low depreciation in Asia was Japanese Yen.

Table 1.1 Macroeconomic and financial indicators of major developed economies in 2015 (%)

Indicator	First quarter of 2015			Second quarter of 2015		
	January	February	March	April	May	June
The United States						
Actual GDP growth rate (annualized)	0.6			3.9		
Unemployment rate	5.7	5.5	5.5	5.4	5.5	5.3
CPI	−0.2	−0.1	0	−0.1	0	0.2
The United Kingdom						
Actual GDP growth rate (annualized)	0.8			0.3		
Unemployment rate	−0.9	0.3	0.2	0.2	0.2	0.05
CPI	5.7	5.6	5.5	5.5	5.6	5.6
Eurozone						
Actual GDP growth rate (annualized)	0.5			0.4		
Unemployment rate	11.3	11.2	11.2	11.1	11.0	11.0
HICP Harmonized Index of Consumer Prices	−0.6	−0.3	−0.1	0	0.3	0.2
Japan						
Actual GDP growth rate (annualized)	4.4			−0.5		
Unemployment rate	3.6	3.5	3.4	3.3	3.3	3.4
CPI	2.4	2.2	2.3	0.6	0.5	0.4

(continued)

Table 1.1 (continued)

	Indicator	Third quarter of 2015			Fourth quarter of 2015		
	Indicator	July	August	September	October	November	December
The United States	Actual GDP growth rate (annualized)	2.0			–		
	Unemployment rate	5.3	5.1	5.1	5	5	5
	CPI	0.2	0.2	0	0.1	0.4	0.7
The United Kingdom	Actual GDP growth rate (annualized)	0.4			0.4		
	Unemployment rate	0.2	0.3	0.2	0.3	0.2	0.3
	CPI	5.5	5.4	5.5	5.4	5.5	5.4
Eurozone	Actual GDP growth rate (annualized)	0.3			0.7 (initial value)		
	Unemployment rate	10.8	10.8	10.6	10.6	10.5	10.4
	HICP Harmonized Index of Consumer Prices	0.2	0.1	−0.1	0.1	0.1	0.2
Japan	Actual GDP growth rate (annualized)	1			–		
	Unemployment rate	3.3	3.4	3.4	3.1	3.3	3.3
	CPI	0.2	0.2	0	0.3	0.3	0.2

Source Zhejiang University CIFI, the World Bank

Table 1.2 Macroeconomic and financial indicators of emerging economies

	Indicator	2011	2012	2013	2014	2015
China	GDP (Current US$ in trillion)	7.573	8.561	9.607	10.482	11.008
	GDP growth rate (%)	9.536	7.856	7.758	7.298	6.914
	Inflation (GDP deflator %)	8.152	2.392	2.225	0.828	−0.435
Russia	GDP (Current US$ in trillion)	2.034	2.154	2.232	2.053	1.331
	GDP growth rate (%)	4.264	3.518	1.279	0.706	−3.727
	Inflation (GDP deflator %)	23.642	8.299	4.770	8.986	7.681
India	GDP (Current US$ in trillion)	1.823	1.829	1.863	2.042	2.095
	GDP growth rate (%)	6.638	5.619	6.639	7.243	7.563
	Inflation (GDP deflator %)	8.54	7.852	6.227	3.300	1.067
Brazil	GDP (Current US$ in trillion)	2.615	2.461	2.466	2.417	1.775
	GDP growth rate (%)	3.910	1.915	3.015	0.103	−3.847
	Inflation (GDP deflator %)	8.318	7.818	7.385	6.865	7.97
South Africa	GDP (Current US$ in trillion)	0.416	0.396	0.368	0.351	0.315
	GDP growth rate (%)	3.284	2.213	2.330	1.629	1.265
	Inflation (GDP deflator %)	6.532	5.287	6.588	5.701	3.957

Source Zhejiang University CIFI, the World Bank

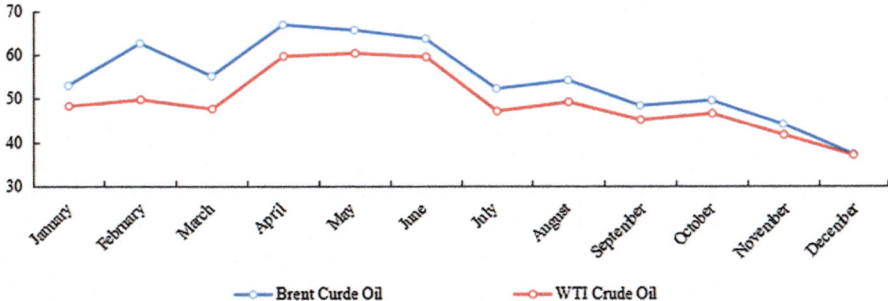

Fig. 1.1 2015 Global crude oil price trend (US Dollar/Barrel). *Source* Zhejiang University CIFI, Wall Street CN

1.2 China's Economy Aligned Stability with Sustainable Progress

In the context of diversified and complex global economy, China stood strong to its principle of aligning stability with sustainable progress. China took the initiative to adapt to and lead a new normal economic development that emphasized on quality improvements and put efficiency of economic development at its core. Adhering to the principles of stabilizing growth, adjusting structure, promoting reform and preventing risks, China implemented a proactive fiscal policy as well as a prudent

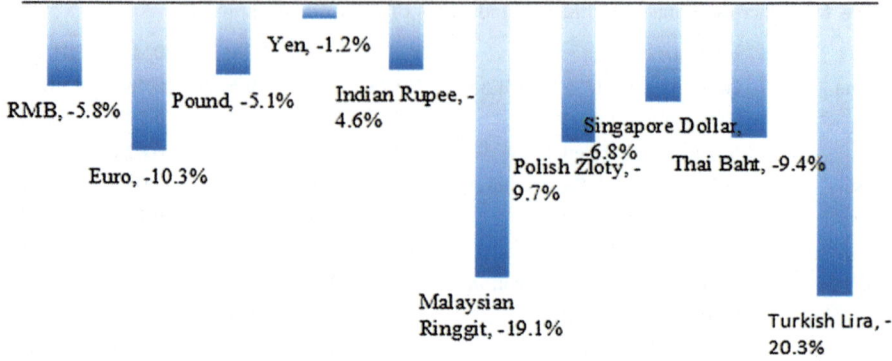

Fig. 1.2 Fluctuations in foreign exchange rate of global major currencies in 2015. *Source* Zhejiang University CIFI, SAFE

monetary policy, in order to continue its structural reform of state-owned enterprises and encourage rising of new entrepreneurs and innovation. The overall economy presented stability with a steady growth rate. In 2015, China's GDP reached 67.7 trillion yuan, increasing by 6.9% compared with 2014. CPI rose by 1.4% in 2015, and the current account surplus increased by 19%, reaching $330.6 billion.

By zooming in, firstly,consumption rose steadily at the annual growth rate of 8% in 2015, with faster development in the tertiary industry and upgrading consumption structure. Secondly, business investment slowed down, whereas the middle western region kept faster growth than the eastern region. Thirdly, China has continually optimized its economic structure. The share of the added value from the tertiary industry improved from 46.9 to 48.2%, with new industries, new forms and new business models constantly emerging. Fourthly, the supply-side structural reform had been accelerated. On one hand, state-owned companies made substantial progress in their restructuring reform. According to statistics, there were totally 12 state-owned companies going through restructuring in 2015, by exploring to avoid the homogeneity competition and improving their market competitiveness. On the other hand, the address overcapacity reform of state-owned companies also yielded notable results. In 2015, 1340 coal mines were obsoleted with eliminating capacity of about 90 million ton. By the end of 2015, there were 10.8 thousand coal mines in China, among which there were 1050 coal mines with capacity of more than 1.2 million ton, increased by 400 compared to 2010. There were more than 7000 coal mines with annual capacity of less than 300 thousand ton, dropped by 4000 compared to 2014. And hence, the total production showed sharp drop from 21.6 to 10% (Fig. 1.3).

Furthermore, the employment market in China was relatively stable with a steady growth in residents' income. According to the National Bureau of Statistics, number of new employments decreased by 100,000 compared with that of 2014, which put to the end of continued growth since 2009. However, the overall demand

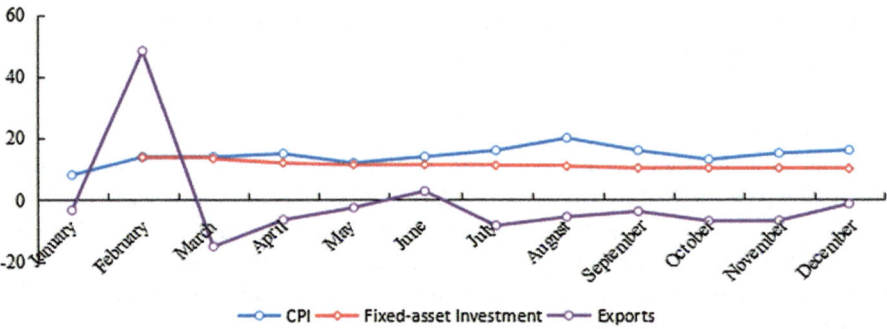

Fig. 1.3 Growth rate of domestic consumption, investment and export in 2015 (%). *Source* Zhejiang University CIFI, National Bureau of Statistics of China

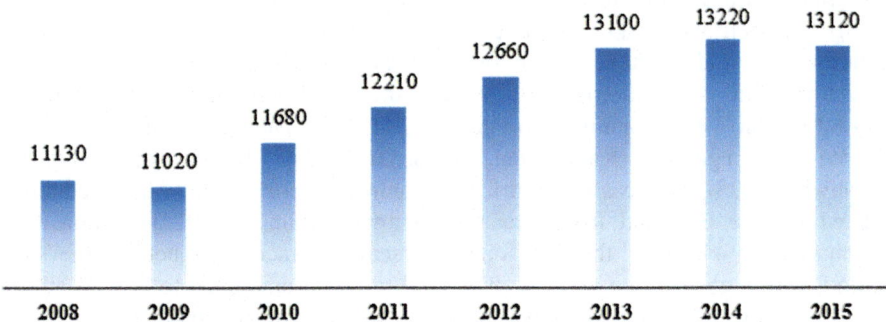

Fig. 1.4 New employment in urban area (in thousand). *Source* Zhejiang University CIFI, National Bureau of Statistics of China

was still greater than the supply in the job market. The rural per capita disposable annual income was 11,422 yuan in 2015 with an annual growth rate of 8.9%, while the per capita disposable income of urban population was 31,195 yuan with an annual growth rate of 6.6%. It can be seen that the growth rate of rural population income was higher than the urban population and the disparity between urban and rural areas would be further reduced (Fig. 1.4).

2015 was the final year of the "12th Five-Year Plan" and was also the vital turning point for the "13th Five-Year Plan". Under the economic background of "new normal", Chinese government's economic policy put more emphasis on structural reforms in order to improve the productivity through address overcapacity and encouraging innovation. Meanwhile, state-owned companies also stepped into a crucial period for reform. In order to achieve the stable economic development under the "new normal", it was essential for government to fully coordinate its regulation with market mechanism.

1.3   "The Belt and Road" Initiatives Yielded Striking Outcomes

China initially proposed the strategy of "the Belt and Road" Initiatives in 2013 as a national strategy from the top governors. Because of the success in "the Silk Road Economic Belt" and "the 21th Century Maritime Silk Road", China was able to win itself the discourse right in the complicated global economy landscape. In 2015, the first batch of infrastructure construction projects kicked off together with numerous international consensus was reached, which showed acknowledgement of this initiative from the neighboring countries.

First of all, economic and trade exchanges gradually increased. In 2015, China signed bilateral currency swap agreements with 15 countries along "the Belt and Road". The overall cross-border settlement amounted to more than 2.64 trillion yuan. From January to October 2015, the bilateral trade volume with countries along "the Belt and Road" amounted to $820.39 billion, accounted for 25.4% of China's total trade volume in the same period. Chinese companies made direct investment in 49 countries, of which the total investment amounted to $14.82 billion with an annual growth rate of 18.2%. Their investments primarily flowed to Singapore, Kazakhstan, Laos, Indonesia, Russia, and Thailand. Meanwhile, 3987 overseas subcontracting contracts were signed with 60 countries related to "the Belt and Road" reached a total amount of $92.64 billion. This accounted for 44.1% of the total new overseas contracted projects in the same period, with a growth rate of 7.4%. The total turnover amounted to $69.26 billion, as 45% of the total turnover over the same period with a growth rate of 7.6%. However, it was still worth being mentioned that the economic and trade cooperation presented regional differences. Compared with Southeast Asian countries, the connections that we have with CIS countries and Central and Eastern Europe remained to be strengthened (Fig. 1.5).

Secondly, financial support was increasingly strengthened for "the Belt and Road". Developmental financial institutions (DFIs) provided financial support to various major projects in accordance with their development strategy. On April 20, 2015, a memorandum was signed by the Silk Road Fund, China Three Gorges Corporation and the Private Power & Infrastructure Board of Pakistan, initiating the first foreign investment. The Silk Road Fund already invested in Italy, Kazakhstan, Russia, Saudi Arabia, etc. Meanwhile, traditional commercial financial institutions dominated by the banking industry reinforced their presence in the countries along "the Belt and Road". By the end of 2015, 56 banks from 20 countries along "the Belt and Road" had established 67 branches in China (including 7 subsidiaries, 18 branches, and 42 offices), whereas 9 Chinese banks opened 56 branches in 24 countries along the Silk Road. In addition, it is worth mentioning that emerging financial business represented by the internet finance rapidly arose, gradually building the online "Silk Road". Ant Financial of Alibaba's group bought shares of commercial platform Lazada in Indonesia, Flipkart and Snapdeal in India. Ant Financial conducted two rounds of stock purchase of Indian largest mobile payment

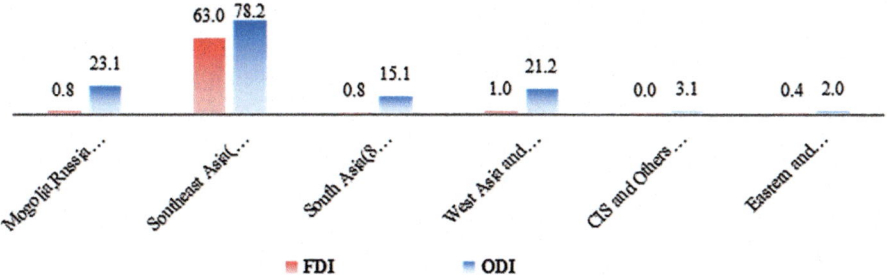

Fig. 1.5 Economic and trade exchanges with countries along "the Belt and Road" (Data was for 2014, partial data missing.) (in '00,000,000 US dollar). *Source* Zhejiang University CIFI, Wind

platform Paytm for its 40% share as well as obtaining the first payment banking license issued by the Reserve Bank of India. This was regarded as a remarkable financial event of the "going global" strategy of Chinese internet finance industry.

1.4 Financial System Continued to Reform

The overall financial market in China functioned smoothly in 2015. Financial reforms kept advancing together with interest rate marketization, RMB internationalization, and Internet finance at the core.

1.4.1 Interest Rate Marketization Achieved Substantial Progress

Since the 1990s, China has continuously promoted a reform with the aim of interest rate marketization. Since 1996, deregulation of interbank market rate and bond repurchase rate had achieved the goal of interest rate marketization in monetary and bond market. On October 29, 2004, China deregulated the lending rate celling and deposit floor rate. Since then, interest rate marketization entered into a crucial stage. In accelerating the course of interest rate marketization, the People' Bank of China (PBOC) had lowered the RMB deposit and lending rates five times (see Table 1.3), and announced that PBOC would no longer set ceiling of the deposit rate on October 23rd, 2015. This marked as a vital progress for interest rate marketization reform in China.

Simultaneously, in order to maintain the order of the financial market, China continued to improve its interest rate pricing mechanism and the members of self-discipline mechanism further expanded. By the end of 2015, the members of the self-discipline mechanism had increased to 643, including 10 core members, 469 fundamental members and 164 observing members. Furthermore, a total

Table 1.3 2015 Adjustments in RMB Benchmark deposit and lending rates (%)

Effective date	Benchmark deposit rate			Benchmark lending rate		
	Before	After	Adjustment rate	Before	After	Adjustment rate
2015-03-01	2.75	2.50	−0.25	5.60	5.35	−0.25
2015-05-11	2.50	2.25	−0.25	5.35	5.10	−0.25
2015-06-28	2.25	2.00	−0.25	5.10	4.85	−0.25
2015-08-26	2.00	1.75	−0.25	4.85	4.60	−0.25
2015-10-24	1.75	1.50	−0.25	4.60	4.35	−0.25

Source Zhejiang University CIFI, PBOC

5.3 trillion yuan of CDs were issued in 2015. Meanwhile, trading volume in secondary market reached 18.4 trillion yuan. The total issuance of large-amount of CD in China achieved 2.3 trillion yuan in 2015. The increase of issuance of CDs also facilitated to expand the range of market-value pricing for debt products. Thus, this created conditions for China to accelerate its interest rate marketization reform.

1.4.2   RMB Internationalization Attained Major Breakthroughs

In 2003, for the first time, China allowed using of RMB as settlement currency for cross-border trading and designated Bank of China (Hong Kong) as the RMB clearing bank in Hong Kong. Since then, RMB internationalization had been carried out for more than 10 years and continued to advance steadily in 2015, specifically in below aspects:

Firstly, RMB's position in global market was continually improved. On November 30, 2015, the Executive Board of IMF decided to include the RMB in the currency basket of SDR as the fifth currency. The weight of the RMB in the SDR basket is 10.92%. The new basket would become effective on October 1, 2016, marking as a major breakthrough of the RMB internationalization (Fig. 1.6).

Fig. 1.6 Currency weight in the SDR basket. *Source* Zhejiang University, IMF

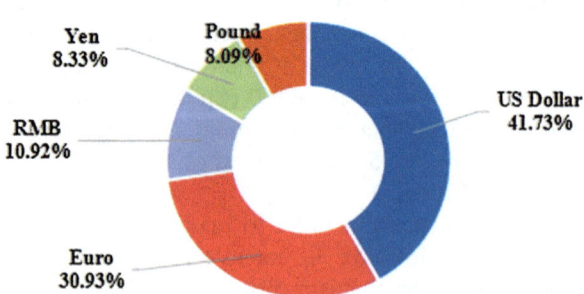

Secondly, RMB was increasingly used as currency for international settlement. According to SWIFT, RMB reached 2.3% of market share in the global payments by December 2015, marking RMB as the world's third most used currency for trade finance, the fifth most traded currency in foreign exchange market and the fifth most used currency for payment. In 2015, the amount of RMB used for cross-border payment totaled as 12.1 trillion yuan with a growth rate of 22%. Additionally, the "China International Payment System" CIPS launched successfully on October 8, 2015, which further improved the efficiency of cross-border settlement and enhanced the use of RMB globally.

Thirdly, China has made outstanding achievements on global cooperation on RMB. By the end of 2015, People's Bank of China, the central bank in China, signed bilateral currency swap agreements with central banks or monetary authorities from 33 countries and regions, with total scale over 3.3 trillion yuan. These swap agreements had a growing substantial effect on accelerating RMB globalization. Moreover, PBOC also signed RMB clearing agreements with 20 countries and regions worldwide. These clearing agreements played a positive role in promoting RMB as a regional settlement currency. On October 20th, 2015, PBOC successfully issued central bank bills in London, as the first issuance of central bank bills dominated in RMB overseas. On November 18th, 2015, the China Europe International Exchange was opened in Frankfurt, with ETF (Exchange Traded Fund) and RMB bonds listed for trading. All of these mentioned events had profound effect on China's offshore corporation via RMB currency, development of offshore RMB market and cross-border investment.

Fourthly, the two-way of cross-border RMB cash pooling business has been upgraded. On September 23, 2015, PBOC announced that it would further lift the net cash inflow limit of offshore RMB as well as lowering the barriers for enterprises participating in RMB cash pooling business. This measure advanced the using of RMB in cross-border settlement, strengthening the interaction between offshore and onshore RMB markets.

Accompanied by the continuous optimization of regulation environment for the cross-border RMB business, the improvements of infrastructure system supported the international use of RMB currency. With growing international acceptance of RMB, it was expected that RMB internationalization would continue to make steady progress.

1.4.3 Internet Finance Presented Diversified Development

In March 2015, the *Report on the Work of the Government* officially proposed "Internet Plus" action plan, which aimed at promoting "small startup business and people's innovation". Chinese government's attitude was shown clearly in the report to push forward the robust development of innovative industries. On July 18th, 2015, PBOC published *Opinions and Guidance on Promoting the Robust Development of Internet Finance* jointly with other 10 ministries, which pointed out that the deep integration of internet and finance was the inevitable trend. Meanwhile, the enormous increase of cumulative data brought by the internet technology advancement gave rise to the development of "cloud computing", "big data" and "block chain", etc. In such circumstances, innovation of internet technologies has penetrated into every financial sector and supply chain. Moreover, the internet technology will connect the supply and demand of products and services, bringing vitality to both traditional finance and internet finance.

(1) **The Impact from Internet Technologies on Traditional Finance Was Notable**

Large commercial banks as the bank industry leaders had yielded promising results on their transformation to internet bank (see Table 1.4). ICBC's three platforms of electronic business platform, mobile phone service platform and direct bank as well as its three major products of payment, financing, and investment have

Table 1.4 Selected banks' transformation to internet bank

Banks	Internet-change progress
Industrial and Commercial Bank of China (ICBC)	Rong e Buy: cumulative trading amount to 204 billion yuan by the end of 2015 Rong e Connection: customers topped 1.3 million by the end of 2015 Direct banking: trading amount exceeded 23 billion yuan in 2015 ICBC e-payment: the number of customers reached 600 million, trading amount exceeded 80 billion yuan by the end of 2015 Internet lending: internet lending of 340 billion yuan to nearly 30 thousand small and micro business customers cumulatively in 2015
China Construction Bank (CCB)	Wechat banking customers: 26 million cumulatively by the end of September 2015 Online banking services for overseas companies: coverage of Asia, Europe, North America, Oceania, and Africa, etc.
Agricultural Bank of China (ABC)	Yin Xun Tong: established 11.3 thousand of service offices by the end of 2015 Data online lending: cumulative released 1179 loans amounted to 363 million yuan to 2 upstream and downstream small and micro distributors qualified as "Data and Internet Financing" client by the end of 2015 E-agricultural Housekeeper: had presence in over 800 large wholesalers in Hubei province, a complete coverage of 69 counties, and was promoted to over 20 thousand farmer shops
Bank of China (BOC)	BOC Yishang Platform: initial issuance of integrated electronic guarantee service in 25 provinces Smart E Community: cumulatively connected to over 10 thousand communities, over 15 thousand merchants, and 1.2 million registered customers

Source Zhejiang University CIFI, Trade Finance Magazine

attained explosive growth throughout all the year round. CCB also built its three platforms of "CCB Buy" "Yue Life" "Hui Life" and three product lines as internet payment, internet wealth management and internet financing. CCB also introduced three new smart technologies of big data, "financial services cloud", and smart customer services, so as to actively develop its finance ecosystem. Meanwhile, ABC took a different path and launched "Data and Internet Financing" aiming to solving the financing difficulties for agricultural enterprises owned by farmers, small and micro businesses. BOC also achieved notable results by developing its internet finance business. BOC expanded its cross-border RMB and foreign currencies electronic payment and settlement business with customers, which covered more than 50 institutions and trading volume to nearly 10 billion yuan.

In terms of internet fund, Tencent, Alibaba, Xiaomi and other internet giants all had launched their own fund products, strengthening the cooperation of internet technologies and fund products in 2015. At the same time, with the Shanghai Composite Index rising and fund booming in the first half year of 2015, these internet fund have experienced significant growth. The fund sales of 1234567.com. cn made by Eastmoney fund was striking with a fund sales of 617.2 billion yuan in the first 3 quarters in 2015, which was up to 363% compared with that of 2014. Additionally, Lufax joined as fund agency in September 2015, and sold more than 2000 funds on a commission basis within 3 months. By the end of 2015, Lufax's daily fund sale exceeded 1 billion yuan, going to become the "black horse" of internet fund business in 2015.

The development of internet insurance also kept a fast pace in 2015. Although the market share of internet insurance only accounted for 4.7%, it had great potential for further growth. By the end of the third quarter of 2015, more than 100 insurance companies launched their internet business in China, and the number of investments on internet insurance also went up by about 185% compared to last year. Moreover, the total investment amount on internet insurance was 59 times higher compared to 2014 in total, and 11 times higher even excluding the large-amount investment funding made by Zhongan Insurance.

(2) **Development of Internet Hinance Diverged**

In 2015, Chinese internet finance developed rapidly and healthily, particularly in areas such as internet payment and internet wealth management. Chinese internet finance companies also became leaders globally in internet finance business. However, it cannot be neglected that there existed notable phenomenon of divergent development in different internet finance areas, specifically as follows:

Number of problematic internet lending platforms had been sharply increasing, becoming the "hard-hit area" of Internet finance development in China. According to the statistics from Zhejiang University Academy of Internet Finance, the total number of internet lending platforms kept rising. However, the growth rate took a big drop and the problematic platform ratio increased (see Fig. 1.7). By the end of 2015, there were 3333 internet lending platforms cumulatively with the growth rate of 48.4% compared to 2014, which was far below the average annual growth rate of

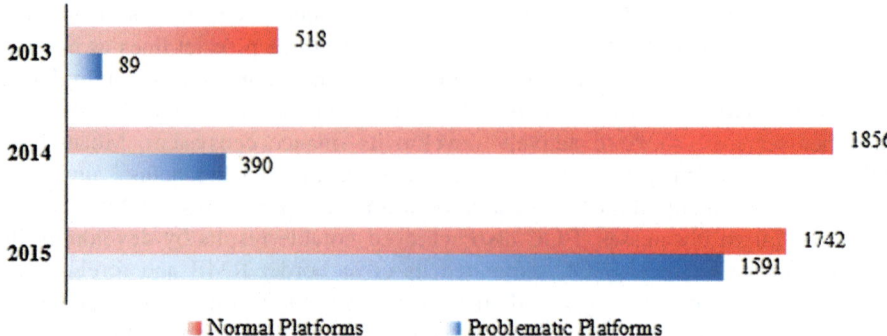

Fig. 1.7 Number of internet lending platforms in China from 2013 to 2015. *Source* Zhejiang University CIFI, AIF

188.9% since 2007. Furthermore, the number of normally operating platforms declined for the first time compared with 2014, showing the inflection point of the industry. As for those problematic platforms, the problematic ratio of internet lending has been increasing every year, intensifying the reshuffle of the industry. In 2015, there were 1450 problematic platforms operating in China with the problematic ratio[1] of 47.7%, whereas the problematic ratio was only 17.4% in 2014 and 14.7% in 2013. In terms of the regional distribution, the internet lending platforms mainly operated on the east coast of China such as Guangdong, Shandong, Beijing, Zhejiang, and Shanghai (these five provinces amounted to 62.7% of the total internet platforms in China). This showed a regional characteristic and stepwise expansion to inland regions year by year. As for the overall industrial trend, frequent occurrence of internet lending incidents such as e-Zubao being suspected of illegal fund-raising in 2015, 250 million yuan bad debt of Lufax and Hongling Capital "Anhui No. 9" project's borrower escaping, showed internet lending "plague" already spreading from small to large platforms. Expecting the official launch of internet lending regulation policy in the upcoming future, internet lending industry would face their biggest challenge and lead to the industry reshuffle. In addition, fraud on internet lending platforms also showed an intensifying trend, accounting for 8.3% of the total problematic platforms. The "Internet fraud" warned us that it became urgent to clarify the "negative list", and regulate the development of the internet finance.

Crowdfunding achieved explosive development and the internet giants actively participated in the competition. According to the iResearch's annual report on crowdfunding, equity crowdfunding reached 2.9 billion yuan in 2015, increased by 625% compared to 400 million yuan in 2014 and increased by 1350% compared to 200 million yuan in 2013. The reason behind this rapid growth was that internet

---

[1]Problematic ratio equals to number of problematic platforms divided by number of total platforms.

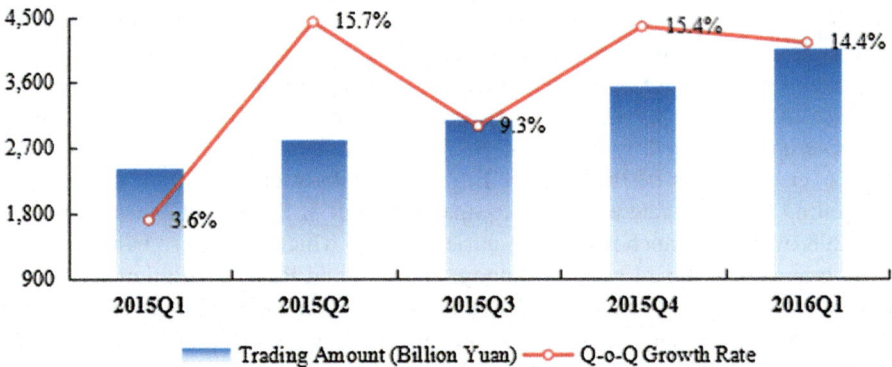

Fig. 1.8 Transaction volume of third-party internet payment in China from 2015Q4 to 2016Q4. *Source* Zhejiang University CIFI, iResearch Inc

giants such as Joybuy and Alibaba utilized their internet platforms to expand their financial business. Other industries such as cultural and entertainment industries were involved in the crowdfunding in order to seek for business breakthrough by cross-industry development.

Third-party payment transactions rose steadily with increasing industry concentration. Specifically, the transaction volume of third-party internet payment grew by 46.9% in 2015 compared with 2014 (see Fig. 1.8). The competition in third-party payment market became progressively fierce with intensified industry concentration. O2O mode had become the main strategy for future companies under the evident trend of online and offline integration. Cross-border payment would also provide opportunities for further business development. Mobile payment would become the focus where internet giants strive to compete.

In addition, the emerging innovative financial models such as digital currency, big data finance, internet banks were on the track for business blossom. Internet finance had played a progressively important role in many aspects including promoting efficiency of financial activities, financial costs reduction, and expansion of client base. This had made a step forward to the vision of human equality in financial services sector.

1.5 Financial Institutions Embraced the World

In 2015, Chinese banks' overseas expansion was led by the policy of "the Belt and Road" along with higher risk management needs arisen while furthering their own development.

On one hand, financial institutions such as banks, securities, and funds management companies continuously advanced their internationalization progress under the guidance of "the Belt and Road". This has formed a multilevel international development trend with joint efforts from banks, securities companies, insurance companies, funds and other financial institutions.

First of all, Chinese banks remained being mainstay of Chinese financial institutions. According to the *2015 Annual Report on Chinese Banks' Social Responsibilities* issued by the China Banking Association, by the end of 2015, the total overseas assets of the China's Big Five Banks was about 9.87 trillion yuan generating a growth rate as 14.2% compared to that of 2014. 22 Chinese banks set up 1298 overseas branches in 59 countries, among which 9 Chinese banks open 56 main branches in the 24 countries along "the Belt and Road". Additionally, PBOC issued a total of $4 billion "the Belt and Road" bonds in Dubai, Singapore, London, Hong Kong SAR and Taiwan in China in 2015, with the goal of meeting the funding need for "the Belt and Road" Initiatives.

Secondly, the overseas development of Chinese securities companies also yielded remarkable results. For instance, CITIC Securities completed 15 IPOs, 24 refinancing, and 19 offshore RMB and US Dollar bonds issuance in Hong Kong. CITIC also utilized its overseas branches and network of CLSA to expand its coverage of European customers. China International Capital Corporation was listed in Hong Kong SAR of China in 2015, setting off its internationalization plan. The overseas expansion of Chinese securities companies were mainly achieved through setting up subsidiaries in Hong Kong or Singapore, establishing joint venture securities companies in the Asia-Pacific region and acquiring European investment banks. For example, Everbright Securities acquired 70% equities of Sun Hung Kai Financial Group, the largest securities broker in Hong Kong, by paying 4.10 billion Hong Kong Dollar. On September 7, 2015, Soochow Securities completed its first overseas branch registration of asset management subsidiary in Singapore. Also in September, Haitong Securities completed its acquisition of Banco Espírito Santo de Investimento, and the Banco Espírito Santo de Investimento officially changed its name to Haitong Bank.

Moreover, the asset structure of insurance companies was further internationalized. Statistics showed that by the end of December 2015, a total number of 49 insurance companies obtained approval to invest in overseas market, with the investment amount to $36.23 billion. The investment volume in 2015 increased by 51.23% compared to $23.96 billion by the end of 2014, and was up to 273.47% compared to $9.7 billion by the end of 2012. In June 2015, China Life Insurance Company set up its first overseas branch in Singapore, becoming the first Chinese insurance company with overseas branches since the launch of the *No. 10 National Notice on Insurance Industry*.

Lastly, Chinese fund management companies also made continuous progress in their overseas development. By the end of March 2016, the total number of qualified foreign institutional investors (QFII) reached 296 with the amount totaling to 80.7 billion yuan. The total number of RMB qualified foreign institutional investors (RQFII) rose up to 189 with the total amount of 470 billion yuan since the pilot phase in 2011.[2]

On the other hand, with the accelerating progress of Chinese financial institutions' overseas expansion, more attention was put on the establishment of risk mechanism and risk prevention. Taking BOC as an example, in 2015, in the context of economic "new normal", BOC developed its rating model for global large enterprise, and set up global credit facility management system, and promoted the integration of its domestic and foreign systems. BOC also strengthened its management of country, market, liquidity, and reputation risks. BOC also implemented a vertical management style on domestic and overseas branches through its internal control and compliance department. CITIC Securities actively managed the exchange rate risk via its unified management conducted through multiple aspects including asset limits, VaR, sensitivity analysis, and stress testing, in order to ensure sufficient fund for its overseas business investments. Insurance companies' assets allocation to overseas countries experienced a gradual transition from direct to indirect investments, with diversified investment fields and strengthened risk management. Fund companies optimized their asset allocation and risk management through diversified investment. Guangfa International Asset Management, the subsidiary of Guangfa Fund Management, accumulated diversified investment projects including global long-short hedging and multi-factor quantitative stock selection.

In general, under the circumstance of growingly complex domestic and foreign economy, Chinese financial institutions closely followed national strategies and made steady progress in their overseas development.

---

[2]Data was retrieved by the end of March, 2016.

Chapter 2
Status of Chinese Banks' Internationalization

In 2015, facing an increasingly complex domestic and international environment, Chinese banks, including commercial banks and development banks, still promoted their internationalization. Following "the Belt and Road" Initiatives, most banks strengthened their financial cooperation with the countries along "the Belt and Road" Initiatives countries by establishing overseas operations, providing loan products, diversifying their financial services and so on.

By the end of 2015, Chinese banking industry had 3.8 million employees, total assets of RMB 199.3 trillion and 4262 legal entities, among which there were 3 policy banks, 5 big state-owned banks, 12 joint-stock banks, 133 city banks, 5 private banks and 859 rural banks, etc. Big state-owned banks, joint-stock banks, small rural banks and city banks ranked the top four in terms of asset share with 39.2, 18.6, 12.9 and 11.4% of the whole industry respectively (see Fig. 2.1).

In the above-mentioned several banks, China's Big Five Banks took a more comprehensive approach in their internationalization, including asset accumulation, operating performance, distribution network and talent hiring. While the scale and coverage of joint-stock banks' internationalization was relatively smaller, and their overseas business was mainly focused on Hong Kong market. Some top city banks such as Bank of Beijing, Bank of Shanghai and Bank of Ningbo, also actively looked for opportunities in their international expansion. Besides, Chinese development banks, most of which are policy banks, kept exploring their own internationalization path by leveraging their funding and policy advantages.

© Zhejiang University Press and Springer Nature Singapore Pte Ltd. 2018
B. Shenglin et al., *In Pursuit of Presence or Prominence?* Current Chinese
Economic Report Series, https://doi.org/10.1007/978-981-10-7730-2_2

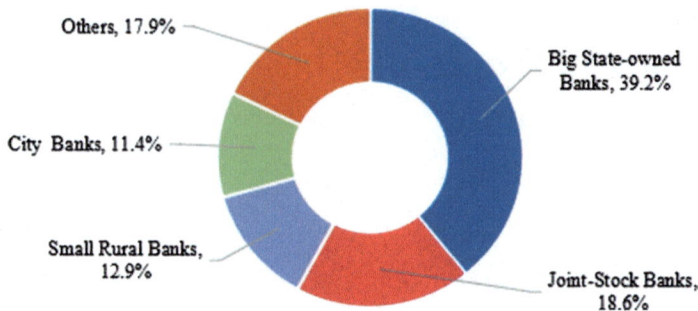

Fig. 2.1 Distribution of Chinese banks' assets. *Source* Zhejiang University CIFI, 2015 annual report from CBRC

2.1 Status of Chinese Commercial Banks' Internationalization

Chinese commercial banks, mostly represented by China's Big Five Banks and joint-stock banks, furthered their development of internationalization during 2015 and achieved a higher level of overall internationalization. These banks continued to expand their overseas business scale, increase focus on overseas business development along "the Belt and Road" Initiatives, improve organization structure, and enhance their international influence. During this process, several risk events occurred, which urged Chinese banks to improve their risk management.

2.1.1 Growth Rate of BII Slowed and the Gap Between China's Big Five Banks and Joint-Stock Banks Narrowed

In order to evaluate the level of Chinese banks' internationalization in a more comprehensively and directly way, this report selected 8 indicators based on the Chinese Bank Internationalization Index (CBII), which was first put forward in 2015. The 8 indicators are: overseas assets to total assets ratio, overseas revenue to total revenue ratio, overseas deposits to total deposits ratio, overseas loans to total loans ratio, overseas profits to total profits ratio, number of countries with operation networks to number of world's major countries ratio, overseas branches to total branches ratio, and overseas employees to total employees ratio. Based on the evaluation given by our experts, this report determined the weight for each indicator and eventually built the Bank Internationalization Index (BII) using Analytic Hierarchy Process (AHP) method. Besides our analysis of the international progress of Chinese banks, this report also rated 16 selected Global Systemically Important Banks (G-SIBs) with relatively complete data, to review and compare the divergence in their internationalization path, explore the internationalization route for Chinese banks and analyze the risks during the process, so as to provide valuable references for Chinese banks' international development.

(1) The Overall Level of Chinese Banks' Internationalization Increased While the Growth Pace Slowed

Our model measured the BII of China's Big Five Banks[1] and five joint-stock banks in China separately, and then derived the consolidated BII[2] as the average level for these two bank types.

Overall, the current internationalization pattern of Chinese banks was still led by China's Big Five Banks. From 2008 to 2015, the respective consolidated BII of China's Big Five Banks and the joint-stock banks kept growing. However, the growth rate had declined (see Fig. 2.2). The consolidated BII of China's Big Five Banks was 8.90 in 2015 with a growth rate of 4.1% compared to 8.54 and 12% in 2014. The 2015 consolidated BII of the five joint-stock banks was only 2.7 (1/3 of China's Big Five Banks' BII) and the growth rate was 10.1% which was much lower than 2014 (20.7%). In addition, according to the BII result of each bank (see Fig. 2.3), the Agricultural Bank of China (ABC), Bank of Communications (BOCOM), Industrial and Commercial Bank of China (ICBC), China Everbright Bank (CEB) and Shanghai Pudong Development Bank (SPDB) reached their highest point in 2015 among all 10 banks, while the BII of the other Five Banks declined slightly compared to the previous year. Such decline in BII implied that the development of internationalization had slowed down.

Such downward trend in globalization can be seen with following reasons. Firstly, it was influenced by the domestic and international economic environment. Particularly, the strengthening of the dollar increased the costs and pressure to overseas investments for Chinese banks. Furthermore, the growth rate of the Chinese economy slowed down under the "new normal", which also lowered banks' motivation for business expansion. Secondly, the external pressure from financial systemic risk and Chinese banks' attention to international operational risks strengthened their risk awareness and adopted prudent development policies while going global.

In recent years, most banks are inclined to put more focus on the transformation of the profit model and the diversification of overseas business. In 2015, besides continuously expanding overseas business and establishing more overseas

---

[1]China's Big Five Banks: Industrial and Commercial Bank of China, Agricultural Bank of China, Bank of China, China Construction Bank and Bank of Communications.

[2]Five joint-stock banks included China CITIC Bank (CITIC), Shanghai Pudong Development Bank (SPD), China Merchants Bank (CMB), China Guangfa Bank (CGB) and China Everbright Bank (CEB). These banks were ahead of other joint-stock banks in terms of globalization level, and their data were both representative and relatively available.

Consolidated BII adopts the same concept as "consolidated financial statements". For example, the consolidated BII of China's Big Five Banks was measured with taking the Five Banks as one entity.

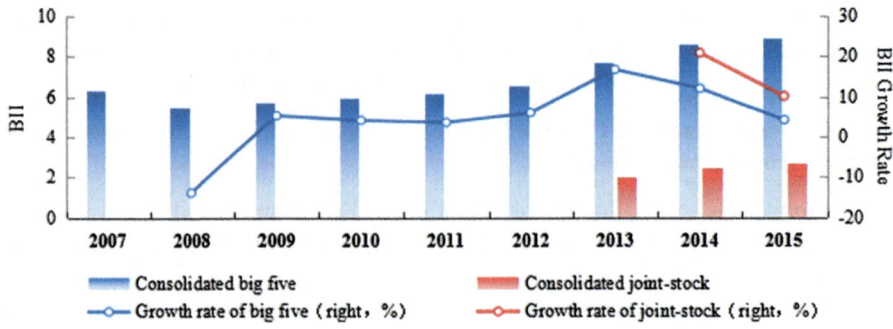

Fig. 2.2 Changes in BII of Chinese banks. *Source* Zhejiang University CIFI

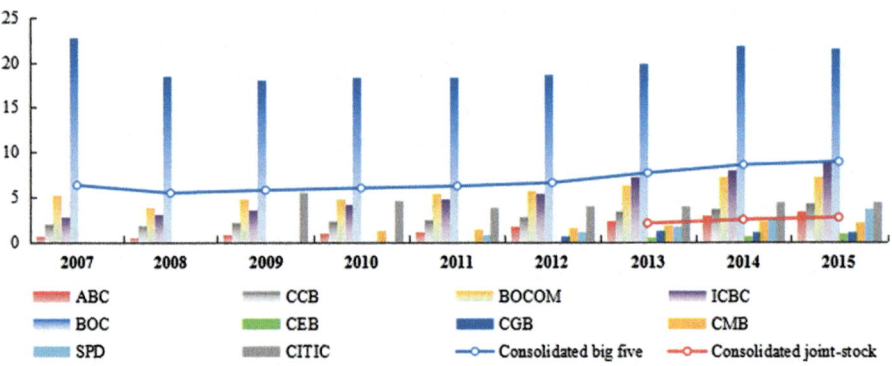

Fig. 2.3 BII of individual Chinese banks. *Source* Zhejiang University CIFI

branches, Chinese banks actively implemented their integrated strategy for overseas business and adopted a unified operating mode by enhancing their capabilities of intermediary businesses such as trading, investing and finance leasing. These intermediary business could effectively make up narrowing interest margins and enabled banks to pro-actively cater for client's future requirements. Although these strategies essentially enhanced Chinese banks' competitiveness in international market and improved their service quality for overseas clients, such transformation and service upgrade would be a long time and impose various challenges and hurdles to Chinese banks. Along with the large gap between Chinese banks and top international banks in their competitiveness in intermediary business, it was expected to see a slowed development pace in Chinese banks' internationalization during this business transformation compared to the earlier stage.

(2) The BII of China's Big Five Banks Diversified, and Joint-Stock Banks Caught Up in Globalization

The gap in BII between China's big five banks and joint-stock banks had been narrowing and the development pattern of Chinese banks' internationalization would be more balanced.

BOC, ICBC and BOCOM were the top three members among China's Big Five Banks who maintained their leading positions in globalization (see Table 2.1). Specifically, BOC demonstrated the highest level in internationalization with the average BII of 19.76 from 2007 to 2015. Although the BII of BOC in 2015 dropped 1.0% to 21.57 compared to 2014, its BII was still 2.4 times higher than the consolidated BII (8.90) of China's Big Five Banks. This decline in BOC's BII was mainly due to the proportion of foreign assets, foreign deposits and foreign loans dropped compared to 2014, which was not significant and could be influenced by the internal and external economic environment as well as its own adjustments on business strategies on international markets. ICBC was the runner-up with its BII of 8.94 and gained a substantial increase of 11.5% compared to 2014. This was the first time that ICBC achieved a BII above the consolidated level since 2007 showing an outstanding growth trend. In particular, out of its eight indicators for BII, only one indicator, proportion of foreign deposits, decreased in 2015. BOCOM took the third place with its BII of 7.15 and a slight decline of 0.8%. Meanwhile, although CCB and ABC only ranked fifth and seventh, which lagged behind CITIC and SPDB respectively, their annual growth rates in BII were up to 17.7 and 19.9% in 2015. Both banks remained strong in internationalization development and their active adjustment of international strategy resulted in the acceleration of their overseas expansion. Take CCB for example, since its adjustments on business strategies in 2006, CCB had started to focus on the wholesale and retail banking

Table 2.1   Ranking of 2015 Chinese banks' BII

Ranking	Chinese banks	2015 BII	2014 BII	Rate of change (%)
1	BOC	21.57 ↓	21.79	−1.0
2	ICBC	8.94 ↑	8.02	11.5
3	BOCOM	7.15 ↓	7.21	−0.8
4	CITIC	4.36 ↓	4.51	−3.3
5	CCB	4.33 ↑	3.68	17.7
6	SPDB	3.66 ↑	2.43	50.5
7	ABC	3.41 ↑	2.85	19.9
8	CMB	2.11 ↓	2.24	−6.0
9	CGB	1.12 ↓	1.15	−2.5
10	CEB	0.87 ↑	0.64	35.4
	Consolidated China's big five banks	8.90 ↑	8.54	4.1
	Consolidated five joint-stock banks	2.70 ↑	2.45	10.1

Source Zhejiang University CIFI

business, develop both loan and intermediary business for profit generation, and accelerated its expansion of overseas business.

The international strategy of China's Big Five Banks was clear. Although certain banks had their BII decreased while others' BII increased in 2015, the scale expansion and business development in their overseas business was continuously pushed forward. On one hand, with RMB joining the Special Drawing Rights (SDR) basket and the internationalization of RMB, banks actively sought for obtaining qualification as offshore RMB clearing bank. On the other hand, China's Big Five Banks made full use of their advantages in business scale and branding. They acted as underwriter for issuance of overseas RMB bonds and enhanced the diversification of their business while further expanding their international operations.

Ranking of joint-stock banks in BII overlapped with China's Big Five Banks, reflecting that a few joint-stock banks caught up with the Five Banks in internationalization by maintaining great developing trends and achieving outstanding performance. Among them, CITIC and SPDB ranked fourth and sixth respectively with their BII of 4.36 and 3.66 in 2015, which were at the same level of ABC and CCB. In addition, BII of these 2 banks were respectively 1.6 times and 1.4 times higher than the consolidated BII of joint-stock banks. CMB, CGB and CEB ranked eighth, ninth and tenth respectively with BII of 2.11, 1.12 and 0.87. The overall growth rate in BII for joint-stock banks declined from 20.7% in 2014 to 10.1% in 2015. Among them, the drop in BII of CITIC, CMB and CGB reached up to 3.3, 6.0 and 2.5% respectively, which were much higher than decline in BOC and BOCOM. SPDB and CGB achieved an outstanding growth rate in BII up to 35% in 2015 and their indicators, including proportion of foreign deposits, foreign loans and foreign profits, all substantially rose. From this, we can see as the business scale of the joint-stock banks was relatively small, their stability of BII was weaker and hence diversified greatly. Moreover, the overseas development of most joint-stock banks was still at a preliminary stage, thus they are way behind of China's Big Five Banks in terms of the steadiness in overseas business strategies and performances.

Besides, other joint-stock banks not included in BII system also attempted to explore opportunities and promoted themselves actively in overseas market. Take China Zheshang Bank Co., Ltd. (CZB) for example. CZB, a joint-stock bank headquartered in Hangzhou, was listed in the Hong Kong Stock Exchange on March 30, 2016. Its listing at overseas stock market made more overseas investors know CZB, which laid a good foundation for its overseas business expansion.

(3) **Internationalization Indicators Varied a Lot and the Business Structure Need to Be Strengthened**

This report used various indicators to estimate BII, and the different indicators of Chinese banks reflected some features of their internationalization.

In the aspect of indicators of these two types (see Fig. 2.4), the proportion of countries, foreign assets and foreign loans of China's Big Five Banks were more outstanding, which were all above 10%. Among them, the number of countries was

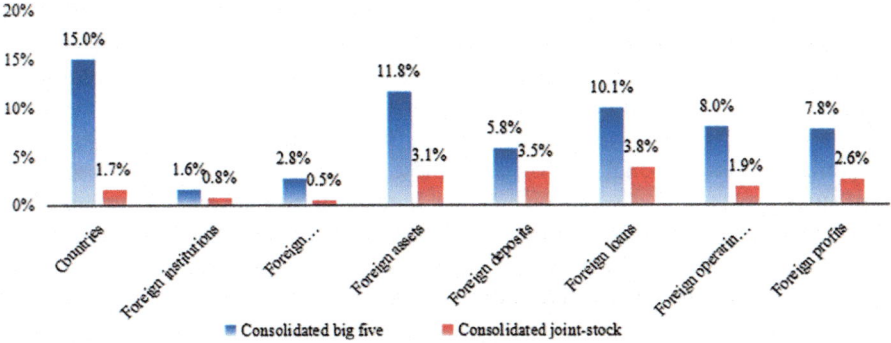

Fig. 2.4 2015 Detail information of BII of Chinese banks. (All data was proportion for overseas indicators.) *Source* Zhejiang University CIFI, annual reports of each bank

particularly prominent in stark contrast to the number of overseas institutions. It meant that although China's Big Five Banks established branches in many countries, the number of institutions in each country was usually only one or two, and thus their ability to attract local clients was limited. For joint-stock banks, they had better performance in the proportion of foreign deposits and loans, which continued to play a key role in their overseas business.

In the aspect of time period, the changes experienced by these two types of banks were quite different (see Table 2.2). On one hand, most of the indicators of China's Big Five Banks maintained growth. Among them, the number of countries where institutions located increased rapidly, which reflected their ability to strengthen the horizontal expansion of internationalization. At the same time, the proportion of foreign profits greatly increased by 0.7%, which meant that the profitability of overseas business was improved. On the other hand, each indicator of the joint-stock banks performed differently. The establishment and expansion of

Table 2.2 Historical changes in BII of Chinese banks (%)

	Consolidated China's big five banks		Consolidated joint-stock banks	
Indicator	2014	2015	2014	2015
Proportion of countries	13.7	15.0 ↑	1.6	1.7 ↑
Proportion of overseas institutions	1.5	1.6 ↑	1.0	0.8 ↓
Proportion of overseas employment	2.5	2.8 ↑	0.5	0.5
Proportion of overseas assets	11.6	11.8 ↑	2.8	3.1 ↑
Proportion of overseas deposits	5.9	5.8 ↓	2.8	3.5 ↑
Proportion of overseas loans	10.0	10.1 ↑	3.2	3.8 ↑
Proportion of overseas revenue	7.3	8.0 ↑	1.9	1.9
Proportion of overseas profits	7.5	7.8 ↑	2.7	2.6 ↓

Source Zhejiang University CIFI, annual reports of each bank

institutions in 2015 was equal to that in 2014. However, the proportion of foreign deposits and loans increased greatly, reflecting the attention and expansion of overseas business for joint-stock banks. The proportion of foreign revenues and profits was still low with no significant changes compared to 2014. It is clear that overseas business did not play a key role in their current development.

Comparing the two major types of Chinese banks, China's Big Five Banks and joint-stock banks, China's Big Five Banks had significant advantages in a number of countries where institutions were located, the proportion of overseas assets and operating performance. In addition, they had richer experience in internationalization. These showed that China's Big Five Banks had more powerful capabilities in expanding their overseas networks, accumulating assets and operating internationally.

2.1.2 The Scale of Overseas Business Continued to Expand with Increasingly Diversified Services

Overall, the scale and expansion of Chinese banks' overseas business maintained a high speed of growth compared to 2014 and achieved a breakthrough in total amount.

(1) **Business Scale Maintained a Steady Growth and BOC Made Up Half of China's Big Five Banks' Overseas Assets**

Compared to 2014, Chinese banks' internationalization further developed with growing overseas assets and profits. By the end of 2015, the total overseas assets of China's Big Five Banks were 9.87 trillion yuan with a growth rate of 14.2%. Overseas assets contributed 11.8% of their total assets. Among them, BOC stood strong with its 4.83 trillion yuan overseas assets, accounting for 48.9% of all China's Big Five Banks. ICBC also reached 2.45 trillion yuan in its overseas assets, which made up a quarter of total overseas assets of China's Big Five Banks.

As for business performance in overseas markets, the total amount of China's Big Five Banks' overseas revenues in 2015 was 201.69 billion yuan with an increase of 17%. The proportion of overseas revenue rose up to 8% of total operating revenue for China's Big Five Banks. For the first time, their total overseas profits exceeded 100 billion yuan with an increase of 6.7%, which made up 7.8% of the total profits from domestic and foreign markets. Although the proportion of overseas revenues and profits was still lower when comparing to the proportion of overseas assets, the profitability in overseas business kept growing with strengthened internationalization level. Being at preliminary stage of globalization, BOC took the lead over other Chinese banks with its outstanding developments in overseas markets. Meanwhile, other banks actively tried to catch up with BOC, among which, ABC achieved an overseas profits of over 50 billion yuan for the first time in 2015 with a stunning growth rate of over 30% (Fig. 2.5).

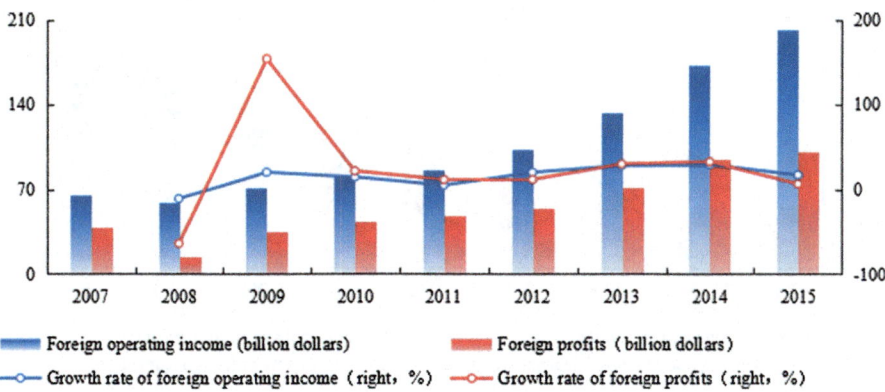

Fig. 2.5 Overseas operating performance of China's big five banks. *Source* Zhejiang University CIFI, annual reports of each bank

The overseas development of the joint-stock banks was also noticeable. CITIC outperformed among all joint-stock banks, in which its overseas assets reached 241.4 billion yuan in 2015 and accounted for 4.7% of its total assets. The overseas revenues and profits of CITIC respectively achieved a record of over 5 and 2.21 billion yuan in 2015. Another joint-stock bank with equally good performance in internationalization is CMB, of which the overseas profits amounted to nearly 1.8 billion yuan and the overseas assets were worth 142.2 billion yuan with a growth rate of 12%.

(2) **Diversification in Overseas Business Enhanced and Integrated Operation Model Promoted**

Generally speaking, during the early stage of international development, banks paid more attention to support their domestic companies going global and provide financing support to multinational corporations. Gradually, their offering of global business grew more comprehensive and serving capabilities were strengthened.

The total overseas deposits of China's Big Five Banks were nearly 3.5 trillion yuan by the end of 2015 with an increase of 5.1%. Their total overseas loans grew to 4.5 trillion yuan at 9.9%. Accordingly, their overseas loan-to-deposit ratio was 128%. By analyzing the development trend of the overseas deposits and loans (see Fig. 2.6) for China's Big Five Banks, it demonstrated that the growth rate of loan business was significantly more prominent by surpassing the deposit amount from 2010. In addition, the faster growth in overseas loans reflected that financing needs from Chinese companies during their globalization substantially increased. Financing support from Chinese banks to these companies became essential.

In order to embrace the trend of establishing integrated business model worldwide, Chinese banks have also put more focus on building an internationally diversified business platform. Firstly, international settlement business for most Chinese Banks experienced substantial growth. In 2015, the international settlement

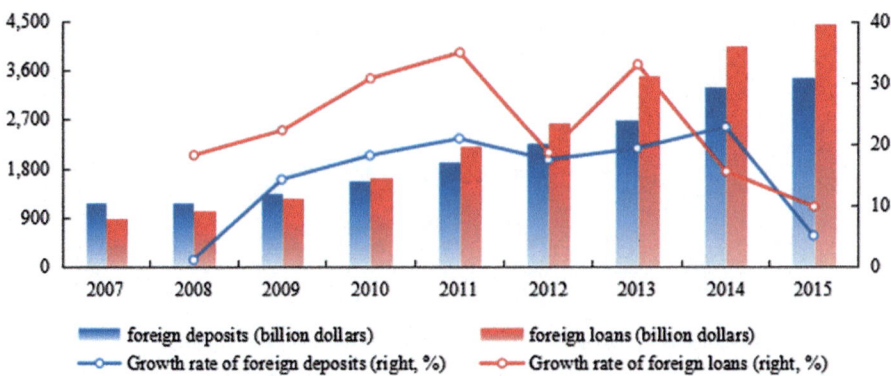

Fig. 2.6 Overseas deposits and loans of China's big five banks. *Source* Zhejiang University CIFI, annual reports of each bank

amount of ICBC was $2.6 trillion and its total cross-border RMB business was 4.41 trillion yuan. Intermediary business has become the new growth point for the whole industry. On February 1, 2015, ICBC successfully acquired 60% stake in Standard Bank Plc, which would facilitate ICBC to build up a global trading platform. Standard Bank Plc possessed category 2 membership in the London Metal Exchange (LME), which is the largest futures and options market of base metals market globally. Also, its matured industry experience and outstanding qualifications in the trading business were also attractive for ICBC to acquire Standard Bank Plc. Along with the completion of this acquisition, ICBC would be able to provide transaction services with underlying assets including commodities, foreign currency, interest rates, credit, equity, etc. through its global network, which increased its service capabilities in the area of international trading. On August 7, 2015, the China Insurance Regulatory Commission (CIRC) officially approved BOC's acquisition of a 51% stake in Samsung Air China Life Insurance Co., Ltd. through its subsidiary, BOC Insurance Co., Ltd. Subsequently, on October 21, BOC-Samsung Life Insurance Co., Ltd. was officially founded. This acquisition was a substantial move by BOC to deepen its comprehensive business strategies and also facilitate BOC to better plan its insurance business distribution in PRC Mainland, Hong Kong SAR and Macao SAR of China as a whole. Other Chinese banks also actively upgraded and diversified their global business. BOCOM continued to promote business by extending overseas business networks and selected Hong Kong SAR of China to establish the business sub-center of asset custody, global market and asset management. CCB achieved a breakthrough in its RMB clearing network establishment, by obtaining the qualification of RMB clearing bank in Switzerland and Chile besides the United Kingdom. ABC also furthered its development of a cross-border comprehensive business model for investment banking, funds, insurance, leasing and so on. In addition, CTBC's equity investments in CITIC Investment Co., Ltd. also facilitated CITIC to build up a full-license platform for overseas investment banking.

As an important player in Chinese banking industry, city commercial banks emerged in the 1980s with their predecessor as urban credit cooperatives and have grew together with the Chinese financial system. By the end of 2015, the total assets of 133 city commercial banks reached 22.7 trillion yuan, accounting for 11.4% of whole banking institutions. Most existing city banks were still small in business scale and their business development was limited by geographical restrictions. However, with the openness of China's financial markets continuing to improve and the related policies more relaxed in recent years, a few city commercial banks have made attempts to expand their overseas business and have achieved some progress.

Column 1 The International Status of the Bank of Shanghai

The Bank of Shanghai (BOSH), founded in 1995, adhered to its strategies by forming a unique business model with different focus cross regions and positioned itself as providing the "best financial service platform covering the Mainland, Hong Kong SAR and Taiwan." By the end of 2015, BOSH's exchange assets amounted to $9.3 billion at a growth rate of 12%, and its total amount of international settlements was $105.1 billion with an increase of 40%. In addition, BOSH maintained its role as an agency bank for over 1500 domestic and overseas banks and their affiliated agencies in more than 120 countries and regions.

BOSH's wholly-owned subsidiary, Bank of Shanghai (Hong Kong) Co., Ltd., specializes in providing high-quality cross-border financial services to Chinese companies during their globalization. Its deposit amounted to 7.915 billion HK Dollars by 2015 and the amount of loans reached 7.95 billion HK Dollars.

By being the frontier among Chinese city commercial banks, BOSH utilized its geographical advantages and actively expanded overseas through its Hong Kong subsidiary. With the internationalization trend of the RMB intensifying, BOSH responded positively by continuously promoting its branding globally, participating in international financial markets and exploring new areas of profit generation.

2.1.3 Global Coverage Achieved and Higher Focus on "The Belt and Road" Initiatives

The overseas distribution of Chinese banks relies on China's Big Five Banks as the main force, which covers nearly 50 major countries in Asia, Europe, North America, Latin America, Oceania and Africa (see Fig. 2.7). The joint-stock banks chose Hong Kong SAR, Macao SAR, Taiwan and parts of Southeast Asia as their main platform for international business development.

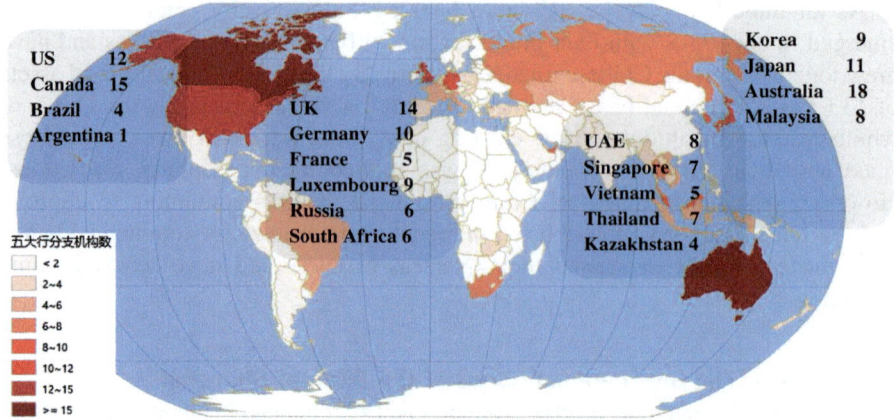

US   12
Canada   15
Brazil   4
Argentina 1

UK   14
Germany   10
France   5
Luxembourg 9
Russia   6
South Africa 6

Korea   9
Japan   11
Australia 18
Malaysia   8

UAE   8
Singapore   7
Vietnam   5
Thailand   7
Kazakhstan 4

五大行分支机构数
<2
2~4
4~6
6~8
8~10
10~12
12~15
>= 15

Fig. 2.7 The distribution of China's big five banks' overseas institutions. (The data in the figure represents overseas branches, subsidiaries and representative offices.) *Source* Zhejiang University CIFI, annual reports of each bank

Among all China's Big Five Banks, BOC and ICBC dominated in terms of the number of overseas network and covered countries. BOC had 644 overseas branches and subsidiaries by 2015 with 14 established after 2014, covering 47 countries and regions including new places such as Laos, Myanmar and the Czech Republic. In June 2015, BOC opened a branch in Durban, which became its second branch in South Africa. BOC also established a new branch in Morocco and entered the local market. By the end of 2015, the number of overseas branches and subsidiaries of ICBC reached 404 with a growth rate of nearly 20% compared to 2014. ICBC had gained presence in 43 countries and regions by setting up business network and in June 2015, its Riyadh branch in Saudi Arabia was officially established and opened for business.

From perspective of geographic layout, China's Big Five Banks all follow the strategy "from Near to Far; from the Developed Countries to Developing Countries" when planning their overseas network path. Hence, the number of overseas branches in Asian countries is much larger than other regions (see Table 2.3). By the end of 2015, the proportion of overseas network in Eurasia accounted for 71.3%, nearly three-quarters of all countries. Also, the proportion of branch network in Asia was already 44.4%. Overall, BOC was still solid in its leading position in internationalization and its overseas branches accounted for more than half of all China's Big Five Banks combined.

Meanwhile, China's Big Five Banks continued to enhance their distribution in "the Belt and Road" countries. Chinese banks accelerated their establishment of new branches in "the Belt and Road" countries. In 2015, BOC set up five branches in Southeast Asia along the "Maritime Silk Road". Among them, 3 new branches were opened in Thailand while others were in Laos and Myanmar. Furthermore, the financial industry along the Silk Road and Eurasia was in full swing. CCB also

Table 2.3 Chinese banks' overseas distribution by the end of 2015[a]

2015	BOC	ICBC	CCB	ABC	BOCOM	Total	Proportion (%)
Asia	51 ↑	23 ↑	12	9 ↑	9	104	44.4 ↓
Europe	31 ↑	14 ↑	10 ↑	5	3 ↑	63	26.9 ↑
North America	19	5	2	2	3	31	13.2 ↓
Oceania	11	2	4	1	2 ↑	20	8.5 ↓
Latin America	2	3	1	0	0	6	2.6 ↓
Africa	6 ↑	2	2 ↑	0	0	10	4.3 ↑
Total	120	49	31	17	17	234 ↑	
Proportion (%)	51.3 ↓	20.9 ↓	13.2 ↑	7.3 ↓	7.3 ↑		
2014	BOC	ICBC	CCB	ABC	BOCOM	Total	Proportion (%)
Asia	46	22	12	8	9	97	45.3
Europe	29	12	5	5	2	53	24.8
North America	19	5	2	2	3	31	14.5
Oceania	11	2	4	1	1	19	8.9
Latin America	2	3	1	0	0	6	2.8
Africa	5	2	1	0	0	8	3.07
Total	112	46	25	16	15	214	
Proportion (%)	52.3	21.5	11.7	7.5	7.0		

[a]The data in the table represents overseas branches, subsidiaries and representative offices
Source Zhejiang University CIFI, official websites and annual reports of each bank

established five new branches in Europe, including UK, France, Spain, Italy and Netherlands. Chinese banks actively explored markets of the "Belt and Road" countries and regions by leveraging with various financial instruments to enrich their product offerings as well as providing financing support to large infrastructure projects. BOC issued the "the Belt and Road" bond in RMB, USD, EUR and SGD currency through its subsidiaries in Abu Dhabi, Hungary, Singapore, Taipei and Hong Kong SAR of China. The total underwriting amount of this bond reached $4 billion.

In addition, joint-stock banks had a stronger presence in overseas countries as well. CITIC Bank International Limited, a wholly-owned subsidiary of CITIC Bank, had branches in Hong Kong, Macao, New York, and Los Angeles, Singapore and so on. CMB also had several branches and representative offices in Hong Kong, US, Singapore, London, Taipei and Luxembourg, together with 1963 domestic and overseas agency banks in 111 countries and regions. China Zheshang Bank Co., Ltd. was successfully listed in the Hong Kong Stock Exchange on March 3, 2016.

2.1.4 Human Resources Was Better Structured and Talent Training Was Significantly Strengthened

Given the fact that banks do not specifically disclose the education level of their overseas employees, we can see from Table 2.4 that the overall level of academic qualifications was increasing. Among the 9 Chinese banks selected in our study, employees with the bachelor's degree or above in the joint-stock banks accounted for over 80% of all employees and this proportion was higher than China's Big Five Banks. China's Big Five Banks being lower in their employees' education level may be due to their huge staff base and competitive recruitment mechanisms. However, by offering a broader platform for career development, China's Big Five Banks are very attractive to high-end financial talents. The number of employees with higher education level in big five banks grew faster than that in joint-stock banks.

Internal training and re-education programs are also important ways to cultivate talents. Financial practitioners have high demands for relevant knowledge in order to keep themselves updated and well equipped. Training programs provided by banks are specifically conducted to achieve their business strategies, in order to make a more positive impact on the development of banks and enhance its competitiveness. In 2015, Chinese banks combined their talents developments with the current economic situation and policy. BOC offered training programs with focus on the "the Belt and Road" Initiatives, free trade zone, RMB internationalization, global financial services and others. BOCOM built a talent team of more than 1100 experts and hired over 70 international talents. CCB organized several on-site and online training sessions, which were mainly about internationalization and emerging business transformations. Joint-stock banks like CITIC and CMB actively enhanced their training for international talents with eyes on the future.

Table 2.4 2015 Ranking of Chinese banks in human resource structure

Ranking	Name of bank	Bachelor or above (%)	Growth rate (%)
1	CITIC	84.31↓	−2.7
2	CMB	82.78↓	−2.0
3	CEB	80.88↑	2.5
4	SPD	80.06	0.0
5	BOCOM	78.24↑	3.3
6	BOC	69.89↑	2.6
7	CCB	62.69↑	3.7
8	ICBC	53.60↑	3.5
9	ABC	47.20↑	4.2

Source Zhejiang University CIFI, annual reports of each bank

2.1.5 International Influence Was Strengthened and Global Recognition Was Achieved as G-SIBs Banks

Internationalization level for banks is not only reflected in their proactive strategies in overseas expansion and participation in various international projects, but also in the recognition of their international influences.

In order to avoid the recurrence of financial crisis, the Financial Stability Board (FSB) and Basel Committee on Banking Supervision (BCBS) announced the first list of Global Systemically Important Banks (G-SIBs) in 2011. This list imposed different supplementary capital requirements from 1.0 to 3.5% based on the significance of different banks (see Table 2.5). This first G-SIBs list chose 28 banks, including BOC, which achieved the highest level of internationalization among the Chinese banks. Subsequently, along with further development of Chinese banks and continuous adaptation of G-SIBs, another 3 China's banks became qualified as G-SIBs: ICBC, ABC and CCB. G-SIBs list is a comprehensive evaluation system adopted by global banking regulators to assess major banks' systemic importance. Hence, being included in this list shows Chinese banks' international influence being recognized, which is an objective evaluation of their achievements in internationalization.

It should be noted that the additional capital requirements for G-SIBs are divided into five tiers. However, no banks have been selected for the highest tier with additional capital requirement of 3.5%. All 4 Chinese banks were categorized in Tier 1 with an additional capital requirement of 1%. As can be seen from Table 2.5, Tier 1 had the largest number of banks, accounting for 63.3% of the whole list. There were 11 banks from Tier 2 to Tier 4, including top global banks such as HSBC, JPMorgan Chase and Citigroup. Thus, though being included in G-SIBs list, these 4 Chinese banks still had a long way to go compared to these top overseas banks with many years of experiences in international market and the international influence of Chinese banks was still limited.

2.1.6 Risk Events Occurred, and Robust Risk Management Is Critical for Banks' Success in Internationalization

Although the international development of Chinese banks is universally recognized, an unfamiliar business environment, international competitors and different legal and culture environment make the development in overseas countries more challenging and could cause various risks. Since the early 21st century, the Chinese banks experienced many challenges in their global expansion including operational risk, market risk, legal risk, political risk and so on. In 2002, BOC New York Branch was fined by the US Office of the Comptroller of the Currency (OCC) and PBOC over a loan fraud case. In 2007, China Development Bank's $2.2 billion investment in Barclays lost 50% in value within 1 year. From 2007 to 2009, after

Table 2.5 2015 Basic information of G-SIBs

Tier	Additional capital requirement (%)	Number of banks	Proportion (%)
5	3.5	0	
4	2.5	2	6.7
3	2.0	4	13.3
2	1.5	5	16.7
1	1.0	19	63.3
Total		30	100.0

Source Zhejiang University CIFI, FSB

two attempts to acquire UCBH Holdings Inc., CMB was eventually declined by the American authorities. In 2016, executives of ICBC Madrid Branch were accused of money laundering. These various types of risk events tested the capability of Chinese banks' international risk management.

It was frequently reported in the media that financial institutions suffered great losses, lawsuit or penalties due to all kinds of risk incidents. Due to the complexity of global economy and high frequency in financial activities, even large multinational financial groups with strong position in market competition faced the same challenges when expanding their overseas business. During the wave of multinational operations in the 20th century, many overseas banks were forced to adjust their business strategies and even went bankrupt. Since Chinese banks are lack of operational experience and resources in foreign countries, they are more vulnerable to risks during their international expansion (Table 2.6).

Firstly, Chinese banks are enthusiastic about going global, however, they are often stuck in the dilemma due to lack of strategic planning and ignorance of risk management. Secondly, operational loopholes in overseas business, weak risk control systems and inadequate internal control make banks more difficult to respond to irregular operations in a timely manner. Thirdly, when facing different political, legal and cultural environments, Chinese banks who were used to domestic business often underestimate the compliance risks in their international operations with weak consciousness in legal and regulations. For example, BOC was accused of helping clients evade tax by the US government in 2003. BOC paid $5.25 million for settlement and this incident was concluded with an "out-of-court settlement". In 2012, ICBC's acquisition of the Bank of East Asia led to a demonstration by the All-America Asian Union, as the acquisition involved discrimination against minority communities and resulted in an adverse social impact. Finally, overseas banking regulators incline to closely supervise Chinese banks, given the fact that Chinese banks are normally weaker in risk management compared to their business scale and lack of experience in international operation.

According to ranking of Top 1000 World Banks published by *The Banker* magazine in 2015, Chinese banks performed well in terms of Tier 1 capital. Among top 20 banks, ICBC and CCB ranked 1st and 2nd respectively while BOC, ABC and BOCOM ranked 7th, 9th and 19th. However, with aspect of comprehensive

Table 2.6 Number of cases and the amount of fine that American financial giants suffered (number of cases, million US Dollars)[a]

Year	JPMorgan Chase		Citigroup		Goldman Sachs	
	Case	Amount	Case	Amount	Case	Amount
2008	1	25	5	1811	2	34
2009	4	76	4	5	3	65
2010	2	49	4	77	3	578
2011	3	453	3	286	2	20
2012	9	806	11	793	9	107
2013	6	15,709	6	1650	2	660
2014	4	2884	4	8211	4	583
Total	29	20,001	37	12,834	25	1551
Year	Bank of America		Wells Fargo		Total	
	Case	Amount	Case	Amount	Case	Amount
2008	0	0	0	0	8	1870
2009	1	33	2	42	14	220
2010	5	995	4	463	18	1666
2011	5	9580	9	1074	22	12,088
2012	5	2972	6	342	40	5021
2013	9	15,172	3	2846	26	36,036
2014	3	26,627	1	625	16	38,930
Total	28	55,379	25	6067	144	95,832

[a]The table didn't include penalties shared by several financial institutions
Source Zhejiang University CIFI, *THE BIG RESET: War on the Gold and the Financial Endgame*

strength, although Chinese banks are large in business scale, they are short of high-end financial talents and hence weak in financial innovation, risk control and internal management. In addition, as the domestic financial market and the related policies are still inadequate, Chinese banks do not have strong legal awareness while the overseas legal system is much tougher. Besides, after the financial crisis, international financial supervision has been steadily strengthened and protectionism has been escalating in various countries. Chinese banks are more likely to become the focus of overseas banking regulators. This inevitably becomes a major risk and disadvantage for Chinese banks' internationalization and must be considered.

2.2 Status of Chinese Development Banks' Internationalization

During 2015, Chinese development banks'[3] financial support for the "the Belt and Road" Initiatives was significantly strengthened. Many institutions, in accordance with their own development strategies, provided financial support to various large cooperation projects. Besides signing several multilateral and bilateral cooperation agreements, in the domestic market, China Development Bank (CDB) facilities significant provinces and cities along "the Belt and Road" Initiatives. CDB also supported construction of "the Silk Road Economic Belt" in Shanxi and the "21st-Century Maritime Silk Road" area in Fujian. The Export-Import Bank of China (China EXIM Bank) provided various loans to related projects including the China-Laos railway project and China-Pakistan Economic Corridor. Asian Infrastructure Investment Bank (AIIB), which is led by China, aims to promote inter-connectivity and economic integration in the Asia region, with its investment focused on energy and power, transportation and telecommunications, agricultural development and urban development. AIIB adopted the Silk Road Economic Belt as its first-phase investment objectives, such as the Beijing-Baghdad railway project which mainly covered Tajikistan, Pakistan, Indonesia and Bangladesh.

2.2.1 China Development Bank Plays an Important Role in Global Development Financing

With its development strategies to "build a world-class development financial institution and support the sustainability of economy and society development", the internationalization of China Development Bank (CDB) is mainly shown in the expansion of its overseas business (see Table 2.7), support for large international projects, and its cooperation with top global institutions.

Firstly, during its internationalization, CDB expanded its overseas network by opening branches. By the end of 2015, with the addition of the London Representative Office, the CDB's overseas distribution had matured by having one offshore branch in Hong Kong and five representative offices in Egypt, Russia, Brazil, Venezuela and the UK. In addition, CDB entered into an agency relationship with 747 banks from 104 countries and regions.

Secondly, CDB facilitated Chinese companies in expanding their overseas operations and RMB internationalization by providing various cross-board

---

[3]In this report Chinese development banks mainly consist of 3 policy banks (Export-Import Bank of China, Agricultural development Bank of China and China Development Bank) and 2 international development financial organization leading by China (New Development Bank and Asian Infrastructure Investment Bank). And since Agricultural development Bank of China was less involved in international business, we did not analyze it specifically.

Table 2.7   Overseas operating information of CDB

	(Up to) 2015 (million yuan)	(Up to) 2014 (million yuan)	Growth rate (%)
Net profits	48,915	43,501	12.4
Non-current assets	39,005	25,503	52.9
Long term investments	63	5	1160
Financial assets	1,397,453	1,057,792	32.1

Source Zhejiang University CIFI, annual report of CDB

financing loans. As the CDB continued to maintain its leading role in funding China's foreign investment and financing, the balance of CDB's foreign currency-denominated loans amounted to $276 billion by the end of 2015, and the balance of its offshore RMB loans reached 69 billion yuan. In its overseas development during 2015, by standing firms on its commitment to support the "the Belt and Road" Initiatives, CDB extended $14.9 billion loans to fund the Sino-Russian and Oil and Gas Cooperation project, Sino-Turkmenistan Gas Cooperation project and many other Chinese enterprises' M&A projects. In addition, CDB focused on countries along the "the Belt and Road" Initiatives route and organized 37 conferences which attracted 799 foreign participants from these countries.

Finally, through active cooperation with other national financial institutions or international development financial organizations, CDB was able to gather relevant experience and strengthen its international competitiveness. On one hand, CDB furthered its support on domestic companies' growth by leveraging experience learned from these overseas financial institutions on development finance. As early as in 2004, CDB started its cooperation with the World Bank and KfW Bankengruppe. They launched the pilot run of a business model combining technology and fund in micro-business financing. In 2 years, they cumulatively provided over 4000 loans to micro-businesses with an average amount of 50,000 yuan and default rate below 1%. On the other hand, CDB attempted to go global by supporting fund for overseas projects. CDB had a cumulative lending of $206 million to cotton farming, processing and procurement projects in Africa by the end of 2015, among which its subsidiary China-Africa Development Fund invested $31.08 million. CDB also issued $300 million loans to support for Central Asia Energy Company's project to build an 800,000 ton/year Refinery Construction in Kyrgyzstan. This not only symbolized the internationalization of Chinese development institutions, but also showed the significant role they played in promoting local economic development and improving local employment market.

2.2.2   The Export-Import Bank of China Helps Chinese Enterprises Go Global

In 2015, the Export-Import Bank of China (China EXIM Bank) conducted a comprehensive reform on its internal management. With its capital based business management philosophy, China EXIM Bank enhanced its global cooperation and centered its working mechanism on "the Belt and Road" Initiatives. China EXIM Bank proactively built business platforms to boost international industrial capacity and equipment manufacturing cooperation. In addition, it also assisted Chinese companies in expanding their overseas operation and supported multilateral cooperation projects.

China EXIM Bank has accelerated its financing support to Chinese companies in their globalization and promoted various cross-border cooperation projects. In 2015, all of its 4 loan products achieved a growth rate over 10%. And among them the outstanding balance of its loans on overseas development projects increased more than 30%, which demonstrated the great support from China EXIM Bank to development companies or projects which had high degree of openness (Table 2.8).

The internationalization of China EXIM Bank is also its way of actively adapting to China's new normal economic conditions. China EXIM Bank has made great contributions by implementing China's overseas development strategy and promoting China's import and export optimization. In the course of implementing the "the Belt and Road" Initiatives, China EXIM Bank enhanced its cooperation with countries in Central and Eastern Europe, Latin America and Oceania in various fields. It improved the management and operation of its international investment funds and facilitated constructions of railway, highway and regional aviation networks and industrialization in Africa. China EXIM Bank also strongly supported the export of assembled equipment, innovative technologies Chinese products, and "2 owns and 1 high" products.[4] Priority was given to manufacturing and relevant technologies and export of relevant service, so as to help China's shipbuilding and aviation industries to develop independent brands.

In general, compared to CDB's focus on developing financial functions, China EXIM Bank's business is more closely related to openness. In 2015, China EXIM Bank conducted $165.733 billion in international settlement, letters of guarantee and trade finance transactions, thus playing an essential role in stabilizing foreign trade, promoting cross-border investment, advancing RMB internationalization, supporting SMEs business and economic openness.

---

[4]"2 owns and 1 high" refers to products with own copyright, own branding and high value-add.

Table 2.8 Loans from China EXIM Bank

	2015 (billion yuan)	2014 (billion yuan)	Growth rate (%)
Foreign trade loans	891.387	801.294	11.2
International cooperation loans	571.919	465.900	22.8
Overseas investment loans	206.349	167.814	23.0
Overseas development loans	478.522	362.863	31.9

Source Zhejiang University CIFI, annual report of China EXIM Bank

Table 2.9 Basic information of AIIB

Opening date	2015.12.25
Headquarter	Beijing, China
Authorized capital	$100 billion
Governance structure	Board of Governors (the highest decision-making body, one Governor and one Alternate Governor for each member state)
	Board of Directors (12 governors, 9 of them from the Asia-Pacific region and 3 representing members outside the region)
	Senior Management (1 president, 5 vice presidents from China, UK, Germany, India, Korea and Indonesia)
Prospective founding members	57:37 from the Asia-Pacific region, 20 representing members outside the region
Initial investment aspects	Energy and power, transportation and telecommunications, rural infrastructure and agriculture development, urban development and logistics, etc.

Source Zhejiang University CIFI, news reports

2.2.3   Asian Infrastructure Investment Bank Links Asia and Promotes Cooperation

As the first multilateral financial organization initiated by China, Asian Infrastructure Investment Bank (AIIB) aims at promoting inter-connectivity in Asia by supporting infrastructure construction projects. By April 15, 2015, China's initiative of forming AIIB confirmed 57 prospective founding members, including 37 from Asia and 20 outside the Asian region. AIIB started its operation along with the agreement entered into force on December 25, 2015. The five aspects of AIIB's initial investment include energy and power, transportation and telecommunications, rural infrastructure and agriculture development, urban development and logistics (see Table 2.9).

As AIIB was formally established around the end of 2015, its main cooperation projects were carried out in 2016. From June to September in 2016, by cooperating with the World Bank, the European Bank for Reconstruction and Development, the Asian Development Bank and other international financial organizations, AIIB has

Table 2.10 Main projects of AIIB

Time	Location	Cooperation organizations	Content
2016.1.6	Indonesia	World Bank	National Slum Upgrading Project
2016.7.6	Tajikistan	European Bank for Reconstruction and Development (EBRD)	Dushanbe-Uzbekistan Border Road Improvement Project
2016.7.6	Bangladesh	–	Distribution System Upgrade and Expansion Project
2016.7.6	Pakistan	Asian Development Bank (ADB)	National Motorway M-4 (Shorkot-Khanewal Section) Project
2016.7.7	India	–	Transmission System Strengthening Project
2016.7.25	Pakistan	–	Tarbela 5 Hydropower Extension Project
2016.9.5	Kazakhstan	–	Kazakhstan Center South Road Corridor Project

Source Zhejiang University CIFI, official website of AIIB

financed numerous infrastructure projects covering several Asian countries like Indonesia, Tajikistan and India (see Table 2.10).

Unlike Chinese policy banks, AIIB is a regional multilateral financial institution with a higher financing capacity. It is able to provide more financing support to its projects and achieve higher international influence. Moreover, as a China-initiated multilateral financial institution, the operation and development of AIIB demonstrate the power of the Chinese financial industry and the intelligence of Chinese financial talents.

2.2.4 New Development Bank Establishes a Safe Financial Network Among the BRICS States

After the initiative of establishing the New Development Bank (NDB) first proposed in 2012, the BRICS states actively facilitated its establishment. NDB was formally established on July 15, 2014 and opened on July 21, 2015. NDB is headquartered in Shanghai and its first president is K. V. Kamath (see Table 2.11).

According to the *Fortaleza Declaration*, "based on sound banking principles, the NDB will strengthen the cooperation among our countries and will supplement the efforts of multilateral and regional financial institutions for global development" and "with the purpose of mobilizing resources for infrastructure and sustainable development projects in BRICS and other emerging and developing economies." Moreover, building up an integrated financial infrastructure helps improve the efficiency of resources allocation and financial operations among the BRICS states.

Table 2.11 Basic information of NDB

Opening date	2015.7.21		
Headquarters	Shanghai, China		
Initial authorized capital	$100 billion		
Initial members	BRICS States		
Governance structure	B	Brazil	The First Chair of Board of Governors
	R	Russia	The First Chair of Board of Directors
	I	India	The First Elected President
	C	China	Headquarters
	S	South Africa	African Center
Objectives	Facilitate settlements and lending among BRICS states to reduce reliance on the Dollar and the Euro, and effectively protect the capital flows and trade between member States		

Source Zhejiang University CIFI, news reports

At present, NDB is not active in participating multinational projects, as its establishment is aimed at resolving short-term financial crises in BRICS states. As the Contingency Reserve Arrangement has only symbolic meaning, NDB's remediation mechanism is more efficient.

In addition to actively embracing competition from foreign financial institutions as well as learning from them, Chinese banks become more active in going global. Especially, establishing various multilateral and bilateral cooperation agreements shows China's attention and responsibility to the international financial market. China is trying to build a more effective communication mechanism with the world and position itself strongly in the international financial market through international development institutions such as AIIB and NDB.

Chapter 3
Status of Foreign Banks' Internationalization

For a comprehensive understanding of foreign banks' internationalization, this report selected 30 most representative "Global Systemically Important Banks" (G-SIBs) as our research subjects, among which we completed BII calculation and analysis of 16 most representative foreign G-SIBs. Furthermore, this report combined theories on banks' internationalization with case studies for a better analysis of the internationalization history and current situation of foreign banks. This provided valuable references for Chinese banks for their internationalization development. For detailed information of these 16 selected foreign banks for readers' references, the report introduced their basic information in Appendix B.

Evaluation criteria of Global Systemically Important Banks include bank operation scale, interrelations with other banks, importance in certain business or market, activeness in cross-border transactions, global influence, etc. The G-SIBs have extensive impact on the financial system. Sometimes they even bring systematic risks to the global economy, if they suffer major risk incidents or operating failures. Thus, the G-SIBs are regarded as the "stabilizers" in the global banking sector.

Table 3.1 displayed the latest list of G-SIBs in 2015, in which banks were classified into 5 groups according to their supplementary capital requirements. Banks with higher importance are imposed with higher supplementary capital requirements. Among all 30 G-SIBs from 11 countries or regions, 8 banks were from the US, accounting for 26.7%, far ahead of the rest of the countries. China had 4 banks recognized as G-SIBs, accounting for 13.3% of the total number of G-SIBs. China has the same number of G-SIBs as France and the United Kingdom (see Table 3.2).

© Zhejiang University Press and Springer Nature Singapore Pte Ltd. 2018
B. Shenglin et al., *In Pursuit of Presence or Prominence?* Current Chinese Economic Report Series, https://doi.org/10.1007/978-981-10-7730-2_3

Table 3.1 List of G-SIBs

Supplementary capital requirement	G-SIBs	Country
5 (3.5%)	(Empty)	
4 (2.5%)	HSBC	The United Kingdom
	JPMorgan Chase	The United States
3 (2.0%)	Barclays	The United Kingdom
	BNP Paribas	France
	Citigroup	The United States
	Deutsche Bank	Germany
2 (1.5%)	Bank of America	The United States
	Credit Suisse	Switzerland
	Goldman Sachs	The United States
	Mitsubishi UFJ FG	Japan
	Morgan Stanley	The United States
1 (1.0%)	Agricultural Bank of China	China
	Bank of China	China
	Bank of New York Mellon	The United States
	China Construction Bank	China
	Groupe BPCE	France
	Groupe Crédit Agricole	France
	Industrial and Commercial Bank of China	China
	ING Bank	The Netherlands
	Mizuho FG	Japan
	Nordea	Switzerland
	Royal Bank of Scotland	The United Kingdom
	Santander	Spain
	Société Générale	France
	Standard Chartered	The United Kingdom
	State Street	The United States
	Sumitomo Mitsui FG	Japan
	UBS	Switzerland
	UniCredit Group	Italy
	Wells Fargo	The United States

Source Zhejiang University CIFI, FSB

3.1 Foreign Banks Had Overall High BII Level but Slower Growth in Past Decade

In order to have a comprehensive understanding of foreign banks' internationalization level, this report is based on the list of G-SIBs released by Financial Stability Board and selected G-SIBs with relatively more accessible data in order to conduct BII calculation.

3.1.1 Foreign Banks Showed Overall High Level of Internationalization and All Top 8 Banks with Highest BII Ranking Were European Banks

Table 3.3 displayed 16 foreign banks' BII and their rankings over the years, demonstrating the development level of internationalization of these foreign banks which had greater global significance.

Table 3.2 Number of G-SIBs by country

Country	Number of G-SIBs
The United States	8
France	4
The United Kingdom	4
China	4
Japan	3
Switzerland	2
The Netherlands	1
Germany	1
Spain	1
Italy	1
Sweden	1

Source Zhejiang University CIFI

From the table above, foreign banks achieved generally higher internationalization level with their average BII result above 20. And all top 11 foreign banks had their BII above 50 in 2005. Compared to 2014, there were 9 out of 16 foreign banks experienced a drop in their BII, reflecting that the current global economy recovery created pressure for banks' international development.

By examining these banks individually, Standard Chartered Bank ranked top among all 16 foreign banks with its BII of 88.84, which was far higher than Santander who ranked second (76.74 in 2015) and gained a notable growth of 4.7% compared to 2014. The reason behind was associated with the history of Standard Chartered Bank. In 1969, the Standard Bank of British South Africa merged with Chartered Bank of India, Australia and China, and the merged bank became known as Standard Chartered Bank. Since its establishment, Standard Chartered Bank had served the British government for its ambition to colonize the world. With its "internationalization gene", Standard Chartered Bank's international expansion started at an early stage and developed fast with perfect timing.[1] Santander and Nordea, who ranked second and third respectively with their BII of 76.74 and 69.48, showed mild fluctuation compared to 2014. BII of Santander increased by 2.6% while Nordea declined by 3.0%. Although Mitsubishi UFJ FG ranked 12 with its BII of 40.66 in 2015, its growth rate reached as high as 40.6%. The reason could be that Japanese banks were able to sustain strong stability as their financing structure was dominated by deposits. Their rich experiences in dealing with defaulted assets and bad debt ratio were not severely affected by either the 2008 global financial crisis or the deteriorating Japanese economy. Therefore, Japanese banks could actively leverage their advantages and expand their overseas business after the financial crisis. By the end of the first quarter in 2015, the total foreign debt balance of Japanese banks reached $3.53 trillion, ranked top in the world, which exceeded the United States. Over the past five years, Japanese

---

[1]Please refer to Sect. 3.3.1 for the international development route and mode analysis of the Standard Chartered Bank.

Table 3.3 Selected foreign banks' BII ranking[a] in 2015

Ranking	Foreign bank	BII in 2015	BII in 2014	Change (%)
1	Standard Chartered	88.84 ↑	84.83	4.7
2	Santander	76.74 ↑	74.77	2.6
3	Nordea	69.48 ↓	71.64	−3.0
4	ING Bank	67.43 ↓	68.17	−1.1
5	Credit Suisse	65.92 ↑	60.47	9.0
6	HSBC	62.65 ↑	62.16	0.8
7	UBS	55.16 ↓	56.83	−2.9
8	UniCredit Group	54.59 ↓	55.09	−0.9
9	Deutsche Bank	54.22 ↑	53.80	0.8
10	Citigroup	53.58 ↑	53.37	0.4
11	BNP Paribas	52.50 ↓	58.19	−9.8
12	Mitsubishi UFJ FG	40.66 ↑	28.92	40.6
13	Groupe Crédit Agricole	36.16 ↓	36.82	−1.8
14	Bank of New York Mellon	33.98 ↓	34.63	−1.9
15	Mizuho FG	26.02 ↓	26.09	−0.3
16	JPMorgan Chase	20.45 ↓	22.42	−8.8
	Average	53.65 ↑	53.01	1.2

[a]The financial year of Mitsubishi UFJ FG and Mizuho FG is from April 1 to March 31
Source Zhejiang University CIFI

banks' foreign debt balance was on the rise track by $1.12 trillion with the annual compound growth rate of 6.18%, which ranked second in the world and only behind the increment and growth rate of the United States.

We also noticed that banks with headquarters in Europe generally had a higher level of internationalization. Specifically, among the 16 selected banks, there were 11 European banks, 3 American banks and 2 Japanese banks. All 9 banks with highest BII were all from Europe. Financial industry in Europe has been active with a long history. With numerous countries and their close connections, the platform of financial cooperation among the members was established particularly after the establishment of European Union. Even though quite a few European banks have their headquarters located in one European country, their extensive branches in the neighboring countries have enabled them to have overall high level of internationalization.

3.1.2 *Foreign Banks' Internationalization Reached Its Mature Stage and Remained Stable in the Recent Decade*

According to BII for previous years (see Table 3.4), all the 16 selected foreign banks experienced relatively mild fluctuations in their BII, while the BII of most

Table 3.4 BII trend of selected foreign banks

Year	2007	2008	2009	2010	2011	2012	2013	2014	2015	Ranking in 2015
Standard Chartered	–	–	–	–	83.42	81.46	83.79	84.83	88.84	1
Santander	67.65	69.96	72.24	75.53	78.31	77.71	74.84	74.77	76.74	2
Nordea	63.00	72.55	72.30	70.83	70.59	70.06	71.79	71.64	69.48	3
ING Group	68.67	70.46	60.78	67.83	65.09	65.52	63.08	68.17	67.43	4
Credit Suisse	64.61	24.93	60.89	60.53	60.38	52.19	58.97	60.47	65.92	5
HSBC	57.86	48.59	54.39	59.62	60.17	64.4	60.11	62.16	62.65	6
UBS	–	–	76.53	52.12	50.23	76.96	50.4	56.83	55.16	7
UniCredit Group	66.8	60.36	61.3	70.97	71.14	93.44	65.2	55.09	54.59	8
Deutsche Bank	–	–	–	–	–	–	–	53.8	54.22	9
Citigroup	68.31	54.52	60.54	58.46	58.62	57.34	56	53.37	53.58	10
BNP Paribas	–	–	–	–	–	–	–	58.19	52.5	11
Mitsubishi UFJ FG	30.05	−181.57	24.18	28.37	30.77	27.73	32.2	28.92	40.66	12
Groupe Crédit Agricole	–	–	–	–	–	36.94	38.61	36.82	36.16	13
Bank of New York Mellon	35.02	36.19	28.15	35.35	31.72	32.87	33.11	34.63	33.98	14
Mizuho FG	62	15.99	14.23	19.47	20.49	21.06	23.32	26.09	26.02	15
JPMorgan Chase	–	–	–	–	–	–	–	22.42	20.45	16
Average								53.01	53.65	

Source Zhejiang University CIFI, annual reports of banks

banks plunged in 2008 or 2009, which were affected by the global financial crisis in 2008.

These selected foreign banks had quite long history since establishment. Their headquarters are mostly located in countries or regions where financial industry has a long history of development and maintain at an advanced level. After a major wave of internationalization in the 20th century, foreign banks reached their mature stage of internationalization and it became more challenging for them to find new areas of growth. This resulted in a relatively stable trend of their international development. With the growing complexity in the global economy after financial crisis, US economy was still in recovery and European economy suffered frustrations, and emerging economies also faced uncertainties. In this context, many banks chose to adjust their strategies of global asset allocation, optimize their business model, and focus their business in priority countries or regions.

Column 2 Citigroup's "Trend of De-internationalization"

Affected by the global financial crisis, Citigroup slashed its overseas investment since 2009 and the trend of de-internationalization became increasingly notable. Volatility in the financial markets, economy downward pressure, etc., have all led to the contraction of Citigroup's overseas footprint (see Fig. 3.1).

In 2009, Citigroup sold its Japanese brokerage department to Sumitomo Mitsui Financial Group as well as its 64% share of Nikko Asset Management Company to Sumitomo Trust & Banking Company. On December 5th, 2012, Citigroup announced a layoff plan of 11,000 employees worldwide due to its failure to balance the cost and profit for overseas retail banking business. In 2014, Citigroup abandoned its plan of focusing on the "global 150 major cities" and shifted to the 100 cities with the greatest potentials. Citigroup exited from markets including Tokyo, Lima and Panama.[2] In 2015, Citigroup sold its Japanese credit card business to Sumitomo Trust & Banking Company. At the end of February, 2016, Citigroup sold 20% shares of Guangdong Development Bank and ended 10-year partnership with Guangdong Development Bank. Moreover, within the first half of 2016, Citigroup closed 5 branches in China.

Along with its strategies of transformation, Citigroup showed a notable declining trend in internationalization during the recent decade with its BII as 53.58 in 2015, decreased by 11.5% compared to 60.54 in 2009. In 2010, Citigroup had 3200 overseas branches in total and dropped to 2214 overseas institutions in 2015, displaying a noteworthy downtrend by years. The total overseas assets remained relatively stable as $183 billion in 2015 and $192 billion in 2010, which proved that their strategies of closing branches to

---

[2]Some resource was from http://www.huanqiu.com.

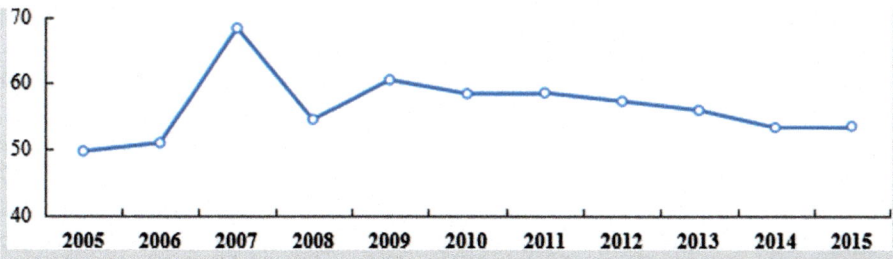

Fig. 3.1 Citigroup's BII. *Source* Zhejiang University CIFI

stabilize assets and income were effective in the short term. However, the negative impact along with network reduction shall not be neglected.

3.2 Factors that Affect Banks' Internationalization in View of BII

With the deepening of economic integration and financial globalization, the internationalization has become an irreversible trend for banks. This report analyzed relevant factors that affect banks' internationalization combining with detailed case studies.

3.2.1 Territory Size and Economy Scale—ING Group

In general, with all other factors being equal, the smaller territory size of the country is, the higher degree of internationalization for their banks will be.

Countries with smaller territory normally face issues of scarce resources, and hence are more inclined to trade with other countries for resources in need. Being the vital part of the national financial system, banks also ask for support in funding and clients. When their potential domestic clients could not meet their financing needs, banks chose to accelerate the pace of internationalization in order to seek for potential clients worldwide.

Moreover, the larger economy scales of a country is, the greater benefits to their banks' international development will be. Domestic market has become the solid foundation to build up the internationalization of commercial banks. The expansion of the national economy scale also attracts more investments. With increasing market size and development potentials, it also brings greater attraction for overseas clients. Meanwhile, banks are more interested in choosing relatively developed economies as their target country for international development. Hence, the scale of national economy expansion would facilitate banks' internationalization progression.

Internationale Nederlanden Groep (ING Group) is a typical case demonstrating such effect from the territory size and economy scale on banks' internationalization. In 1991, the banking business of NMB Postbank Group and the insurance business of Nationale-Nederlanden were merged to form an integrated financial group, ING Group. ING Group has been committed to expand its international market since its establishment (see Table 3.5). In August 2007, ING Group was ranked 81st of the "Global Top 100 Brands" with an estimated value of $388 million.

The territory size of Netherlands is 41,864 km^2, ranked 129th globally. However, according to the BII ranking of foreign banks (see Table 3.4), the BII of Netherlands was as high as 67.43 in 2015. Other banks with comparatively higher BII such as Nordea, Santander, and Standard Chartered Bank are all from countries with relatively smaller territory size. Citigroup with its headquarters located in the US was ranked

Table 3.5 History of ING bank's internationalization

Year	Critical events
1995	Announced to merge with Barings Bank, becoming the first step of its international development
2000	Announced to buy the international and financial service units from Aetna Inc., marking its completion of its integrated financial service system for America and Asia
2005	Announced to acquire 19.9% shares of Bank of Beijing for 1.78 billion yuan at 1.79 yuan per share
2006	ING Bank announced to ABN AMRO's local mutual funds business in Taiwan of China
2007	Acquired Oyak Bank at 1.99 billion Euro ($2.673 billion), which was founded in 1984, and was the 9th largest commercial banks in Turkey with about 360 branches; in the same year, ING Bank acquired 13.11 billion new shares of Thai Soldiers Bank, its holding shares increasing to 30% after the purchase
2008	Acquired Aetna Life Insurance at 15.2 yuan per share
2009	Announced to sell its reinsurance business in the US to the Reinsurance Group of America, as part of its global restructuring plan, it also sold its private banking business in Asia to the OCBC Bank in order to release funds to support this restructuring
2011	Sold its internet banking business in the US to the Capital One Financial Corp. at $9 billion and sold majority of its insurance business in Latin America to Grupo de Inversiones Suramericana SA
2012	ING Asia insurance sold all of its shares of ING Malaysia, transferred 33.3% of China Merchants Fund shares, and sold its insurance business in Hong Kong, Macao and Thailand with value of $2.14 billion
2013	ING announced to sell its life insurance business in Korea to the private equity firm, MBK
2014	ING announced to sell 33.50 million shares of its US branch, after the share transfer, ING's holding of its US branch dropped from 57% by the end of 2013 to 45%

Source Zhejiang University CIFI, ING's annual reports and news

Table 3.6 GDP ranking of major countries or regions worldwide in 2015

GDP ranking	Country	GDP ($ in billion)	GDP rank	Country	GDP ($ in billion)
1	The United States	17,968.195	11	Korea	1392.952
2	China	10,864.877	12	Russia	1311.371
3	Japan	4120.083	13	Australia	1240.803
4	Germany	3358.052	14	Spain	1199.594
5	The United Kingdom	2849.278	15	Mexico	1141.975
6	France	2422.767	16	Indonesia	861.770
7	India	2059.899	17	The Netherlands	752.005
8	Italy	1819.047	18	Turkey	722.219
9	Brazil	1799.612	19	Switzerland	676.979
10	Canada	1572.781	20	Saudi Arabia	653.219

Source Zhejiang University CIFI, IMF

behind most European banks. Hence, we could conclude that a bank's internationalization level had certain correlations with the territory size of the country.

Table 3.6 showed the GDP ranking of selected countries in 2015, among which the Netherlands ranked 17th with its GDP of $752 billion. Compared with its territory size, the Netherlands had comparatively large economy scale and its economic development was far advanced compared to global average level, whilst other banks of top rankings in BII were also from countries with top rankings in GDP. Accordingly, with other factors being equal, banks from countries with larger economy scale had higher level of internationalization.

3.2.2 Level of Development in the Domestic Economy— HSBC

A developed country is a sovereign state that has a highly developed economy, advanced technological infrastructure and higher living standards. Higher level of economic development has become the strong facilitator for the domestic banks' international development.

(1) Developed countries have overall sound economic environment, which facilitate banks' international development. On one hand, developed countries had comparatively matured economic operation mechanism, robust market system and more effective macroeconomic regulation system. These formed a solid basis for their financial development and fastened the advancement of banks' internationalization. On the other hand, when the domestic development of commercial banks reached a certain point, banks have stronger motives to expand their financial services overseas out of their profit-driven nature. The

overall strong economy, highly internationalized financial market, active and stable national economy of developed countries stimulated their banks to further their overseas development.

(2) The governments of developed countries always attach great importance and support to their domestic banks' internationalization. A bank's internationalization does not entirely depend on its own market behavior, but also relies on other non-market factors including international status, discourse power and international relations of its home country. In general, a bank's international operation brings benefit to the improvement of the country's economy and international influence. Hence, the government inclines to introduce policies such as preferential tax in order to encourage and support domestic banks' overseas expansion.

(3) Developed countries have been focused on the cultivation of innovative and international talents. Since the 1990s, developed countries had begun to improve and reform their training models and teaching techniques in order to cultivate international talents. This impressively enhanced the countries' international competitiveness, and also supported and fused financial enterprises' internationalization progression.

In the G-SIBs list, all the foreign banks are from developed countries. It could be seen that the internationalization level of a bank is closely related to the economic development level of a country. HSBC group (Hongkong and Shanghai Banking Corporation, HSBC) built its global business network by relying on the advanced financial system of the UK at the early stage of its development. Now HSBC is still positioned as one of the world's largest financial institutions (see Table 3.7).

The striking achievement that HSBC obtained in the process of internationalization relies greatly on the advanced economy of the UK. As a significant economy power and the world's financial center, the UK is one of the world's most developed countries with most advanced technology and economy as well as its highest living standards. Financial institutions from the UK have been the global leaders with their extensive branch networks all around the world and maintain high proportion of overseas assets. To some extent, these banks gained their advantage of internationalization with benefits from the UK's own development history. In a sense, the British colonial domination had played as stimulator in UK banks' overseas development.

Figure 3.2 showed the GDP per capita in UK and BII of HSBC in recent years. GDP per capita is one of the most commonly used indicators to measure the economic development level of a country. The GDP per capita in UK has been at the forefront in the world and their GDP per capita during past 5 years (2011–2015) was all above $40,000. UK ranked 14th in 2015 with GDP per capita of $43,734. Correspondingly, financial institutions in UK (including HSBC) overall remained a comparatively higher level of internationalization. The BII of HSBC was maintained above 60 in recent 5 years and achieved BII of 62.65 in 2015, ranked 6th among the 16 selected foreign banks. HSBC came up to the 1th and 3rd in overseas deposits   (513.78 million yuan)   and   overseas   loans   (345.51 million yuan)

Table 3.7 History of HSBC's internationalization

Year	Critical events
1865	HSBC was founded in Hong Kong and extended to Shanghai where branches were first opened in the same year, was the first local bank under the principles of Scottish banks
1875	HSBC set up branches in 7 countries and regions in Asia, Europe, North America, etc.
1900	Operation was expanded to 16 countries and regions, and provided financial, foreign exchanges, and commercial banking business worldwide
1959	HSBC acquired Chartered Mercantile Bank of India, London and China and Bank of England Middle East
1992	Established HSBC Holdings Co., Ltd., and acquired Midland Bank
2000	Acquired Credit Commercial de France, changed its name to HSBC France and was listed in Paris Stock Exchange
2002	Acquired Grupo Financiero Bital, changed its name to HSBC Mexico
2004	Acquired Bank of Bermuda and was listed in Bermuda Stock Exchange, purchased 19.9% of the Bank of Communications in the same year
2005	Acquired Metris Inc. and 70.1% of Dar es Salaam Investment Bank of Iraq
2007	Increased its stake in Techcombank of Vietnam from 10 to 20%, and acquired the Chinese Bank in Taiwan
2008	Announced to sell its 18.68% of Financiera Independencia in Mexico and acquired 88.89% of Bank Ekonmi, one of the largest commercial banks in Indonesia. At this point, HSBC had 190 branches and offices in 24 cities of Indonesia, becoming the third largest foreign bank after Standard Chartered Bank and Citigroup
2009	Increased its share of Bao Viet from 10 to 18%, sold its Auto financing department to Santander, and sold the headquarters of HSBC France
2010	Sold 20% common shares and 100% preferred shares of its Wells Fargo HSBC Trade Bank to Wells Fargo
2011	Announced that HSBC sold its general insurance business including Assicurazioni Generali and AXA
2013	HSBC sold HSBC Panama to the largest bank in Colombia at $2.1 billion
2015	Announced that HSBC sold all its business in Brazil to Banco do Estado de Sao Paulo S.A., strengthened its presence in Asia with the intention to restructure its global branches and optimize the asset structure

Source Zhejiang University CIFI, HSBC's annual reports and news

respectively.[3] Figure 3.2 displayed that the BII trend of HSBC was roughly consistent with the GDP per capita trend in UK in recent years. Thus, the internationalization level of a bank is proven to have certain correlations with the economic development level of its home country.

---

[3]For convenience of analysis, this report converted USD to RMB for rankings of domestic and foreign banks. Please see Tables 4.5 and 4.6 for deposits and loans ranking.

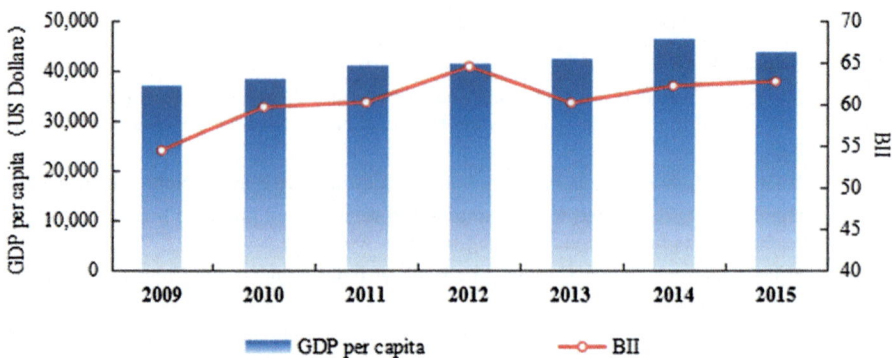

Fig. 3.2 GDP per capita in UK and BII of HSBC. *Source* Zhejiang University CIFI, the World Bank

3.2.3   Level of Internationalization in Domestic Economy—Citigroup

The internationalization of a country's economy implies to ease the economic barriers and financial regulation against other countries or regions. It opens up economic business, trades, financial services, capital projects management by allowing the free flow of the domestic capital in the global market. The internationalization of an economy is the fruit from the internationalization of trade and manufacturing industry, which plays an equally important role in promoting domestic banks' internationalization. Specifically, in following aspects:

(1) The higher internationalization of the domestic economy will lead to the higher trade openness. By following their trading companies' footprint in internationalization, banks would be able to set up branches in overseas countries in order to provide trade settlement and payment more conveniently.

(2) Along with the improvement of the domestic economy in global stage, the country's restrictions of capital flow would be relaxed. As a result, banks could have easier access to global fund and are able to optimize its global resource allocation to further their international development.

Taking Citigroup as an example, Citigroup is one of the world's largest bank and financial institutions with its headquarters located in New York. It is also the first integrated financial group offering services including commercial banking, investment banking, insurance and fund, etc. By tracing Citigroup's history back to its establishment, the predecessor of Citibank was City Bank of New York, which was founded on June 16, 1812. After its development over 200 years, Citibank has earned

Table 3.8 History of Citigroup's internationalization

Year	Critical events
1897	Citigroup as the first American bank setting up the foreign business department, started to develop foreign currency trading business
1902	Business expanded to Asia and Europe, and opened offices in Shanghai and London, etc.
1914	Set up branches in Argentina, became the first American Bank setting up overseas branch
1939	Citigroup had 100 overseas offices globally, becoming the world's largest international bank
1979	Citigroup became the world's primary agency bank for foreign currency trading
1995	Opened its first branch in China, Vietnam and South Africa
1996	Citigroup had the largest number of credit cards holders in Asia, Taiwan of China became Citigroup's the first foreign region exceeding 1 million credit cards issuance outside the US
2003	One of the first batch banks obtaining custody license for QFII with approval from the People's Bank of China, China Securities Regulatory Commission and State Administration of Foreign Exchange
2004	Began to carry out risk management and financial derivatives business in China, and Became the first foreign bank that obtained financial derivative license issued by China Banking Regulatory Commission
2007	Acquired the third largest securities company in Japan by increasing its stake from 4.9 to 61.1%. Citigroup acquired Banco De Chile, the second largest bank in Chile, in the same year
2009	Citigroup sold its Japanese brokerage department to Sumitomo Mitsui Financial Group, and it sold 64% stake of Nikko Asset Management Company to Sumitomo Trust & Banking Company
2012	Through the block trades, Citigroup transferred 506.16 million shares of Shanghai Pudong Development Bank to China Pacific Insurance (Group) Co., Ltd. and its subsidiary, China Pacific Insurance Company, accounting for 2.714% of the total shares issued by SPDB. Citi Orient officially went into business in the same year
2013	Citibank China was one of the first batch banks setting up branches in Shanghai Free Trade Zone, was in the lead to promote its new account receivable solution "mobile payment service" by implementing the global digital development strategy of Citibank
2015	Citigroup sold its Japanese credit card business to Sumitomo Trust & Banking Company and underwent negotiation of selling its 20% stake of China Guangfa Bank

Source Zhejiang University CIFI, Citi's annual reports and news

its position as one of the most known banks worldwide for its foreign exchange and retail business as well as its extensive global branch network (Table 3.8).

The broad concept of economic internationalization for a country should include openness of its economy and trade business, relaxation of its restriction on its financial markets and increasing of foreign investment etc. This report used the degree of openness in foreign trade to represent a country's level of economic

Table 3.9 Degree of foreign trade dependence for different countries in 2015 (%)

Country	China	France	Germany	Japan	The Netherlands	Switzerland	The United States
Percentage (%)	35.9	43.7	70.7	30.9	154.1	114.1	27.8

Source Zhejiang University CIFI, The World Bank

Table 3.10 Degree of foreign trade dependence of the United States from 2006 to 2015 (%)

Year	2006	2007	2008	2009	2010	2011	2012	2013	2014	2015
Foreign trade dependence	26.5	27.7	29.8	24.6	28.1	30.9	30.8	30.2	30.1	27.8

Source Zhejiang University CIFI, US Bureau of Economic Analysis (BEA)

internationalization, specifically measured by using foreign trade dependence of a country. By comparing data in Table 3.9 and BII of financial institutions from different countries, it could be seen that the Netherlands ranked top in terms of foreign trade dependence, whilst the BII of ING Group was also positioned in the forefront (see Table 3.4). Furthermore, Switzerland and Germany both had comparatively higher foreign trade dependence, and their banks, Credit Suisse and Deutsche Banks, also retained comparatively higher BII level. However, as for countries with relatively lower degree of foreign trade openness, such as China, Japan, and the US, their banks including Mizuho FG, and JPMorgan Chase all ranked at the bottom for their BII. Thus, we could draw a conclusion that a bank's internationalization level is strongly connected to its country's economic internationalization level.

Economic internationalization level's impact on its banks' globalization could also be seen from time dimension. Taking at the US as example (see Table 3.10), its foreign trade dependence steadily rose from 2006 to 2008, whereas the US economy experienced a significant decline affected by the global financial crisis from 2008 to 2009. Although there was a temporary fallback from 2009 to 2011, the overall trend of the US economy in 2015 still presented a downward tendency. Table 3.4 showed that the BII of Citigroup experienced a big drop in 2009 comparing to 2007, then continuously fell afterwards. Compared these two sets of data, the BII of Citigroup was highly correlated with the foreign trade dependence of the US. Some academic research also indicated that the country's foreign trade dependence has a greater impact on its banks' internationalization during the early stage. However, such impact diminishes as the overseas development became gradually mature and banks have more complex motivations for its business expansion.

3.2.4   Internationalization Level of the Currency—UniCredit Group

In general, internalization level of a currency refers to not only its role in its own country, but also its significance in global transaction as reserve currency and trading currency. The improvement of a country's currency internationalization would affect the internationalization of the country's banks through the following aspects.

(1) Reduce transaction costs and break trading barriers. Once the currency of a country becomes an international currency, it would greatly reduce the frequency of currency exchanges when companies conducting cross-border transaction. This leads to efficiency improvement of the international capital flows thanks to lower transaction costs. Additionally, internationalized currency breaks the monopoly of the banking industry in other countries. It would also remove various types of trade barriers built by different currency systems, which would benefit the international operation of the home country's financial institutions.

(2) Reduce currency conversion and avoid exchange rate risk. When the currency of a country retains at a high level of internationalization, it could be freely converted, traded and circulated globally. This effectively lowers banks' exchange rate risk caused by currency conversion while conducting their multinational business. As banks are no longer bounded by the currency conversion, they would be able to adapt to global markets more efficiently with lower costs, which effectively remove obstacles in their international operation and improve the efficiency of international business development.

(3) Strengthen its international influence and expand overseas markets. When the currency of a country achieves a high level of internationalization, thanks to its high using frequency, the currency conversion costs will be reduced with faster currency circulation. This would be beneficial for the country's banks while conducting their pricing and settlements when conducting international trading business. Meanwhile, the currency internationalization also plays a significant role to enhance the country's international influence, which would pave the way for the banks to set up their overseas branches.

Hence, the improvement of a currency's internationalization would effectively promote the international development of the country's banks. According to Table 3.11, among the ranking based on the number of overseas branch networks by the end of 2015, the top 10 banks were all from countries where their currencies have been recognized as international currencies, including US Dollar, Euro, Pound, etc. On November 30, 2015, RMB was included in the currency basket of SDR. The accelerating progress of RMB internationalization will also actively facilitate the international development of Chinese banks.

On January 1, 2002, the single currency in Europe–Euro notes and coins were put into circulation, marking the official launch of the Euro currency. Euro is the

Table 3.11 Ranking by number of countries where selected banks located by the end of 2015

Ranking	Bank	Number of countries	Ranking	Bank	Number of countries
1	Citigroup	93	6	JPMorgan Chase	60
2	BNP Paribas	75	7	Groupe Crédit Agricole	52
3	HSBC	71	8	Credit Suisse	50
4	Deutsche Bank	70	9	UBS	50
5	Standard Chartered	67	10	Bank of China	47

Source Zhejiang University CIFI

most significant outcome of the European monetary reform since the Roman Empire, not only by improving the Europe's unified market and the convenience of free trade, but also becoming a critical part of the EU integration process. Therefore, we take UniCredit Group as an example to analyze the correlation between the internationalization level of a currency and the international development of the country's banks. UniCredit Group is one of the oldest and largest global banking groups in Europe, with its headquarters located in Milan, Italy. UniCredit Group has more than 8400 branches and 147,000 employees worldwide. In 2015, the BII of UniCredit Group was 54.59, ranking 8th among the 16 selected foreign banks. Its BII was once as high as 93.44 in 2012.

By judging its regional distribution of revenue, it could be seen that Euro has played a key role in UniCredit Group's internationalization. Based on Table 3.12, 98.3% of UniCredit Group's operating revenue was generated in Europe, specifically 43.5% from Italy, 14.0% from Germany, 9.5% from Austria, and 31.3% from other European countries and regions. There was no doubt that Euro has maximized its potentials of the currency internationalization. First of all, Euro has broken a variety of barriers among different economic bodies and financial systems in these countries as well as greatly reduced costs of cross-border transactions. Secondly, Euro has fundamentally eliminated the uncertainties in currency exchange rates by reducing interest rate and exchange rate risks for banks in the region. It also

Table 3.12 Regional distribution of UniCredit Group's operating revenue in 2015

Country/region	Operating revenue (€ in million)	Regional operating revenue ratio (%)
Italy	9278.61	43.5
Germany	2985.91	14.0
Austria	2028.24	9.5
Other European countries	6683.38	31.3
America	295.73	1.4
Asia	55.59	0.3
Other countries/regions	0.01	0.0

Source Zhejiang University CIFI, UniCredit Group's 2015 annual report

provided strong support for steady operations of banks. Thirdly, countries' adopting the same currency policy has strengthened the public's trust on the currency policy, and hence produced positive effect to improve the international status of Euro. The prominent advantage of Euro has provided great advantage for UniCredit Group's overseas business.

3.2.5 International Level of Domestic Companies—Deutsche Bank

The internationalization of domestic companies also plays a role in banks' internationalization. Enterprise internationalization refers to enterprises that achieve internationalization through production factors such as capital, equipment, and talents in the form of export, joint venture, technology transfer, and overseas subsidiaries or branches establishment. In addition to financial institutions, the higher level of their internationalization has notable positive impact on the internationalization of banks, specifically in the following aspects:

(1) The improvement of enterprises' internationalization increases potentials of overseas clients and capital for domestic banks. When domestic companies set up overseas subsidiaries, in convenience of conducting economic exchanges with parent companies, they are more inclined to deal their deposit and loan business with domestic banks, particularly when involving some illiquid currencies. Therefore, when the internationalization level of domestic companies gets enhanced, domestic banks would be able to attract more overseas clients by setting up overseas branches, which also motivates more banks to expand abroad.

(2) Multinational corporations actively conduct transaction worldwide in multiple aspects including capital, product, human capital, technology, and information. Through the emerging of new technology and products in order to maintain their status in market competition, the increasing of multinational corporations has narrowed the gap between domestic and global markets. The exchanges between domestic and global financial market also keep growing, setting an ideal international platform for financial institutions to expand.

Deutsche Bank is the largest bank in Germany with its headquarters located in Frankfurt. Deutsche Bank has branches and subsidiaries around the world, and provides financial services including loan, securities trading, foreign exchange trading and financial derivatives to individual, companies, and government clients. It has a long history of internationalization. In 1996, Deutsche Bank had 780 overseas branches in cities such as Luxembourg, Moscow, Madrid, and London, etc. Deutsche Bank is also the European bank with the most branches in Asia and Pacific region. By the end of June 1996, there were over 4900 overseas employees in Asia-Pacific region, mainly distributed in 18 countries including Japan, China and Australia (Table 3.13).

Deutsche Bank's internationalization was already at mature stage, and was benefited from the internationalization of German enterprises. Table 3.14 demonstrated exports of goods and services to the country's GDP ratio of selected countries. This ratio reflects the internationalization level of a country.

By comparing Tables 3.14 and 3.4 of foreign banks' BII, we noticed that countries whose enterprises have higher internationalization level, such as Germany, Spain, and the Netherlands, etc., the BII of their domestic banks all ranked in the forefront, including ING Group, Santander, and Deutsche Bank. This reflects a close correlation between the internationalization level of domestic companies and the internationalization level of the financial institutions.

By comparing the internationalization level of German enterprises in history (see Table 3.15) with the internationalization level of Deutsche Bank (see Table 3.16), we could find that the proportion of exports of goods and services was on the rise from 2005 to 2008, but experienced a plunge in 2009. It slowly picked up from

Table 3.13 History of Deutsche Bank's internationalization in China

Year	Critical events
1872	Set up branches in Shanghai and Yokohama, then closed both branches in 1875
1981	Set up Beijing Representative Office, becoming the first Germany bank in Beijing
1995	Set up Guangzhou Representative Office, upgraded to branch in 1999
2006	Made joint investment of 2.64 billion yuan with Luxembourg company to acquire part of Huaxia Bank's shares
2010	Deutsche Bank (China) Co., Ltd. announced that Tianjin Branch was officially established
2013	The Qingdao Branch of Deutsche Bank (China) Co., Ltd. officially opened
2014	Shanghai Free Trade Zone Sub-branch of Deutsche Bank was established

Source Zhejiang University CIFI, Deutsche Bank's annual reports and news

Table 3.14 Exports of Goods and services to country's GDP ratio of selected countries (%)

Country	China	France	Germany	Japan	The Netherlands	Spain	The United Kingdom	The United States
Proportion	22.4	30	46.9	17.9	82.8	33.1	27.4	12.6

Source Zhejiang University CIFI, The World Bank

Table 3.15 Exports of goods and services to german GDP ratio from 2005 to 2015 (%)

Year	2005	2006	2007	2008	2009	2010	2011	2012	2013	2014	2015
Proportion	37.7	41.1	43.0	43.4	37.8	42.2	44.8	45.9	45.4	45.7	46.9

Source Zhejiang University CIFI, the World Bank

Table 3.16 Overseas assets to total assets ratio of Deutsche Bank from 2005 to 2015 (%)

Year	2005	2006	2007	2008	2009	2010	2011	2012	2013	2014	2015
Overseas assets to total assets ratio	78	79	80	81	72	71	62	64	65	66	67

Source Zhejiang University, Deutsche Bank's annual reports

Table 3.17 German enterprises in the fortune Global 500 list in 2015

Ranking	Company name	Ranking	Company name
8	Volkswagen	178	Bayer
17	Daimler	179	Thyssenkrupp
22	E.ON	197	Deutsche Bahn
32	Allianz	233	Continental
56	BMW Group	285	Lufthansa Group
63	Siemens	292	Talanx
76	Basf	295	DZ Bank
97	Metro	314	Edeka Zentrale
102	Deutsche Telekom	387	Fresenius
103	Munich Re Group	405	Phoenix Pharmahandel
111	Deutsche Post	424	Energie Baden-Württemberg
150	Robert Bosch	469	TUI
154	RWE	488	ZF friedrichshafen
164	Deutsche Bank	489	Landesbank Baden-Württemberg

Source Zhejiang University CIFI, Fortune China

2010 to 2012, and then gradually rose from 2013 to 2015. Meanwhile, the proportion of Deutsche Bank's overseas assets gradually increased from 2005 to 2008, but sharply fell in 2009 with the downward trend continuing from 2010 to 2011, and slowly rose in 2012. The trends of the two ratios were basically identical, demonstrating a strong connection between the internationalization in the banks and enterprises for a country (Table 3.17).

Many established German enterprises have a long history of internationalization and played a profound influence in the global market. Among the "Fortune Global 500 List", there were totally 28 German enterprises whose international development was overall at mature stage. Volkswagen, for example, its products successfully entered into 18 countries and regions back in 1950. During that time, Volkswagen exported its products mostly to Sweden, the Netherlands, and other European countries, whilst American countries such as Brazil, the US also became its focus of the major export markets. In 1953, Volkswagen stepped into a critical turning point of its global expansion. With its competitive advantages, Volkswagen entered into America, Africa, and Asia-Pacific markets, forming an all-embracing and multilevel business pattern. This forward-looking international roadmap of Volkswagen also optimized financial market in Germany. Besides Volkswagen, BMW, Siemens and a number of enterprises with major international influence also provided foundation to support German financial institutions' overseas expansion including Deutsche Bank.

3.2.6 Positioning in Banking Business—Credit Suisse and Wells Fargo

The positioning of the business also has a great impact on banks' internationalization process. In general, universal banks and wholesale banks[4] have higher level of internationalization compared to retail banks. Universal banks refer to those banks that not only provide banking business but also securities, insurance, derivatives and other emerging financial business. Diversification in their banking business facilitates their international development, such as:

(1) Diversified business model could better meet customers' requirements and reduce service costs through customer resources sharing. Under such diversified business system, potential customers of different departments could overlap in different degree. Through sharing and integrating customer resources, banks could take the advantage of the holistic information in order to provide comprehensive, multi-area, and customized financial services. Meanwhile, cross-selling among different departments also creates new business opportunities for banks, helping to improve its profitability and efficiency of economic system.

(2) Diversified banking operation could bring the connection between banks and its customers closer as a way to enhance customer stickiness. On one hand, with the development of diversified business, especially the investment banking business, banks begin to underwrite corporate bonds, and even exercise shareholder rights as agents (e.g. German and Japanese banks). This resulted in a closer and stronger relationship between banks and their customers. On the other hand, there are multi-aspects in business cooperation between banks and customers, so both sides have the incentives to maintain a good credit-ability and effectively establish a trust mechanism between banks and customers.

(3) Diversified operation also enhances banks' resistance ability to risks. Product diversification provides strong support for banks to develop new financial product and business expansion. This further improves banks' risk prevention and self-adjustment abilities to changes in financial markets. Banks could adapt

---

[4]Wholesale banking refers to banking services between merchant banks and other financial institutions. This type of banking deals with larger clients, such as large corporations and other banks, whereas retail banking focuses more on the individual or small business.

Table 3.18 BII comparison between Credit Suisse and Wells Fargo in 2015

	BII (Ranking)	Overseas deposits to total deposits ratio (%)	Overseas loans to total loans ratio (%)	Number of countries with branches
Credit Suisse	65.92 (5)	38.12	43.15	50
Wells Fargo	–	8.76	12.7	36

Source Zhejiang University CIFI

faster and more efficiently to volatilities in the financial market, and quickly fit to the foreign financial environment.

Taking Credit Suisse and Wells Fargo for example, Credit Suisse was founded in 1856, as one of the world's largest consortium with its headquarters located in Zurich, Switzerland. Its comprehensive financial business has been a major feature of Credit Suisse. In addition to traditional retail banking business, Credit Suisse also offers individual and corporate financial services, pension, insurance, etc. Credit Suisse has taken advantage of its high-level professional knowledge, high level of accumulated capital, and their detail-oriented attitude in order to provide high-quality services for their clients.

Meanwhile, Wells Fargo is a distinctive bank with focusing on retail banking business. Its business structure is mainly divided into community banking, wholesale banking and wealth management, of which the community banking business (mainly retail banking business) accounted for the largest proportion of the bank's total revenue.

We could see from Table 3.18 that the BII of Credit Suisse in 2015 was 65.92, ranked 5th among the 26 selected Chinese and foreign banks. Its overseas loans accounted for over 40% to its total loans, representing a higher level of internationalization compared to Wells Fargo. There was no BII of Wells Fargo due to data accessibility issue. However, judging by the statistics such as overseas deposits ratio (8.8%), overseas loans ratio (12.7%), and number of countries with branches (36), Wells Fargo lagged far behind Credit Suisse in internationalization level. It also remained at the bottom in its ranking of overseas deposits and loans scale among the 16 selected foreign banks. In conclusion, the banks' business positioning plays a vital part in their international development.

3.3 Banks' International Development Pattern in View of Growing Path

Along with banking business developed over the years, more banks have initiated their internationalization by actively participating in the global financial market, which has affected the world's financial structure. However, due to varied establishment background, differentiated development strategies, and diverse advantages, banks have adopted differentiated internationalization patterns. Through our research, we found that banks are similar to multinational corporations, the internationalization patterns of banks could be mainly divided into organic and traditional.[5]

3.3.1 The Organic Internationalization Pattern—Standard Chartered Bank

A few banks entered into international markets shortly after their establishment, seeking for competitive advantages from resource exploitation and utilization globally. These banks adopted an organic internationalization pattern. The founders of these banks normally had rich knowledge and experiences on foreign markets and hence adopted the concept of global business right from the start. They considered the whole world as one market and didn't limit themselves in one country. Growth of these banks came mainly from global markets instead of domestic markets. Under the organic internationalization pattern, banks may choose to hold relatively small or no share in their domestic market. They focused on setting up extensively and closely connection in global network from the beginning, so as to access to more resources in a short time and expand rapidly worldwide. This organic international pattern requires banks to be equipped with multiple features. Among major large global financial institutions, there are relatively fewer banks being able to adopt this pattern during their international expansion.

Standard Chartered Bank is a leading international banking group with a history of more than 150 years. It does not have a large market share in the UK, whereas about 90% of its revenue and profits are generated from Asia, Africa and Middle East. Standard Chartered Bank brought vitality to investments and trade development in these regions through various types of financial services. This report indicated that the BII of Standard Chartered Bank ranked 1st consecutively from 2013 to 2015, presenting an outstanding performance in internationalization. Standard Chartered Bank was formed in 1969 by a merger of two British overseas banks: the Standard Bank of British South Africa and the Chartered Bank of India, Australia and China. The former bank mainly provided financial services to British business in South Africa, and the latter focused on British business in India, Australia and China. Both banks were highly internationalized banks with limited business operation in the UK (see Table 3.19). Thus, the Standard Chartered Bank was "born" with international characteristics from its establishment.

In 1969, the Standard Bank and the Chartered Bank merged and formed the Standard Chartered PLC, now known as Standard Chartered Holdings Limited, and subsequently acquired Hodge Group and the Wallace Brothers Group. Early from

---

[5]BEN Shenglin, MA Lina *Accelerating Internationalization: A Case Study of Geely.*

Table 3.19 Development of Standard Bank of British South Africa and Chartered Bank of India, Australia and China

Standard Bank of British South Africa	Founded in 1862 in London by John Paterson In 1867, it was prominent in financing and development of the diamond fields of Kimberley In 1886, business network was expanded to Johannesburg In 1953, established over 600 branches in Southern, Central, and Eastern Africa In 1956, merged with Bank of British West Africa with business throughout Africa
Chartered Bank of India, Australia and China	In 1853, founded by James Wilson, under a Royal Charter from Queen Victoria In 1858, opened its first branches in Bombay, Calcutta and Shanghai In 1859, opened branches in Hong Kong and Singapore Mainly to provide funds for traditional trades, including cotton trade in Bombay, tea trade in Calcutta, rice trade in Burma, tobacco trade in Sumatra, and silk trade in Yokohama, etc.

Source Zhejiang University, Standard Chartered Bank's annual reports and news

its establishment, Standard Chartered Bank set up branches in Europe, Argentina, Canada, Panama, Nepal, and the US. In the recent decade, more than 90% of its revenue was from overseas. In 2015, Standard Chartered Bank's number of overseas institutions to the total number of institutions ratio was 86%, while covering 67 countries worldwide with both overseas deposits and loans accounted for more than 85% of the whole group.

The international development of Standard Chartered Bank primarily followed expansion of British neo-imperialism in the Victorian era. From the 1870s to 1914, during the period of the First World War, the European colonial expansion policies and ideology were known as the "neo-imperialism" led by the British Empire. The European powers competed for overseas colonies. During that time, the total area of the European powers in overseas colonies reached 23 million km^2. Particularly, Africa where had rarely been set foot on by the Europeans until 1880s, became the main target of the imperialists. At the same time, the expansion of the British Empire also extended to the Southeast Asia and East Asian coast. The two predecessors of the Standard Chartered Bank realized their international development in Africa and Asia respectively benefiting from the British Empire's expansion.

After its establishment and due to the British overseas colonies hegemony, Standard Chartered Bank had the political advantages while other banks did not have. Risks such as legal and cultural shock that Standard Chartered Bank faced were much less than banks in other countries. Meanwhile, its main business was still to serve the domestic companies and support their global development, so culture gaps in foreign countries did not become the major issue to limit its development at that time. Furthermore, Standard Chartered Bank did not face strong competition from local banks when entering into overseas markets, due to the weak financial systems in Africa and other countries.

3.3.2 The Traditional Internationalization Pattern—Santander

Traditional internationalization pattern refers to banks that firstly choose to develop in their domestic countries. Then, after accumulating a strong domestic market basis, they begin to expand overseas through international activities including overseas branches setup, foreign indirect investment, overseas mergers and acquisitions, and multinational alliance, etc. The key to this pattern lies in knowledge and investment, meaning banks decide to invest more resources in overseas markets according to the extent of their knowledge of these countries. From this perspective, traditional internationalization pattern is a series of progressive decision-making outcomes. Generally, banks adopting traditional international pattern will firstly enter into countries with narrow differences in economy, culture, politics, language, etc., from their home country. Only when their accumulation of international experiences and knowledge reaches a certain point, these banks will step into foreign markets which are significantly different from their domestic markets.

During the booming of banking internationalization in the 1990s, the international strategies of different banks varied enormously and among which, Santander successfully completed its international expansion.

Santander was founded in 1857 with its headquarters located in Santander, Spain. Santander is the largest Spanish bank and the second largest European bank. Its internationalization footprint could be divided into two steps: firstly, developing its domestic business and becoming the leader of banking industry in Spain; secondly, strategically entering foreign markets with smaller differences in region and culture, after fully understanding the market environment, replicating their successful domestic business model in the overseas markets (Table 3.20).

First of all, Santander differentiated itself among banks in the domestic market by reducing operating costs. Spanish banks have been in extreme competition with high degree of market penetration, and even became excessive (95.9 bank branches per 10,000 residents in Spain, compared to 52.1 bank branches in Italy, and 49.4 bank branches in Germany). Such intense competition urged Spanish banks to reduce operating costs to seek competitive advantages by promoting electronic money transfer business, abandoning bank checks, widely setting up ATM machines, and improving risk management system and human resource system.

Table 3.20 Key indicators of Santander (1985–2015)

Year	1985	1995	2005	2015
Number of customers	750,000	–	66,083,199	121,000,000
Net income (€ in million)	133	530	6220	5966
Market value (€ in million)	2500	8268	69,735	65,792

Source Zhejiang University CIFI, Santander's president speech at ESADE, Santander's annual reports

In 1989, Spanish Government deregulated Spanish banks through various methods such as uplifting interest rate limits, stock market reform and pension policy reform. Most large banks considered these reforms as a threat, whereas Santander, who committed to improve its management efficiency and reduce operating costs, saw it as an excellent opportunity to accelerate its expansion. The advantage of low costs allowed Santander to provide higher interest rate for customers and grow its market shares. In 1989, Santander set up the "Supercuenta Santander" with the interest rate of 11%, compared to the average interest rate of 5% offered by other banks. Taking advantage of the high interest rate, Santander was able to attract a huge number of customers, and became the largest commercial bank in Spain.

Secondly, following its successful development in the domestic market, Santander set off to replicate its core business model in its global expansion. For its first attempt of internationalization, Santander cautiously chose Latin America, where there existed the smallest cultural difference. As the former colony of Spain, Latin America had minor barriers in the language and culture. Moreover, the management of Santander was very optimistic about the potential development of Latin America. The local banking industry was still under development and the competition was not severe. Actually, this unique vision brought hefty profits for Santander. As the political environment stabilized, Latin America entered into a rapid growth period, and Mexico, Chile, Argentina, and Colombia became the most profitable sources for Santander.

After entering Latin America, Santander selected other European countries as its next expansion targets. Due to the strict European financial regulation and highly competitive market, Santander chose the consumer credit business as a breaking point, which was comparatively deregulated. In 1999, Santander acquired a Portuguese bank—Tottay Açores and Crédito Predial Protuguês. In 2003, it acquired an Italian bank—Finconsumo, which was mainly engaged in the consumer finance. Afterwards, Santander expanded its branch network to countries such as Poland, Britain, and Norway, and became the second largest consumer credit financial institution in Europe.

At present, Santander is operating in over 40 countries and regions worldwide with its BII gradually rising over the years. Its overseas income ratio reached the highest level of 86% in 2015. With the expansion to the US and Asia, the internationalization of Santander might be further improved.

Chapter 4
Comparison Between Chinese and Foreign Banks on Globalization

In recent years, a lot of foreign banks slowed down their pace of overseas business expansion. Although, they stood stronger in international market compared to Chinese banks, who were still at an early stage. This chapter analyzed and compared the international development achieved by Chinese and foreign banks in respects of BII ranking, scale of overseas business, overseas operation outcome and layout of overseas business network, in order to facilitate Chinese banks to be fully aware of their status quo and current market position. In the meantime, we also followed up the process of internationalization with the real-time data updating, and analyzed the new challenges and opportunities, to help Chinese banks to formulate the next step of internationalization strategy better.

4.1 Big Gap Between Chinese and Foreign Banks in BII Level and Chinese Banks Still Have a Long Way to Catch Up

Comparisons between the BII of Chinese and foreign banks indicate that Chinese banks had significantly lower BII levels than foreign banks, showing that Chinese banks still lagged behind in internationalization (Table 4.1).

4.1.1 Consolidated BII of China's Big Five Banks Was 8.90, Only 1/6 of the Average BII for 16 Foreign Banks

The internationalization level of Chinese banks is relatively lower by comparing against 16 selected foreign banks. The average BII of those 16 foreign banks was 53.65 in 2015, which is 5 times higher than the consolidated average BII for

© Zhejiang University Press and Springer Nature Singapore Pte Ltd. 2018
B. Shenglin et al., *In Pursuit of Presence or Prominence?* Current Chinese
Economic Report Series, https://doi.org/10.1007/978-981-10-7730-2_4

Table 4.1 BII Ranking of selected Chinese and foreign banks

Chinese and foreign banks	Year									2015 Ranking
	2007	2008	2009	2010	2011	2012	2013	2014	2015	
Standard Chartered	–	–	–	–	83.42	81.46	83.79	84.83	88.84	1
Santander	67.65	69.96	72.24	75.53	78.31	77.71	74.84	74.77	76.74	2
Nordea	63.00	72.55	72.30	70.83	70.59	70.06	71.79	71.64	69.48	3
ING Bank	68.67	70.46	60.78	67.83	65.09	65.52	63.08	68.17	67.43	4
Credit Suisse	64.61	24.93	60.89	60.53	60.38	52.19	58.97	60.47	65.92	5
Top-5 Average	57.86	48.59	54.39	59.62	71.56	69.39	70.49	71.98	73.68	
HSBC	57.86	48.59	54.39	59.62	60.17	64.4	60.11	62.16	62.65	6
UBS	–	–	76.53	52.12	50.23	76.96	50.4	56.83	55.16	7
UniCredit SpA	66.8	60.36	61.3	70.97	71.14	93.44	65.2	55.09	54.59	8
Deutsche Bank	–	–	–	–	–	–	–	53.8	54.22	9
Citibank	68.31	54.52	60.54	58.46	58.62	57.34	56	53.37	53.58	10
Top-10 Average	–	–	–	–	–	–	–	64.11	64.86	
BNP Paribas	–	–	–	–	–	–	–	58.19	52.5	11
Mitsubishi UFJ FG	30.05	–181.57	24.18	28.37	30.77	27.73	32.2	28.92	40.66	12
Groupe Crédit Agricole	–	–	–	–	–	36.94	38.61	36.82	36.16	13
Bank of New York Mellon	35.02	36.19	28.15	35.35	31.72	32.87	33.11	34.63	33.98	14
Mizuho FG	25.62	15.99	14.23	19.47	20.49	21.06	23.32	26.09	26.02	15
Top-15 Average	–	–	–	–	–	–	–	55.05	55.86	
BOC	22.73	18.43	18.09	18.33	18.3	18.69	19.94	21.79	21.57	16
JPMorgan Chase	–	–	–	–	–	–	–	22.42	20.45	17
ICBC	2.82	3.12	3.59	4.15	4.79	5.42	7.16	8.02	8.94	18
*BOCM	5.24	3.88	4.80	4.81	5.29	5.63	6.20	7.21	7.15	19
*CITIC	–	–	5.43	4.58	3.88	3.94	4.00	4.51	4.36	20

(continued)

Table 4.1 (continued)

Chinese and foreign banks	Year										2015 Ranking
	2007	2008	2009	2010	2011	2012	2013	2014	2015	
CCB	1.97	1.91	2.14	2.26	2.40	2.76	3.31	3.67	4.33	21
*SPD	–	–	–	–	0.81	1.14	1.66	2.43	3.66	22
ABC	0.67	0.47	0.69	0.94	1.06	1.68	2.25	2.85	3.41	23
*CMB	–	–	–	1.25	1.35	1.52	1.87	2.24	2.11	24
*CGB	–	–	–	–	–	0.69	1.22	1.15	1.12	25
*CEB	–	–	–	–	–	–	0.46	0.64	0.87	26

Banks with * are not in G-SIBs
Source Zhejiang University CIFI

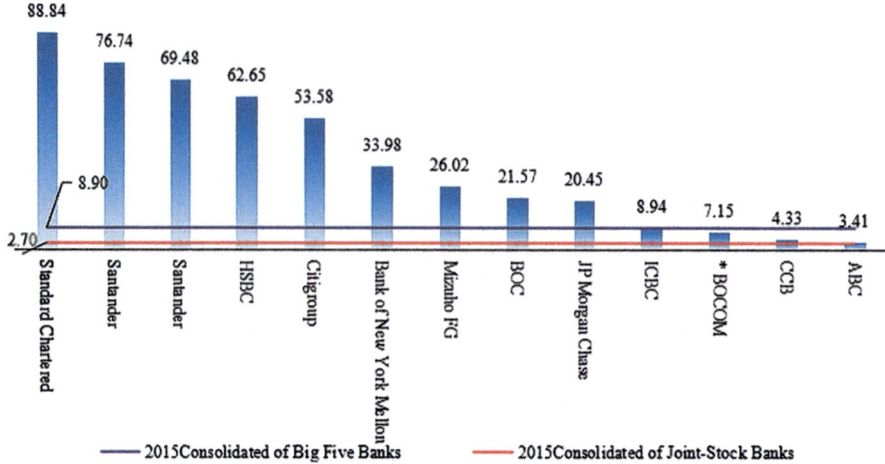

Fig. 4.1 2015 BII of Selected banks. Banks with * are not in G-SIBs. *Source* Zhejiang University CIFI

China's Big Five Banks (8.90) and 18.9 times higher than the consolidated average BII for joint-stock banks (2.70). BOC ranked as 16th among all 26 foreign and Chinese banks, followed by ICBC ranking 18th.

Besides HSBC and Citibank, Fig. 4.1 shows the comparison between the top and bottom 3 foreign banks in BII ranking of China's Big Five Banks. It is quite evident that the average BII of the top 3 foreign banks in 2015 was 78.35, which is 2 times higher than BOC who has the highest rank of BII among all Chinese banks. It is also nearly 9 times and 29 times of BII for the consolidated China's Big Five Banks and Chinese joint-stock banks respectively. Moreover, the average BII of the 3 foreign banks at the bottom reached 26.82, which is still higher than the overall BII of Chinese banks and 2 times higher than the consolidated BII of China's Big Five Banks. To some extent, the main reason of Chinese banks being recognized as G-SIBs is their large operation scale, and the big influence in global banking financial assets, rather than their performance in global markets.

Given the relatively short history of the modern banking industry in China, it has been a remarkable achievement for these leading Chinese banks to be listed as G-SIBs within a few decades. In contrast, after the long-term development and evolution, foreign banks have gained significant prestige through their international expansion and management expertise. Therefore, Chinese banks still have the advantages that they have a large space to promote and experience from foreign banks, although they are in a relative lower level of internationalization. It could also be observed from Table 4.2 that the gap between the average BII level of major Chinese banks (both big five and joint-stock banks) and the average BII level of foreign banks has narrowed in 2015.

Table 4.2   Comparison of BII levels between Chinese and foreign banks

Year	Average of foreign banks	Consolidated China's big five banks	Consolidated Chinese joint-stock banks
2014	53.01	8.54	2.45
2015	53.65	8.90	2.70

Source Zhejiang University CIFI

4.1.2   Chinese Banks Fall Behind in Global Footprint and Need to Upgrade Their Overseas Business Structure

According to Fig. 4.2, Chinese banks are less competitive compared to foreign banks. Taking HSBC and Citibank for example, Their BII ranks were 6th and 10th respectively in 2015. Except for the number of countries with bank located, both banks maintained relatively high level in all indicators of internationalization at a level above 50%. Notably, HSBC had 96.6% of total profit from overseas in 2015. Taking data availability into consideration, we categorized most overseas data of HSBC as "outside of Europe" and overseas data of Citibank as "outside of North America". Consequently, the actual level of internationalization for these two banks could be even higher.

In terms of their global footprint of overseas branch network (see Table 4.3), the geographical distribution of Chinese banks has extended widely but insufficient in penetration. This is mainly due to the fact that Chinese banks developed their business network in foreign countries mainly by establishing branches, sub-branches or representative offices, hence their overall presence in a single country is quite limited and sometimes only located in China-towns. For example,

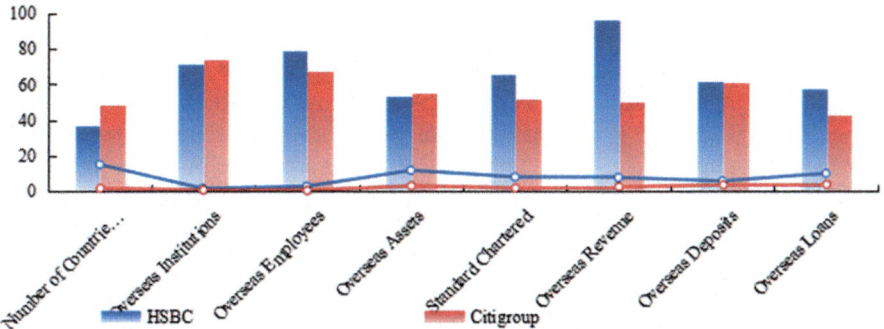

Fig. 4.2   Comparison of BII indicators of Chinese and foreign banks in 2015 (%). (These figures reflect the proportion of each indicator in the foreign region. Most indicators from HSBC refer to the portions measured "outside of Europe"; Citibank's overseas revenues and profits are measured "outside North America".) *Source* Zhejiang University CIFI, annual reports of banks

Table 4.3 Comparison of the indicators between Chinese and foreign banks in 2015

	HSBC/ Consolidated China's big five banks	Citi/ Consolidated China's big five banks	HSBC/ Consolidated Chinese joint-stock banks	Citi/ Consolidated Chinese joint-stock banks
Proportion of countries with presence	2.4	3.2	21.3	27.9
Proportion of overseas institutions	43.7	45.4	85.4	88.6
Proportion of overseas employees	28.5	24.3	162.8	138.8
Proportion of overseas assets	4.5	4.7	17.0	17.6
Proportion of overseas revenues	8.2	6.4	34.6	27.2
Proportion of overseas profits	12.4	6.5	36.7	19.1
Proportion of overseas deposits	10.5	10.4	17.4	17.2
Proportion of overseas loans	5.7	4.3	15.0	11.1

Source Zhejiang University CIFI, annual reports of banks

the number of countries where HSBC operates is about 2.4 times as much as all China's Big Five Banks combined. And its proportion of overseas branches is even 42.7 times higher than China's Big Five Banks as a whole. A widespread bank network can greatly accelerate banks to penetrate local market and bring convenience to their clients, which can be seen from the high proportion of overseas revenue for foreign banks. Given that Chinese banks are far behind foreign banks in breadth and depth of market penetration and business development in foreign countries, they should therefore put this as their primary target on future business agenda.

From the perspectives of overseas operations, Chinese banks ought to further strengthen their capability of business development and improve profitability. Compared with foreign banks, as we can see from Table 4.3, Chinese banks fell behind in overseas revenues and profits. For example, the contributions from overseas revenue for HSBC and Citibank are 8.2 times and 6.4 times as much as

China's Big Five Banks combined as well as 34.6 times and 27.2 times as much as joint-stock banks combined. The gap between Chinese and foreign banks in overseas profit generation remained large. In contrast, among all indicators, Chinese banks have the smallest gap on the proportion of overseas loans if compared with foreign banks, which indicates that their overseas business model is rather concentrated on deposit and loan business with similar operating models originated from their domestic market, instead of applying a more dynamically different strategies by adapting to foreign financial environment. At the meantime, the financial condition of foreign countries or regions is quite different from that of China, for example, the degree of interest rate liberalization in many developed countries or regions is much higher than China, which means that Chinese banks ought to evolve and get rid of their excessive reliance on interest income. Only with in-depth assessment of local market conditions, Chinese banks could fasten the development of diversified business models and enhance their operation capacity. This will enable them to relocate their unique advantages and targets as well as actively seek new frontier for business growth.

4.2 Chinese Banks' Total Overseas Assets Kept Growing While Foreign Banks Slowly Declined

As the footstone of overseas business operations, a bank's scale of overseas assets not merely exhibits its business size in foreign countries but also reflects its capability of generating future cash flows. In addition, as an essential traditional banking business, a bank's overseas deposits and loans can be used to directly measure its performance in global business expansion. Meanwhile, the number of a bank's foreign employees is also a key indicator demonstrating a bank's scale of overseas operation.

It's important to point out that only the 16 selected foreign banks had completed and accessible data to compute all 8 indicators, which formulated our calculation and analysis of BII for foreign banks. Throughout the remaining chapter, we would further elaborate our analysis by presenting their overseas business scale, operation performance and layout of overseas branch network. And we put some available data of foreign G-SIBs into our rankings too. For example, Wells Fargo was not included in BII computation, due to the lack of data related to its overseas assets, overseas revenues and overseas profits, while data on its overseas deposits and loans abroad were available. Accordingly, this report incorporated Wells Fargo only in relevant sections where ranking and analysis were performed based on banks' overseas deposits and loans. Secondly, among these 26 foreign and Chinese banks selected for BII computation, certain banks had unavailable data for consecutive years. To overcome such data problems, this report used two estimation methods as described in Appendix A "Data Processing for BII" for details. Meanwhile, estimated data were not considered in relevant ranking or analysis. For example, CITIC

Bank was excluded from the ranking of overseas employees and the computation of average level of this indicator, given the fact that the number of overseas employees was estimated for CITIC Bank. Thirdly, as one graphic figure couldn't accommodate all foreign banks, the remaining chapter would show the most representative foreign bank in relevant aspects for analysis.

4.2.1   The Gap Between Chinese and Foreign Banks in Total Overseas Assets Was Narrowing and Chinese Banks Were Progressing Rapidly

The following ranking was made in accordance of total overseas assets, proportion of overseas assets and the growth rate of overseas assets in 2015 (Table 4.4).

(1) **The Overall Scale of Chinese Banks in Overseas Assets Still Couldn't Catch Up with Foreign Banks, But the Gap Was Reducing**

The average value of overseas assets for China's Big Five Banks was nearly 2000 billion yuan by the end of 2015, about 14 times higher than the average level of the 5 selected joint-stock banks (128.66 billion yuan) (see Fig. 4.3). BOC topped all Chinese banks with its overseas assets as 4830.8 billion yuan, which was 1.5 times higher than the average level of all China's Big Five Banks. BOC was followed by ICBC with its overseas assets as 2450.56 billion yuan and roughly the average level of China's Big Five Banks. ABC was placed at the bottom among all China's Big Five Banks with its 780 billion yuan in overseas assets and that was nearly 40% of the average level. Among all selected Chinese joint-stock banks, CITIC Bank scored the highest by having the largest overseas assets of 241.41 billion yuan. Though this was only 1/3 of ABC's total overseas assets, it was roughly as 1.9 times as the average of Chinese joint-stock banks. The scale of overseas assets for CCB was merely 22.79 billion yuan, which placed it at the very bottom in the list. In general, China's Big Five Banks were far ahead of joint-stock banks with astonishing speed of asset accumulation in overseas markets.

Compared with foreign banks, Chinese banks still had lower scale of overseas assets, however, this gap had narrowed in recent years. Among 25 Chinese and foreign banks, Deutsche Bank, HSBC and Santander were the top 3 foreign banks in respect of overseas assets. The average overseas assets of the 15 foreign banks was about 4350.1 billion yuan, almost doubled the average level of China's Big Five Banks or 33 times higher than the average level of Chinese joint-stock banks. From the view point of individual banks, BOC was the only Chinese bank exceeding the average overseas assets of foreign banks and climbed into top 10. All other Chinese banks were far behind in their overseas assets compared to foreign banks. Even being placed at the 7th, BOC's scale of overseas assets was less than 60% of Deutsche Bank's, which ranked 1st. This indicated a huge gap between Chinese banks and foreign banks. However, this gap was reducing, which could be

Table 4.4 Ranking of overseas assets for selected Chinese and foreign banks in 2015[a]

Ranking	Total overseas assets (RMB in billions)		Proportion of overseas assets (%)		Growth rate of overseas assets (%)	
1	Deutsche Bank	8457.83	ING Bank	82.5	*CEB	69.2
2	HSBC	8308.45	Santander	75.6	ABC	32.5
3	Santander	7146.45	Credit Suisse	73.0	ICBC	27.7
4	Citibank	6179.08	Standard Chartered	72.6	CCB	23.2
5	Mitsubishi UFJ FG	5758.85	Nordea	72.2	*CITIC	21.5
6	ING Bank	4873.16	Deutsche Bank	67.0	*CMB	12.1
7	BOC	4830.80	UBS	61.2	BOC	6.0
8	Credit Suisse	3881.69	UniCredit	57.8	Mizuho FG	4.9
9	UniCredit	3508.30	Citibank	55.0	*CGB	2.6
10	JPMorgan Chase	3469.15	HSBC	53.1	*BOCOM	2.3
11	Nordea	3293.84	Mitsubishi UFJ FG	39.7	Santander	1.1
12	Mizuho FG	3232.59	Mizuho FG	33.0	Mitsubishi UFJ FG	0.8
13	BNP Paribas	3023.14	BOC	28.7	HSBC	-0.3
14	ICBC	2450.56	Bank of New York Mellon	24.3	Deutsche Bank	-0.9
15	Groupe Crédit Agricole	2070.07	JPMorgan Chase	22.7	Citibank	-1.7
16	Standard Chartered	1427.72	BNP Paribas	21.5	UniCredit	-2.1
17	CCB	1149.54	Groupe Crédit Agricole	19.2	Bank of New York Mellon	-4.2
18	ABC	782.26	ICBC	11.0	Standard Chartered	-8.7
19	*BOCOM	659.61	*BOCOM	9.2	ING Bank	-10.1
20	Bank of New York Mellon	620.94	CCB	5.7	BNP Paribas	-11.4
21	*CITIC	241.41	*CITIC	4.7	Credit Suisse	-12.3
22	*SPDB	191.30	ABC	4.4	Nordea	-13.4

(continued)

Table 4.4 (continued)

Ranking	Total overseas assets (RMB in billions)		Proportion of overseas assets (%)		Growth rate of overseas assets (%)	
23	*CMB	142.22	*SPD	3.8	Groupe Crédit Agricole	-13.4
24	*CEB	45.56	*CMB	2.6	JPMorgan Chase	-16.9
25	*CGB	22.79	*CEB	1.4		
26			*CGB	1.2		

[a]Foreign Banks' overseas assets were all converted to RMB with the spot exchange rate on respective balance sheet date

Due to the significant change in statistic criteria of UBS, UBS was not ranked in total overseas assets and the growth rate in 2015. It was only included in the ranking of overseas assets

We used estimation to compute BII for SPDB with limited data accessibility on their overseas assets during 2010–2014. Hence, SPDB was excluded from the ranking of growth rate on overseas assets

Banks with * are not in G-SIBs

Source Zhejiang University CIFI, annual reports of selected banks

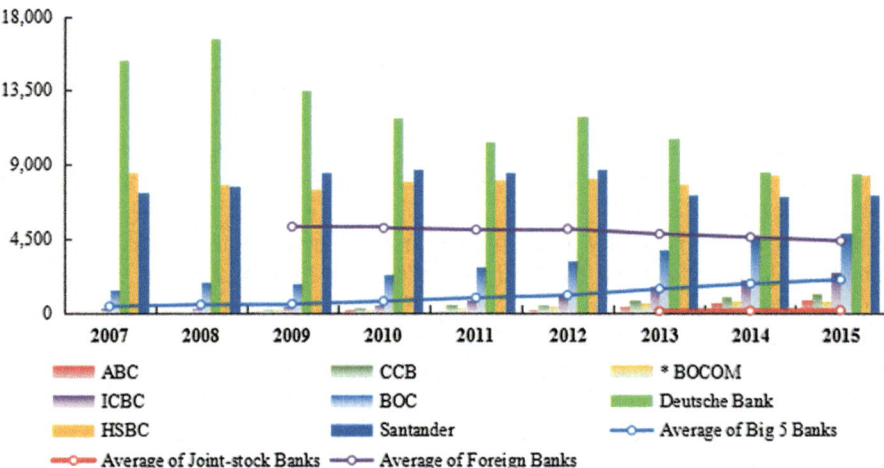

Fig. 4.3   Overseas assets of Chinese and foreign banks (RMB in billions). Banks with * are not in G-SIBs. *Source* Zhejiang University CIFI, annul report of selected banks

clearly observed from Fig. 4.3. The average scale of overseas assets for foreign banks had been decreasing over the years, while China's Big Five Banks continuously increased their overseas assets, making the difference decrease from 10 times in 2009 to 1.2 times in 2015. This once again reflected Chinese banks' achievements in their overseas expansion.

(2) **Average Proportion of Overseas Assets of China's Big Five Banks Measured Up to Only 1/4 of Foreign Banks**

Figure 4.4 showed BOC, CITIC Bank and ING which separately achieved the highest percentage of overseas assets among China's Big Five Banks, Chinese joint-stock banks and foreign banks. The proportion of overseas assets of Chinese

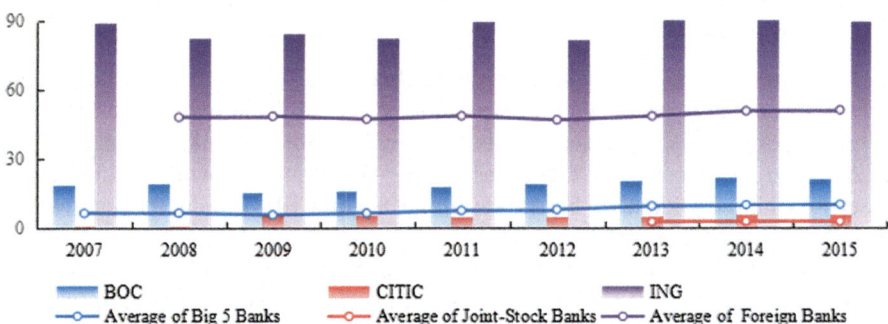

Fig. 4.4   Proportion of overseas assets for Chinese and foreign banks (%). *Source* Zhejiang University CIFI, annul report of selected banks

banks showed an upward trend, but remained at a low level. The average proportion of overseas assets for China's Big Five Banks had increased by 70% since 2007 and rose up to 11.84% in 2015. Being the most outstanding bank, BOC's overseas assets accounted for 28.73%, around 2.4 times that of China's Big Five Banks' average level. CITIC Bank achieved the largest proportion of overseas assets among all joint-stock banks as 4.72% in 2015 and 1.7 times the average level of joint-stock banks (2.76%).

Foreign banks generally were higher in their proportion of overseas assets, which could be concluded by the fact that all top 12 banks of the 26 banks by ranking the proportion of overseas assets were exclusively foreign banks. Furthermore, 10 of them reached more than 50% of their total assets as overseas assets. Even if we took possible errors in statistics criteria or data processing into consideration, most foreign banks maintained higher level in their proportion of overseas assets than their Chinese competitors. From the perspective of historical trend, the average overseas assets of foreign banks remained substantially stable, though the indicator of ING Bank experienced a short period of decline. It can be concluded that when a bank's international development reaches its mature stage, the proportion of its domestic and overseas assets would be relatively balanced.

Chinese banks could not compete with foreign banks in neither the average level nor the highest level in their proportion of overseas assets, and their progress in closing this gap was rather slow compared to the scale of overseas assets. In 2014, the average proportion of overseas assets of foreign banks achieved 51.46%, which was about 4 times the size of the average level of China's Big Five Banks. Among them, ING's overseas assets accounted to 73.14% and this was equivalent to 6 times of China's Big Five Banks' average level. In 2015, the average proportion of overseas assets of foreign banks reached 51.90% and this was 3 times higher than that of China's Big Five Banks. Meanwhile, ING achieved 82.46% in this indicator, which was 6 times higher than the average of China's Big Five Banks. Assuming that the worldwide growth in international expansion remains stable, Chinese banks have a great growth potential as their proportion of overseas assets can be increased by 3 times at least.

(3) **Chinese Banks Outperformed Foreign Banks in the Growth Rate of Overseas Assets**

In contrast to the scale and proportion of overseas assets, Chinese banks had achieved stunning results in the expansion speed of their overseas assets. The average growth rate of overseas assets of China's Big Five Banks reached 18.31% in 2015 and ABC scored the highest as 32.5%. The average growth rate of overseas assets of Chinese joint-stock banks was 26.35% with CEB being in the lead with its growth rate of 69.2% (see Fig. 4.5).

From the figure above, it could be concluded that Chinese banks were among the top players in terms of their expansion rate in overseas countries. By comparing the average growth rate in overseas assets of China's Big Five Banks and foreign banks, China's Big Five Banks had a better performance. Even Mizuho, who had

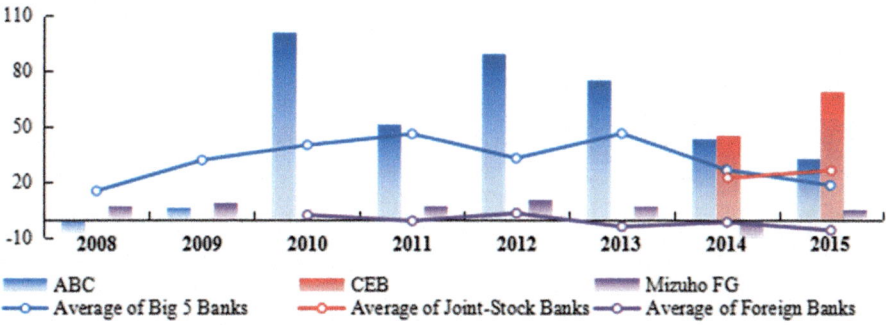

Fig. 4.5 Growth rate of overseas assets by Chinese and foreign banks (%). *Source* Zhejiang University CIFI, annul report of selected banks

the highest growth rate in overseas assets among selected foreign banks, fell behind the average growth rate of China's Big Five Banks. It was noteworthy that in recent years, foreign banks were reducing their expansion of overseas assets and hence, their growth rate became negative and dropped to −5.91% in 2015, indicating a cyclical contraction of overseas assets.

4.2.2 Chinese Banks Continued to Increase Overseas Deposits While Foreign Banks Were Shrinking Their Footprints

Deposit is the foundation of modern banking industry, which serves as an important source of funds for banks to carry out other financial businesses. The basic profile of overseas deposits for Chinese and foreign banks in 2015 could be outlined as follows (Table 4.5):

(1) **Chinese Banks Continuously Increased the Scale of Overseas Deposits, While Foreign Banks Had It Declined Slightly**

The total overseas deposits of Chinese banks kept growing and in 2015 alone, the total overseas deposits of China's Big Five Banks reached 3466.36 billion yuan with a 5.1% growth rate. BOC once again led China's Big Five Banks by having its total overseas deposits as 20,690.92 billion yuan in 2015 and won itself the 7th place. Meanwhile, ABC's overseas deposits only amounted to 89.35 billion yuan and ranked 24th. Among Chinese joint-stock banks, CITIC and CMB[1] ranked 22nd and 23rd respectively according to their amount of overseas deposits as 184.88 and 106.01 billion yuan.

---

[1]Overseas deposits for CMB were offshore deposits.

Table 4.5 Ranking of overseas deposits for selected Chinese and foreign banks in 2015[a]

Ranking	Total overseas deposits (RMB in billions)		Proportion of overseas deposits (%)		Growth rate of overseas deposits (%)	
1	HSBC	5137.80	Standard Chartered	85.1	*CMB	41.5
2	Santander	3585.10	UniCredit	75.1	Bank of New York Mellon	27.1
3	UniCredit	3095.80	Santander	74.4	*CITIC	24.1
4	Citibank	2758.38	Nordea	70.1	ABC	19.5
5	ING Bank	2563.20	ING Bank	66.9	*BOCOM	19.0
6	Mitsubishi UFJ FG	2170.60	HSBC	61.4	Mizuho FG	14.5
7	BOC	2069.92	Citibank	60.9	Groupe Crédit Agricole	10.2
8	Standard Chartered	1983.21	Bank of New York Mellon	47.1	BOC	5.2
9	BNP Paribas	1665.37	UBS	40.3	Mitsubishi UFJ FG	5.1
10	JPMorgan Chase	1647.61	Credit Suisse	38.1	Wells Fargo	4.4
11	Deutsche Bank	1516.99	Deutsche Bank	37.8	HSBC	3.0
12	Groupe Crédit Agricole	1088.10	BNP Paribas	34.4	UBS	2.7
13	Mizuho FG	1082.57	Groupe Crédit Agricole	30.5	BNP Paribas	2.1
14	UBS	1019.88	Mitsubishi UFJ FG	25.6	Santander	1.9
15	Credit Suisse	898.03	JPMorgan Chase	19.6	CCB	1.1
16	Bank of New York Mellon	854.21	Mizuho FG	19.0	JPMorgan Chase	-0.3
17	Wells Fargo	695.27	BOC	18.1	UniCredit	-0.5
18	Nordea	596.00	Wells Fargo	8.8	ING Bank	-0.6
19	ICBC	564.99	*BOCOM	7.8	ICBC	-1.5
20	CCB	392.33	*CITIC	5.8	Citibank	-4.4
21	*BOCOM	349.76	ICBC	3.5	Deutsche Bank	-5.3
22	*CITIC	184.88	*CMB	3.0	Nordea	-7.8
23	*CMB	106.01	CCB	2.9	Credit Suisse	-9.2
24	ABC	89.35	ABC	0.7	Standard Chartered	-11.6

[a]Foreign Banks' overseas deposits value were converted to RMB at the spot exchange rate at the balance sheet date

We used estimation to compute BII for SPDB and CEB due to data availability issue for their overseas deposits in 2015. Hence, SPDB and CEB are excluded from the ranking of total overseas deposits, growth rate and overseas deposits to total deposits ratio

Banks with * are not in G-SIBs

Source Zhejiang University CIFI, annul report of selected banks

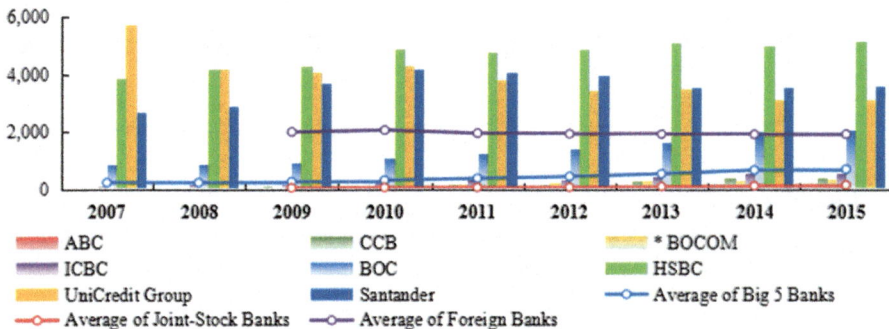

Fig. 4.6 Overseas deposits of Chinese and foreign banks (RMB in billions). Banks with * are not in G-SIBs. *Source* Zhejiang University CIFI, annual reports of selected banks

The average overseas deposits of China's Big Five Banks was nearly 700 billion yuan in 2015, which grew by 5% compared to 2014. At the same time, the average of foreign banks' overseas deposits was around 2000 billion yuan, which was 3 times that of China's Big Five Banks' average level. HSBC won the 1st place with its overseas deposits as 5137.8 billion yuan, which was 2.5 times that of BOC, and ranked 1st among all Chinese banks. It was obvious that HSBC had stronger business capacity in developing deposit business overseas than Chinese banks (see Fig. 4.6).

Viewing from the historical trend, overseas deposits of Chinese banks continued to grow while foreign banks experienced a decline in recent years.

(2) **Both Foreign and Chinese Banks Are Stable in Their Proportion of Overseas Deposits and Standard Chartered Bank Maintained Its Leading Position**

The comparison in the proportion of overseas deposits between Chinese and foreign banks showed that foreign banks were undeniably better positioned to attract overseas clients (see Fig. 4.7). In 2015, the average proportion of overseas deposits of China's Big Five Banks was 6.6%, which was significantly lower than the level of BOC (18.1%) by 65% and was only 1/7 of the average level of foreign banks. BOC, though delivered the best performance in this indicator among all Chinese banks, had its proportion of overseas deposit less than half of the average level of foreign banks, and was only 1/5 of Standard Chartered Bank (who ranked 1st among all foreign banks). CITIC Bank again ranked first in Chinese joint-stock banks with its proportion of overseas deposits as 5.8% in 2015 which was higher than those of ICBC, CCB and ABC.

As Chinese banks were still in their initial stage of globalization, they actively expanded their domestic and overseas business. Among them, China's Big Five Banks managed to maintain their proportion of overseas deposits at a stable level. Influenced by the financial crisis and negative interest rates of major economies, the proportion of overseas deposits of Chinese banks showed a decline followed with a

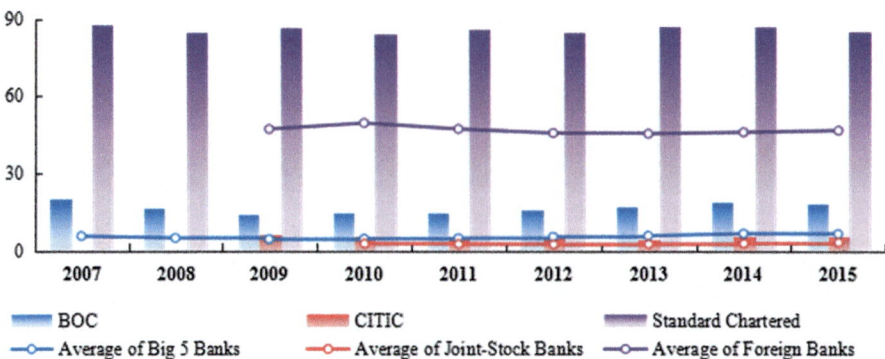

Fig. 4.7 Proportion of overseas deposits for Chinese and foreign banks (%). *Source* Zhejiang University CIFI, annul reports of selected banks

steady recovery from 2008 to 2010. However, the shrinkage in overseas deposits was more substantial and long-term for foreign banks. The average proportion of their overseas deposits continuously declined during 2010–2014 and only made a small recovery in 2015.

In terms of the future competition in banking industry, even though deposits may not be the core business for banks and their main source of profitability, such indicator on overseas deposits still provides a reasonable measurement in banks' market penetration in foreign countries and their capability of attracting new clients.

(3) **Chinese Joint-Stock Banks Progressed Rapidly While Foreign Banks Remained Stable**

The growth of Chinese joint-stock banks in overseas deposits was more significant as a result of their smaller overseas deposits base. Being the representatives of the Chinese joint-stock banks, CMB and CITIC Bank ranked 1st and 3rd of all banks for their full-speed growth in their overseas deposits as 41.5 and 24.1% respectively. ABC had the smallest base of overseas deposits among all China's Big Five Banks and therefore was well positioned in the frontier with its growth rate up to 73.5%. In recent years, ABC had slowed its growth rate in overseas deposits and achieved only 19.5% in 2015, which was still about 2.2 times the average growth rate of China's Big Five Banks (see Fig. 4.8).

Foreign banks had maintained their growth rate of their overseas deposits at a relatively low level for six consecutive years. In 2015, the average growth rate of overseas deposits for foreign banks was 1.8%, which was only 1/4 of average level of China's Big Five Banks. However, Bank of New York Mellon ranked 2nd according to its growth rate in overseas deposits among all banks, which was only lower than CMB but ahead of ABC by 40%.

At present, with Chinese economy entering its "new normal" and global economy undergoing significant transformation, the future business landscape in banking industry will evolve along with the growing complexity in financial

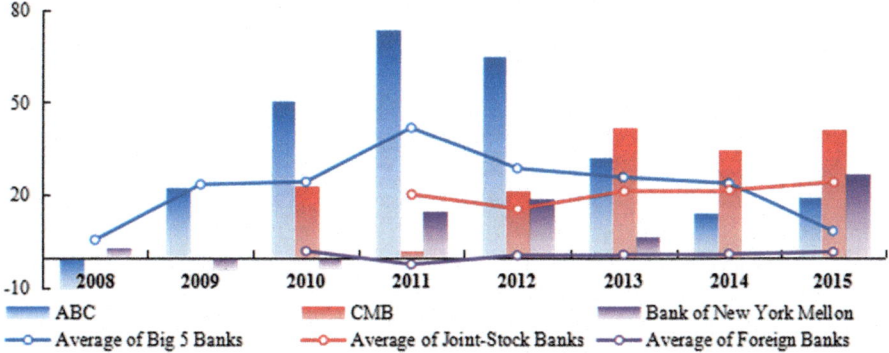

Fig. 4.8 Growth rate of overseas deposits by Chinese and foreign banks (%). *Source* Zhejiang University CIFI, annul reports of selected banks

markets and the volatilities in overseas deposits will grow. Chinese banks need to be fully aware of the distinctly unique characteristics of their domestic and overseas markets. Besides learning from foreign banks for their rich experiences in international market, Chinese banks should also combine their own business characteristics to effectively attract overseas clients when developing their international expansion strategies. By doing so, Chinese banks will be able to fully demonstrate their advantages and explore various types of RMB business in the context of the internationalization of RMB.

4.2.3 Chinese Banks Actively Expanded Overseas Loan Business While Foreign Banks Reduced, and Both of Them Achieved High Level in Proportion of Overseas Loans

At present, interest spread of deposits and loans still brings the main profit for Chinese banks. Hence, during their globalization, overseas loans become their core business sector for profit generation. Table 4.6 displayed a ranking of Chinese and foreign banks based on their scale of overseas loan business.

(1) **Overseas Loans Continued to Grow**

BOC held the top position among Chinese banks and ranked 7th among selected 26 Chinese and foreign banks in 2015 with its overseas loans of 1936.77 billion yuan. ICBC, CCB and ABC ranked after BOC being 2nd, 3rd and 4th. BOCOM had the smallest scale of overseas loans as 326.4 billion yuan, amounting to 1/3 of average level of all China's Big Five Banks. Among all joint-stock banks, only CITIC Bank exceeded 100 billion yuan in overseas loans and ranked 22nd.

Table 4.6 Ranking of overseas loans for selected Chinese and foreign banks in 2015[a]

Ranking	Total overseas loans (RMB in billions)		Proportion of overseas loans (%)		Growth rate of overseas loans (%)	
1	BNP Paribas	7389.88	Standard Chartered	89.9	*CEB	68.0
2	Santander	4483.32	Santander	80.4	*CGB	22.5
3	HSBC	3455.09	BNP Paribas	74.9	Wells Fargo	21.5
4	ING	2517.84	UniCredit	72.1	CCB	21.5
5	Mitsubishi UFJ FG	2512.10	Nordea	72.0	*CITIC	19.5
6	UniCredit	2410.22	ING	62.8	*BOCOM	17.8
7	BOC	1936.77	HSBC	57.6	ICBC	12.8
8	Nordea	1854.03	Deutsche Bank	53.3	ABC	12.6
9	Citibank	1714.67	Groupe Crédit Agricole	51.7	Bank of New York Mellon	11.1
10	Deutsche Bank	1629.56	UBS	49.9	Mizuho FG	10.9
11	Groupe Crédit Agricole	1543.24	Credit Suisse	43.2	Deutsche Bank	4.4
12	Standard Chartered	1525.40	Citibank	42.8	Credit Suisse	4.3
13	Mizuho FG	1248.82	Mitsubishi UFJ FG	41.1	Mitsubishi UFJ FG	4.2
14	UBS	1048.95	Mizuho FG	30.9	UBS	3.8
15	ICBC	1048.58	Bank of New York Mellon	22.5	Santander	3.5
16	Credit Suisse	765.64	BOC	21.2	BOC	3.2
17	CCB	685.24	Wells Fargo	12.7	BNP Paribas	1.8
18	JPMorgan Chase	568.83	JPMorgan Chase	11.1	ING	−0.8
19	ABC	446.63	ICBC	8.8	HSBC	−1.4
20	Wells Fargo	377.15	*BOCOM	8.8	Citibank	−1.7
21	*BOCOM	326.40	CCB	6.5	UniCredit	−5.6
22	*CITIC	139.37	*CITIC	5.5	Groupe Crédit Agricole	−6.6
23	Bank of New York Mellon	93.14	ABC	5.0	Standard Chartered	−8.0
24	*CMB	57.77	*CMB	2.0	Nordea	−10.2
25	*CEB	24.41	*CGB	1.7	JPMorgan Chase	−11.2
26	*CGB	14.77	*CEB	1.6	*CMB	−16.9

[a]Value of overseas loans of foreign banks was converted to RMB by using RMB exchange rate at balance sheet date

We used estimation to compute BII for SPDB due to limited data accessibility on their overseas loans for 2015. Hence, SPDB was excluded from the ranking of total overseas loans, growth rate and overseas loans to total loans ratio

Banks with * are not in G-SIBs

Source Zhejiang University CIFI, annual reports of selected banks

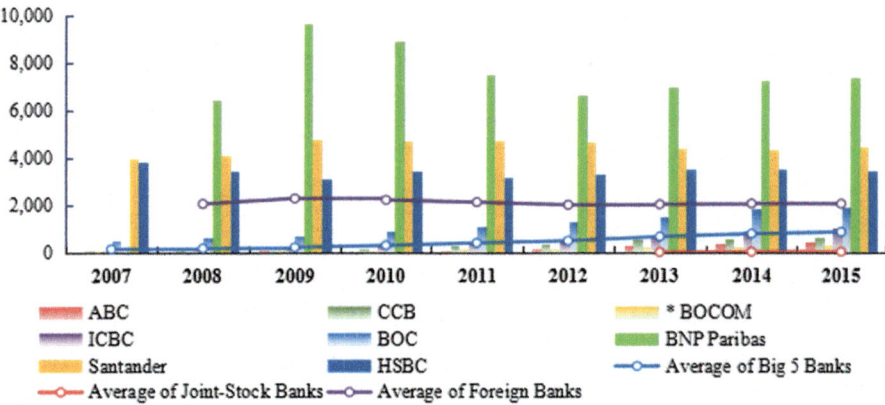

Fig. 4.9 Overseas loans of Chinese and foreign banks (RMB in billions). Banks with * are not in G-SIBs. *Source* Zhejiang University CIFI, annual reports of selected banks

The average level of overseas loans for joint-stock banks reached 59.08 billion yuan and only accounted for 1/15 of the average level of China's Big Five Banks.

Similar to overseas deposits, Chinese banks fell behind foreign banks in terms of the scale of overseas loans. Even BOC, who had the largest overseas loans among all Chinese banks, couldn't compete with the average level of 16 foreign banks. This gap became even drastic when compared with BNP, who ranked 1st. The scale of overseas loans for BNP reached 7389.88 billion yuan, which was 3.8 times of BOC and 8 times of the average level of China's Big Five Banks.

By analyzing the tendency of overseas loans (see Fig. 4.9), Chinese banks demonstrated a continuous growth in their overseas loans, showing the same development pattern as overseas deposits. From 2007 to 2015, the overall scale of the overseas loans for China's Big Five Banks quintupled from 871.81 billion yuan to 4.44 trillion yuan, achieving an annual growth rate of 22.6%. Foreign banks were heavily impacted by global economic downturn and consequently experienced a considerable fall in the scale of overseas loans. However, they had managed to stabilize this business in recent years, which reflects a certain degree of economic recovery.

(2) **As for the Proportion of Overseas Loans, China's Big Five Banks Made a Breakthrough in 2015 by Exceeding 10% While Foreign Banks Remained Above 50%**

According to banks' ranking in 2015 with respect to their proportion of overseas loans, Chinese banks were positioned in the 2nd tier among all banks. BOC was ranked as 16th with its proportion of 21.2%. And the average level of China's Big Five Banks was 10.1% (the highest level since 2007) and was 3.5 times that of average level of joint-stock banks. Except for BOC, all China's Big Five Banks had their proportion of overseas loans below 10%. As for joint-stock banks, CITIC

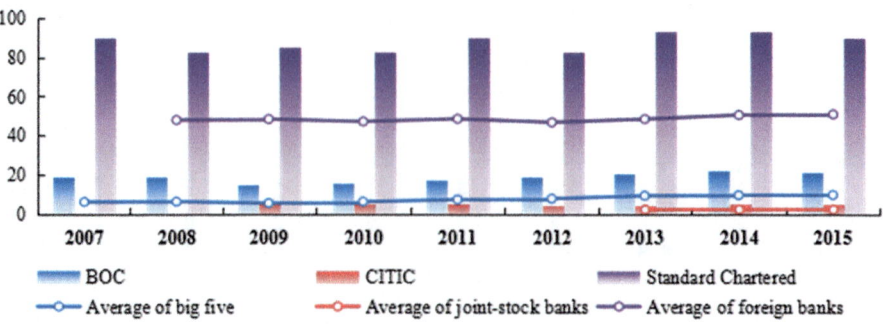

Fig. 4.10 Proportion of overseas loans for Chinese and foreign banks (%). *Source* Zhejiang University CIFI, annual reports of selected banks

Bank had its ratio of overseas assets to total assets greater than 5% and ranked 22nd, which was twice of the average level of joint-stock banks (see Fig. 4.10).

By the end of 2015, the average proportion of overseas loans reached 51.1% for foreign banks, which was also the highest level for past 8 years. More specifically, European banks had higher ratio among all foreign banks. Standard Chartered had its proportion of overseas loans as 89.9% and placed 1st. In addition, it needs to be acknowledged that JPMorgan Chase and Wells Fargo fell behind with lower rankings together with Chinese banks. This could be due to the fact that J. P. Morgan Chase was an integrated financial institution with focusing on various complex financial services instead of traditional loan business. Wells Fargo was positioned as a retail bank with higher degree of localization in their overseas business, hence they didn't put overseas loans as high priority.

(3) **Chinese Banks Achieved High-Speed Growth in Overseas Loans While Foreign Banks Remained Stable**

Chinese banks had higher ranking in 2015 according to their growth rate in overseas loans. Among which, CEB and CGB achieved 1st and 2nd place separately demonstrating great potentials from Chinese banks in this business. In light of the fact that the statistics in overseas business of these two banks only pertained to three years, the volatility of this assessment was enhanced by selecting CITIC Bank (ranked 5th) representing joint-stock banks in Fig. 4.11. CITIC Bank's overseas loans had been subject to a steady and accelerated growth from 2011. Although CITIC Bank was smaller in business scale compared to large Chinese and foreign banks, it managed to secure its leading role among joint-stock banks in overseas expansion. The rapid growth in its overseas loan business in recent years reflected its higher priority in overseas market and accelerated establishment of overseas network. CCB's development in overseas loans could represent China's Big Five Banks to a certain degree, though the volatility in its growth rate was relatively high but remained above 15% with its average level as 28.9% for the past 8 years. Meanwhile, it showed that China's Big Five Banks retained high growth in their overseas loans with average growth rate as 30.6% for the past 8 years, though

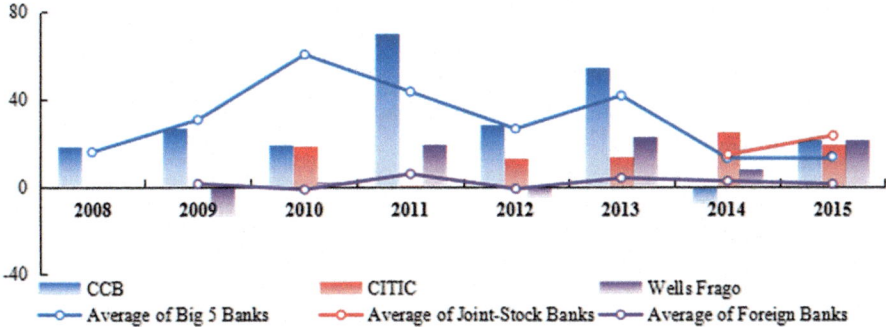

Fig. 4.11 Growth rate of overseas loans by Chinese and foreign banks (%). *Source* Zhejiang University CIFI, annual reports of selected banks

the growth rate dropped to 13.6% in 2015. By contrast, foreign banks had lower growth rate and only Wells Fargo which topped all foreign banks made its growth rate above 20% in 2015. And the runner-up New York Mellon only achieved 11.1%, which was only 1/2 of CCB. Given that the average growth rate was low for foreign banks, the fluctuation of their overseas loans was gentle in the past. Their average growth was 1.2% in 2015, which was close to the average growth rate of 1.8% in the past 7 years.

4.2.4   Chinese Banks Had Lower Number of Overseas Employees but Its Growth Rate Entered Top 5

From the perspectives of overseas employees, Chinese bank demonstrated again a lower ranking in overall number but achieved good performance in growth rate (Table 4.7).

Table 4.7 Ranking of overseas employees for selected Chinese and foreign banks in 2015[a]

Ranking	Total number of overseas employees		Proportion of overseas employees (%)		Growth rate of overseas employees (%)	
1	HSBC	208,000	Standard Chartered	97.0	*CMB	24.1
2	Santander	169,647	Santander	87.5	ABC	23.6
3	Citibank	155,157	HSBC	78.8	*CEB	23.0
4	BNP Paribas	131,103	Nordea	76.6	ICBC	17.0
5	UniCredit	88,185	ING Bank	72.3	CCB	15.8
6	Standard Chartered	81,554	UniCredit	70.3	UniCredit	14.7

(continued)

Table 4.7 (continued)

Ranking	Total number of overseas employees		Proportion of overseas employees (%)		Growth rate of overseas employees (%)	
7	Deutsche Bank	55,347	BNP Paribas	69.3	*BOCOM	9.0
8	Mitsubishi UFJ FG	46,035	Citibank	67.2	Credit Suisse	7.3
9	UBS	38,861	UBS	64.7	Santander	7.3
10	ING Bank	38,134	Credit Suisse	63.9	BOC	5.9
11	Groupe Credit Agricole	33,936	Deutsche Bank	54.7	Deutsche Bank	4.9
12	Credit Suisse	30,800	Groupe Crédit Agricole	47.5	Bank of New York Mellon	4.1
13	BOC	24,983	Bank of New York Mellon	45.1	Mizuho FG	3.7
14	Bank of New York Mellon	23,100	Mitsubishi UFJ FG	45.0	Mitsubishi UFJ FG	1.8
15	Nordea	22,724	BOC	8.1	BNP Paribas	0.9
16	ICBC	19,504	Mizuho FG	8.0	UBS	0.7
17	Mizuho FG	4383	ICBC	4.2	Nordea	0.5
18	*BOCOM	2199	*BOCOM	2.4	HSBC	−0.5
19	ABC	722	*CMB	0.4	Groupe Crédit Agricole	−1.7
20	CCB	718	*SPDB	0.3	Citibank	−3.4
21	*CMB	335	*CEB	0.3	Standard Chartered	−7.5
22	*SPDB	131	CCB	0.2	*SPDB	−13.8
23	*CEB	107	ABC	0.1	ING Bank	−17.8

[a]We used estimation to compute BII for JPMorgan Chase, CITIC, CGB due to limited data accessibility on their oversea employees for 2015. Hence, JPMorgan Chase, CITIC, CGB are excluded from the ranking of overseas employees and growth rate, overseas employees to total employees ratio

Banks with * are not in G-SIBs

Source Zhejiang University CIFI, annual reports of selected banks

(1) **Chinese Banks Had Lower Number of Overseas Employees and Fell Out of Top 10**

A bank's number of overseas employees is closely related to its number of overseas branches and the scale of its overseas business. Among Chinese banks, BOC's overseas employees were subject to a steady growth followed by a decline. By the end of 2015, the number of its overseas employees reached 24,983 and ranked 13th among all 23 selected banks. ICBC displayed an outstanding performance in its growth of overseas employees, of which the annual growth rate achieved 35.7% from 2007 to

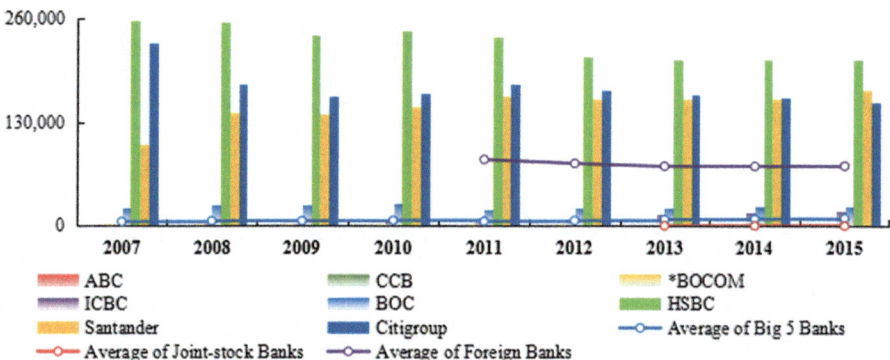

Fig. 4.12 Overseas employees of Chinese and foreign banks. Banks with * are not in G-SIBs. *Source* Zhejiang University CIFI, annual reports of selected banks

2015 and the total number grew up to 24,983 in 2015. Meanwhile, BOCOM had its number of overseas employees surpassed 2000 while both ABC and CCB remained under 1000. For the joint-stock banks, the number of overseas employees was below 500 for CMB, SPDB and CEB. And the average number of overseas employees for joint-stock banks was only 191 in 2015 (Fig. 4.12).

When compared to foreign banks, Chinese banks were greatly short in the total number of overseas employees. The average number of China's Big Five Banks' overseas employees exceeded 9500, which was up to 12.8% of foreign banks. However, the average number of overseas employees for the top 4 foreign banks in 2015 was over 100,000 and among them, HSBC ranked 1st with 208,000 overseas employees even after its cutback in overseas employment by 0.5% in 2015. This indicated that global foreign banks stay in the advantageous position in the international business.

(2) **Chinese Banks' Ratio of Overseas Employees to Total Employees Was Well Below 10%, While Foreign Banks Achieved a Balance Between Local and Overseas Employees**

Both Chinese and foreign banks remained stable in their ratio of overseas employees to total employees with insignificant fluctuation at yearly basis. By the end of 2015, this average ratio was still below 3% for China's Big Five Banks showing their low investment in human resources during overseas business development. However, foreign banks kept their average ratio of overseas employees above 60% as the same level as local employees. Standard Chartered Bank even had 97% of its employees from foreign countries, which put it in the first place (see Fig. 4.13).

By ranking foreign and Chinese banks according to their ratio of overseas employees in 2015, Chinese banks fell behind a long way with the average level below 10%. Such gap indicated that Chinese banks still had their core business operation in domestic markets.

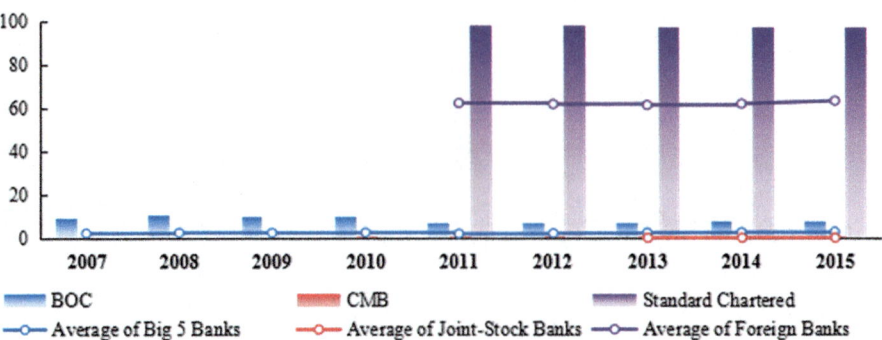

Fig. 4.13 Proportion of overseas employees for Chinese and foreign banks (%). *Source* Zhejiang University CIFI, annual reports of selected banks

(3) **Chinese Banks Actively Increased Their Reserves of Overseas Talents While Foreign Banks Demonstrated a Decline**

As mentioned above, the growth rate in Chinese banks' overseas employees was prominent and secured top 5 among all banks. Though ICBC's number of overseas employees only increased by 17% in 2015, the average growth rate achieved 34% for the past 8 years. CMB managed to maintain an average growth rate as 20.3% since 2011 and reached 25% in 2015. By the end of 2015, the average growth rate for China's Big Five Banks in their overseas employees was 14.3%, which was 14 times that of foreign banks. By analyzing the negative growth in Citibank's overseas employees for 4 consecutive years, we found that as several foreign banks had reduced their business scale in foreign countries, their number of overseas employees declined accordingly (Fig. 4.14).

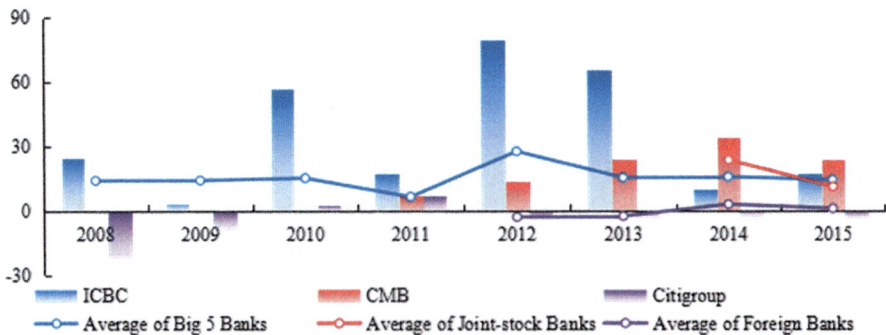

Fig. 4.14 Growth rate of overseas employees by Chinese and foreign banks (%). *Source* Zhejiang University CIFI, annual reports of selected banks

4.3   Chinese Banks Yields Promising Outcome from Their Overseas Expansion, Showing Greater Long-Term Potentials Benchmarking Foreign Banks

Banks attract overseas clients mainly by promoting deposit and loan business or open overseas markets through diversified financial services, and therefore their performance in overseas expansion is ultimately reflected in their business performance and profitability. A bank's profitability in overseas markets can be better measured based on their global operation capacity and management capability.

4.3.1   *Chinese Bank Have Lower Revenue Contribution from Overseas Business but with a Rapid Growth Rate*

Table 4.8 summarized performance of Chinese and Foreign banks on overseas revenue. Compared with foreign banks, Chinese banks have lower level in both amount of overseas revenue and the proportion except for accelerated growth rate.

Table 4.8 Ranking of overseas revenues for selected Chinese and foreign banks in 2015[a]

Ranking	Total overseas revenues (RMB in billions)		Proportion of overseas revenue (%)		Growth rate of overseas revenue (%)	
1	HSBC	304.46	Standard Chartered	93.9	Mitsubishi UFJ FG	89.1
2	Santander	276.43	Santander	86.6	ABC	59.3
3	Citibank	227.50	UBS	76.8	*CEB	37.3
4	BNP Paribas	201.95	Nordea	74.5	CCB	36.1
5	Deutsche Bank	163.90	Deutsche Bank	69.3	ICBC	25.8
6	UBS	152.18	BNP Paribas	66.7	UBS	15.0
7	JPMorgan Chase	144.59	HSBC	66.0	*BOCOM	9.6
8	Mitsubishi UFJ FG	140.52	ING	64.3	BOC	4.9
9	Credit Suisse	98.75	Credit Suisse	64.1	BNP Paribas	4.9
10	Standard Chartered	94.08	UniCredit	56.5	Santander	3.5
11	BOC	93.08	Citibank	51.9	Deutsche Bank	2.8
12	UniCredit	84.98	Mitsubishi UFJ FG	47.4	Mizuho FG	2.3
13	ING	81.68	Groupe Crédit Agricole	47.4	ING	1.0
14	ICBC	66.61	Bank of New York Mellon	35.6	Citibank	0.6
15	Groupe Crédit Agricole	57.47	Mizuho FG	26.4	HSBC	−0.2
16	Nordea	53.25	JPMorgan Chase	23.8	*CITIC	−1.1
17	Mizuho FG	44.48	BOC	19.6	JPMorgan Chase	−3.4
18	Bank of New York Mellon	35.13	ICBC	9.5	UniCredit	−4.7
19	ABC	18.11	*BOCOM	5.2	Bank of New York Mellon	−4.9

(continued)

Table 4.8 (continued)

Ranking	Total overseas revenues (RMB in billions)		Proportion of overseas revenue (%)		Growth rate of overseas revenue (%)	
20	CCB	13.90	*CITIC	3.5	Groupe Crédit Agricole	−7.3
21	*BOCOM	10.00	ABC	3.4	Nordea	−9.2
22	*CITIC	5.08	*SPDB	2.8	Standard Chartered	−10.8
23	*SPDB	4.17	CCB	2.3	*CMB	−11.6
24	*CMB	2.22	*CMB	1.1	Credit Suisse	−12.0
25	*CEB	0.42	*CGB	0.6	*CGB	−15.1
26	*CGB	0.32	*CEB	0.5		

[a]For the sake of comparison, overseas revenue of foreign banks was converted to RMB with the exchange rate at the balance sheet date
We used estimation to compute BII for SPDB due to limited data accessibility on their overseas revenue during 2010–2014. Hence, SPDB is excluded from the ranking of growth rate on overseas revenue
Banks with * are not in G-SIBs
Source Zhejiang University CIFI, annual reports of selected banks

(1) **In Terms of Scale of Overseas Revenue, China's Big Five Banks Didn't Make into Top 10 Even with Their Consolidated Overseas Revenue Exceeded 200 billion yuan**

Firstly, China's Big Five Banks have been increasing steadily on their average scale of overseas revenues for the 8 consecutive years, and hence their average level reached 40 billion yuan and consolidated level achieved 200 billion yuan by the end of 2015. Among them, BOC is always in the lead and topped all other China's Big Five Banks again in 2015 with its overseas revenue of 93.08 billion yuan. This also placed BOC as the 11th among all banks, which successfully defeated UniCredit and ING. In 2015, the overseas revenues of ICBC amounted to 66.61 billion yuan, which was 65% higher than the average level of China's Big Five Banks (40.34 billion yuan) and put ICBC 14th in the ranking. In comparison, ABC, CCB and BOCOM had relatively lower revenue from overseas and ranked from 19th to 21st.

Secondly, the consolidated overseas revenue for large joint-stock banks, including CITIC, SPDB, CMB, CEB and CGB, rose up to 12.22 billion yuan in 2015 with average level as 2.44 billion yuan. This was accounted to only 6% of the average of revenue of China's Big Five Banks. As the joint-stock bank with largest scale in overseas revenue, CITIC only ranked 22nd among 26 banks with its overseas revenue as 5.08 billion yuan in 2015, which was 1/2 of BOCOM who placed at the bottom of China's Big Five Banks. Closely following CITIC, SPDB achieved its overseas revenues of 4.17 billion yuan in 2015. In contrast, the average revenue of CMB, CEB and CGB was less than 1 billion yuan, indicating that they are still at the initial stage of globalization (Fig. 4.15).

In addition, most foreign banks varied in their overseas revenues during 2015 and foreign banks earned top 8 places among all 26 selected banks and achieved their overseas revenue above 100 billion yuan. HSBC topped the chart with an outstanding overseas revenue of 304.46 billion yuan, which was about 3 times

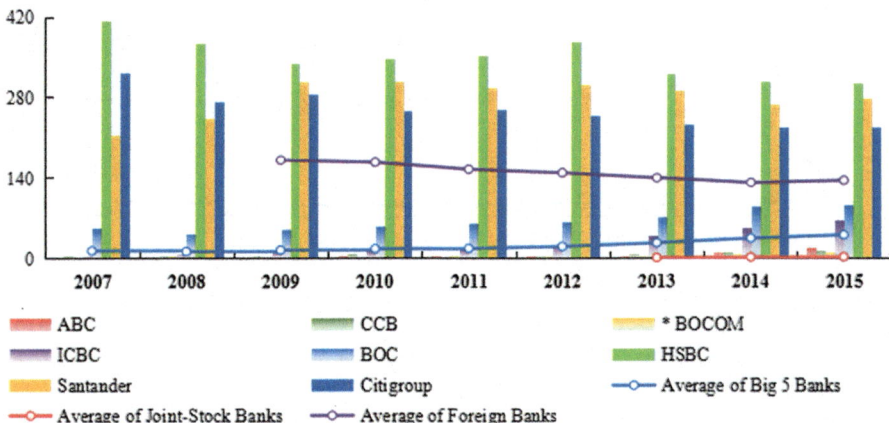

Fig. 4.15 Overseas revenues of Chinese and foreign banks (RMB in billions). Banks with * are not in G-SIBs. *Source* Zhejiang University CIFI, annual reports of selected banks

higher than BOC (who ranked 1st among all Chinese banks). The average overseas revenues of selected foreign banks amounted to 135.08 billion yuan which was 2 times higher than the average level of China's Big Five Banks. It is worth mentioning that foreign banks have reduced their business scale in overseas countries substantially since the financial crisis. And hence, their average overseas revenues dropped by nearly 20% since 2009. At their peak time by taking 2009 as an example, average overseas revenue of foreign banks reached 171.11 billion yuan and this was 12 times the average level of China's Big Five Banks (14.23 billion yuan in 2009). Therefore, it can be concluded that changes in global financial market and international economic situation had great impact on banks' strategies of international business.

(2) **China's Big Five Banks' Average Ratio of Overseas Revenue to Total Revenue Was Only 1/7 of Foreign Banks**

During the past 9 years, Chinese banks remained stable in their proportion of overseas revenues (see Fig. 4.16). BOC was in the leading position among China's Big Five Banks along with its proportion of overseas revenue as 19.6% in 2015 but only placed at 17th among all 26 selected banks. Compared to its ranking on amount of overseas revenue, BOC dropped by 6th place by ranking the proportion of overseas revenue. ICBC only achieved 9.5% in its proportion of overseas revenue, which was only 1/2 of BOC and ranked 18th among all 26 selected banks. Similar to BOC, ICBC descended by 4 places compared to its ranking on amount of overseas revenue. BOCOM's overseas revenues to total revenues ratio was up to 5.2% and placed 3rd among Chinese banks. However, it only ranked 19th among the 26 Chinese and foreign banks.

Among joint-stock banks, CITIC Bank had its overseas revenues to total revenues ratio as 3.5% and ranking 1st in 2015, which even surpassed ABC and CCB.

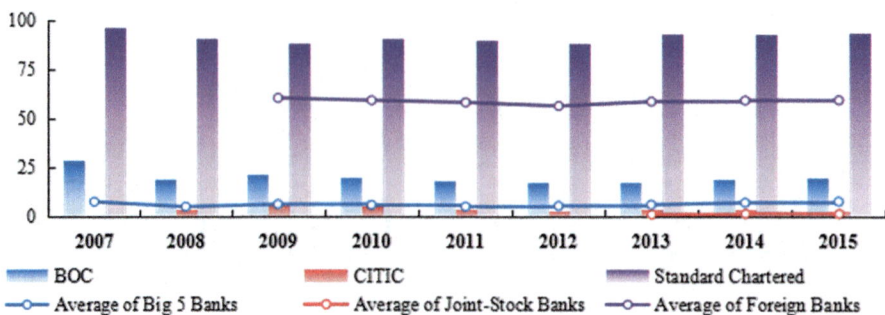

Fig. 4.16 Proportion of overseas revenues for Chinese and foreign banks (%). *Source* Zhejiang University CIFI, annual reports of selected banks

SPDB's overseas revenues to total revenues ratio was 2.8% and achieved higher rank than CCB. In addition, financial crisis also significantly affected Chinese banks by lowering the contribution from their overseas revenues. According to Fig. 4.16, China's Big Five Banks managed to catch up to their peak level in 2007 (7.7%) by realizing a proportion of overseas revenue as 8% in 2015. However, as the best performer in this indicator, BOC still hasn't meet up its level in 2007.

Chinese banks were still far behind foreign banks by measuring their capability of profitability generation. In 2015, the average ratio of overseas revenues to total revenues of China's Big Five Banks (8.0%) was only 1/7 of that of foreign banks (59.4%). Specifically, among 26 Chinese and foreign banks as shown in Table 4.7, Standard Chartered topped with its proportion of overseas revenue as 93.9%, which was 40% higher than the average level of foreign banks. Each foreign bank maintained the proportion of profit from overseas market above 20% and essentially defeated Chinese banks. BOC approached the lowest level of foreign banks with its ratio of overseas revenue up to 20%, while the average level of other Chinese banks was below 10%.

(3) **The Growth Rate in China's Big Five Banks' Overseas Revenues Out-Performed Foreign Banks as 15%**

In recent years, the complexity in Chinese and global economic environment grows while Chinese banks are still at their initial stage in globalization, and the fluctuation in Chinese banks' growth rate of overseas revenue is relatively large and continuously grow. According to Fig. 4.17, ABC, CITIC[2] and Mitsubishi UFJ FG were selected as representatives of China's Big Five Banks, joint-stock banks and foreign banks to demonstrate the volatility in their growth of overseas revenue.

---

[2]Since CEB only had two years data for overseas revenue growth rate, we use CITIC's data for analysis.

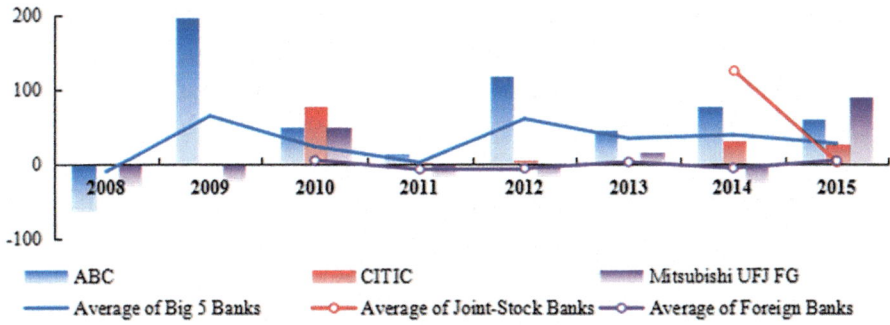

Fig. 4.17 Growth rate of overseas revenues by Chinese and foreign banks (%). *Source* Zhejiang University CIFI, annual reports of selected banks

Although ABC had lower ratio of its overseas revenues to total revenues, but still remained strong in terms of growth rate after the financial crisis during 2007–2009. In which, ABC achieved the highest level as 196% in 2009 and even 14.3% in its worst year of 2011, but still higher than the average level of all other China's Big Five Banks. CITIC had experienced great fluctuation in its overseas revenue and the growth rate reached 77.4% in 2010 then dropped to 0.8% in 2013. Mitsubishi UFJ FG's expansion in its overseas revenue had a certain degree of representativeness that it swayed around the growth rate as zero even with great volatility due to various impacts in recent years.

From the perspective of average growth rate in overseas revenue, it showed a fluctuated but upward trend for Chinese joint-stock banks and China's Big Five Banks. In contrast, foreign banks wavered around zero growth rate. In addition, joint-stock banks achieved higher growth rate in overseas revenue than China's Big Five Banks. Meanwhile, foreign banks had their average growth rate in overseas revenue becoming negative (−1.3%) during 2010–2015, which fell behind China's Big Five Banks.

By concluding, although Chinese bank had greater fluctuation in their growth rate of overseas, the overall trend was still upward. Chinese banks achieved more prominent performance than foreign banks, who stayed stable or even experienced slight shrinkage in their overseas business when entering matured stage of globalization.

4.3.2 Chinese Banks Should Be Acknowledged with Their Profitability Generation Capability in Foreign Countries and Further Their Exploration in New Source of Profit

In this chapter, we performed in-depth analysis on the scale, proportion and growth in banks' overseas revenue. It should be pointed out that the revenue mentioned refers to profit before tax (Table 4.9).

Table 4.9 Ranking of overseas profits for selected Chinese and foreign banks in 2015[a]

Ranking	Total overseas profits (RMB in billions)		Proportion of overseas profits (%)		Growth rate of overseas profits (%)	
1	HSBC	118.26	Credit Suisse	172.1	Mitsubishi UFJ FG	310.7
2	Santander	67.34	Standard Chartered	155.6	BNP Paribas	82.7
3	Mitsubishi UFJ FG	64.98	HSBC	96.6	Groupe Crédit Agricole	61.4
4	BNP Paribas	55.33	Santander	87.3	UBS	40.0
5	BOC	54.75	Nordea	83.6	ABC	30.4
6	Citigroup	51.64	BNP Paribas	80.1	*CEB	24.2
7	JPMorgan Chase	49.71	ING	71.9	ING	20.3
8	ING	37.20	Mitsubishi UFJ FG	55.7	ICBC	19.2
9	ICBC	29.27	Bank of New York Mellon	50.9	Santander	10.5
10	Nordea	27.73	Citigroup	50.3	Citigroup	6.4
11	Mizuho FG	17.08	Groupe Crédit Agricole	43.9	HSBC	5.5
12	Bank of New York Mellon	13.99	UBS	31.6	BOC	2.9
13	UBS	11.24	Deutsche Bank	30.3	Nordea	2.6
14	Groupe Crédit Agricole	10.88	Mizuho FG	26.1	JPMorgan Chase	1.3
15	Standard Chartered	8.42	JPMorgan Chase	24.9	Bank of New York Mellon	−0.3
16	*BOCOM	6.05	BOC	23.6	*BOCOM	−2.5
17	ABC	5.43	UniCredit	11.2	*CGB	−11.5
18	CCB	5.31	*BOCOM	7.0	*CMB	−13.8
19	*CITIC	2.21	ICBC	6.5	CCB	−16.3
20	UniCredit	2.11	*CITIC	4.0	Mizuho FG	−16.6
21	*CMB	1.79	*CMB	2.4	*CITIC	−21.9
22	*CGB	0.23	ABC	2.3	UniCredit	−72.0
23	*CEB	0.20	*CGB	2.1	Standard Chartered	−74.4
24	Deutsche Bank	−13.05	CCB	1.8	Credit Suisse	−234.2
25	Credit Suisse	−26.99	*CEB	0.5	Deutsche Bank	−253.1

[a]For the sake of comparison, overseas revenue of foreign banks was converted to RMB with the exchange rate at the balance sheet date

We used estimation to compute BII for SPDB due to limited data accessibility on their overseas revenue during 2010–2014. Hence, SPDB is excluded from the ranking of growth rate on overseas revenue

Banks with * are not in G-SIBs

Source Zhejiang University CIFI, annual reports of selected banks

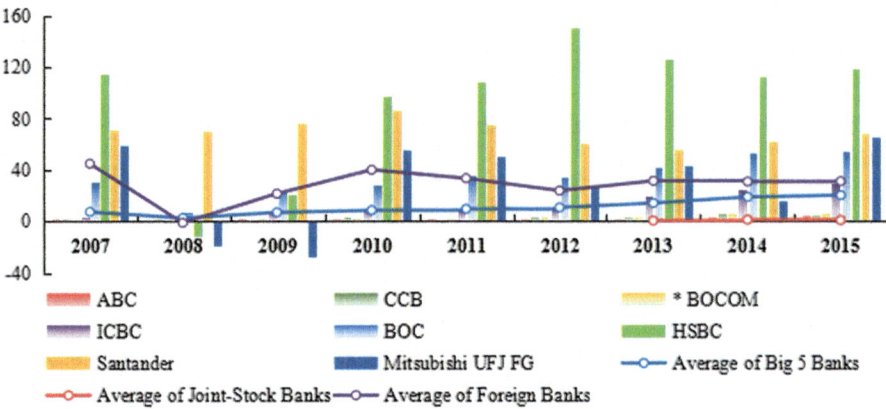

Fig. 4.18 Overseas profits of Chinese and foreign banks (RMB in billions). Banks with * are not in G-SIBs. *Source* Zhejiang University CIFI, annual reports of selected banks

(1) **China's Big Five Banks' Consolidated Overseas Profit Exceeded 100 billion yuan in 2015 with BOC and ICBC Entering Top 10**

According to Fig. 4.18, the total overseas profit of China's Big Five Banks amounted to 100.81 billion yuan in 2015 which marked the milestone of exceeding 100 billion yuan for the first time. Their overseas profit increased by 6.7 and 160% compared to that of 2014 and 2007 respectively. Meanwhile, two Chinese banks entered top 10 among all 25 selected banks by ranking their overseas profits. Among them, the overseas profits of BOC in 2015 ran up to 54.75 billion yuan and earned 1st place among all Chinese banks. Though its growth rate in 2015 was not significant compared to that of 2014, BOC still managed to defeat ICBC (ranked 2nd) by 87% and its ranking among 25 foreign banks rose up to 5th. In addition, BOCOM, ABC and CCB generated similar level of overseas profits in 2015 ranging from 5 to 6 billion yuan. As for joint-stock banks, none was able to have their overseas profit over 3 billion yuan in 2015. Both CITIC and CMB had their overseas profit dropped in 2015 to 2.21 billion yuan and 1.79 billion yuan respectively. CGB and CEB did not even surpass 500 million yuan in their overseas profits in 2015.

The overseas profits of foreign banks showed significant fluctuation in recent 9 years. Their average overseas profits even became negative in 2008 as a result of financial crisis. This was the only time for foreign banks generating lower overseas profits than Chinese banks. Even though foreign banks managed to recover by surpassing Chinese banks since 2008, their average overseas profit only amounted to 30.99 billion yuan in 2015 which was only 60% of BOC's overseas profits. Hence, Chinese banks have the smallest gap compared to foreign banks by measuring their overseas profits. On one hand, this reflected the profound impact from global financial crisis on international financial institutions leading to massive

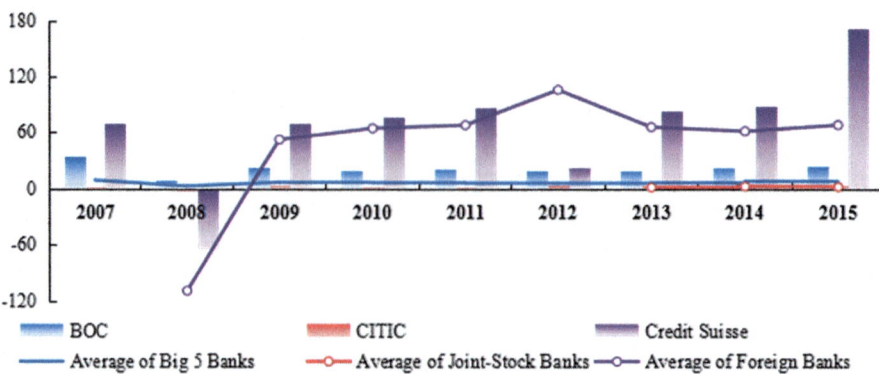

Fig. 4.19 Proportion of overseas profits for Chinese and foreign banks (%). *Source* Zhejiang University CIFI, annual reports of selected banks

reduction in their overseas profitability. On the other hand, it was also an affirmation on Chinese banks' achievements on globalization.

(2) **Chinese Banks' Ratio of Overseas Revenues to Total Revenues Experienced Subtle Fluctuation, While Foreign Bank Fluctuated Greatly**

Firstly, Chinese banks had low proportion of overseas profits and stay involatile, which was similar to their overseas revenue. In 2015, average proportion of overseas profits reached 8.3% for China's Big Five Banks and was still below their level of 2007 (9.1%). BOC ranked 16th among the 25 selected banks with its proportion of overseas profit as 23.6%. Though this did not surpass 33.7% as that in 2007, BOC still topped all Chinese banks and was up to 4 times as the average level of China's Big Five Banks. All other Chinese banks had their proportion of overseas profits below 10% and hence their rankings were lower.

Secondly, foreign banks had experienced great volatility in their proportion of overseas profits. By analyzing their average proportion, we noticed that most foreign banks experienced operation loss in their overseas business in 2008 and hence, the proportion of their overseas profit became −109.6%. Subsequently, foreign banks made a recovery with this ratio returning to positive value. However, by zooming in, there were still a few banks remain loss in their overseas business. As shown in Fig. 4.19, Credit Suisse achieved a proportion of overseas profit as 172.1% in 2015, which indicated that its domestic profits was negative. In addition, the list of banks entered in top 6 in proportion of overseas profits includes Credit Suisse, Standard Chartered, HSBC, Santander, Nordea, BNP Paribas, which all exceeded 80%. It can also be seen from another point of view that internationalization enables banks to allocate their resources globally in order to boost profitability and improve operation stability. Compared with the Chinese banks, the

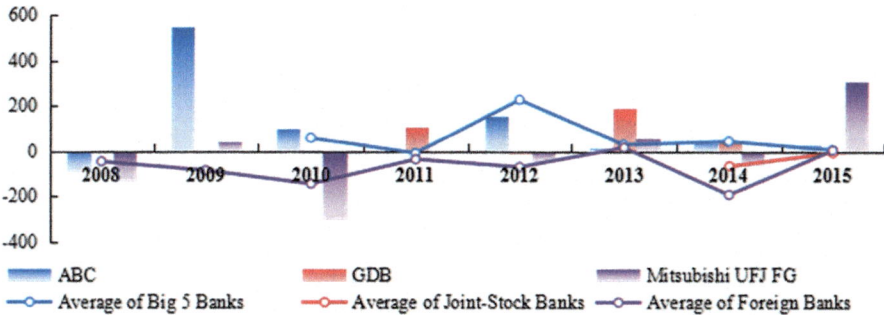

Fig. 4.20 Growth rate of overseas profits by Chinese and foreign banks (%). *Source* Zhejiang University CIFI, annual reports of selected banks

average proportion of overseas profits for foreign banks[3] was up to 68.7%, which was 2.9 times and 8.3 times that of BOC and the average level of China's Big Five Banks.

(3) **Several Chinese Banks Demonstrated Negative Growth Rate in Overseas Profit Due to Instability in Their Source of Overseas Profitability**

The variation in developing overseas profits became complex and showed substantial fluctuation (see Fig. 4.20). ABC achieved a growth rate as 30.4% in its overseas profits in 2015 and ranked 5th. It needs to be pointed out that several Chinese banks experienced lower growth rate in 2015 in their overseas profit and some even became negative. This showed that Chinese banks still have not gained strong position in their overseas business for profit generation. For example, the average growth rate of China's Big Five Banks in 2013 and 2014 were both over 30%, then dropped to 6.8% in 2015 with a decline rate of 80%. Among them, CMB had its growth rate of overseas profit as −13.8% in 2015 while it hit 124.5% in 2014. Due to the fact that Chinese banks are mostly in their initial stage of globalization, their strategies on profit generation are still indistinct. Meanwhile, besides the fact that the economic environment in domestic and overseas markets grow increasingly complex, banks are facing challenges from mixed business model as well as innovative internet technologies, new mindset and new operation models. All of these factors have led to volatility in banks' profit.

By comparing with other indicators of globalization, foreign banks experienced greater fluctuation in their growth rate of overseas profits. This indicated the dominating impact from global economy on the profitability of banks. Ever since 2008, the average growth rate of overseas profits became negative for foreign banks and managed to return to 4.4% in 2015. Mitsubishi UFJ FG topped all 25 banks with its growth rate above 300%. Except for the banks in top 9, all banks had their

---

[3]Deutsche Bank and BNP Paribas were not included due to the lack of data.

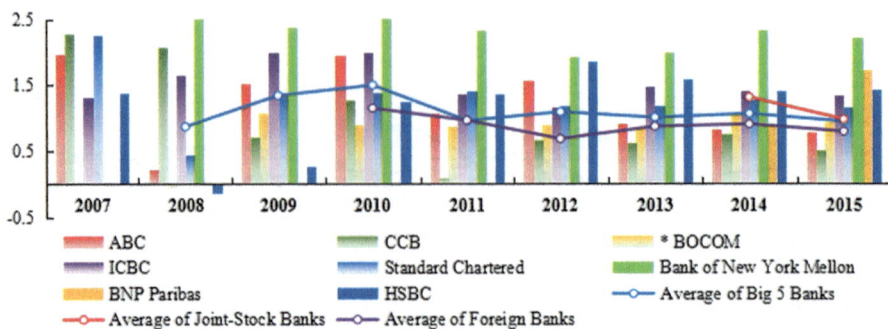

Fig. 4.21 ROA of Chinese and foreign banks (%). Banks with * are not in G-SIBs. *Source* Zhejiang University CIFI, annual reports of selected banks

growth rate below 10% and those placed at the bottom 10 even experienced a negative growth rate in their overseas profits.

However, it brings more challenges for banks to maintain high speed in their business development with volatile growth in overseas profit. As for Chinese banks, they must strive to enhance their operation capacity in order to increase their profitability and sustain their position in global market.

4.3.3 Chinese Banks Managed to Stabilized Their ROA in Overseas Market and Slightly Higher Than Foreign Banks

Return on Assets (ROA) measures the percentage of profit that a company earns in relation to its overall resources, which is computed by dividing total profit with average assets. In order to present Chinese banks' capability of profitability generation at its core, ROA[4] was adopted in this chapter by analyzing outcome of their overseas operation and made comparison against foreign banks (see Fig. 4.21).

In general, Chinese banks maintained their overseas ROA above 1%. Among China's Big Five Banks, ICBC and BOC stood out with their overseas ROA up to 1.2% or higher. The other 3 China's Big Five Banks closely followed with their overseas ROA above 0.5%. In 2015, the average overseas ROA for China's Big Five Banks was only 0.9% and slightly lower than the average level of joint-stock banks. CMB outperformed all other joint-stock banks in 2015 with its overseas ROA as 1.3%.

---

[4]In this report, ROA for a bank's overseas business = overseas profit before tax/average overseas assets.

Compared to other indicators of internationalization, foreign banks maintained relatively lower level in their overseas ROA and even fell behind the average level of Chinese banks. The average overseas ROA for the 13 selected foreign banks[5] dropped below 1% in recent years with only one exception in 2010. Their average overseas ROA in 2015 was only 0.8%, which can be analyzed from below aspects: Firstly, the gap between the overseas ROA of foreign and Chinese banks is as small as 0.1–0.2% during 2013–2015. Secondly, the expansion of business scale is the outcome of accumulation after several year's operation in overseas market. Foreign banks have been ahead of Chinese banks in exploring overseas markets, which facilitated their accumulation of overseas assets and more exposed to the impacts from different financial markets. With their extensive business scope and large operation scale at global platform, foreign banks shouldered greater risks accordingly. Their profitability was substantially affected by the sluggish economy in recent years. Lastly, with Chinese companies actively participating in overseas M&A and the acceleration of RMB internationalization, Chinese banks had been expanding their RMB business after financial crisis and their overseas profit also grown continuously. By concluding, though Chinese banks fell behind in their scale of overseas assets and ROA compared to foreign banks, they demonstrated prominent capability of profitability generation.

Though Chinese banks' maintaining high level in their overseas ROA affirmed their profitability capability at a global scale, they ought to leverage and learn foreign banks' experiences in global market then strive to maintain stable growth in overseas business and revenue.

4.4   Chinese Banks Continued to Expand Overseas Network While the Number of Foreign Banks' Overseas Institutions Dropped

In order to further globalization progress, banks need to leverage their physical network to enhance their presence in overseas markets. This strategy can be achieved by forming agency agreement with other banks, establishing overseas institutions, M&A and equity investments in overseas companies. All these means will facilitate banks to open global markets, expand client base, increase market shares and explore new business opportunities. Therefore, banks' development strategies can be reflected in their layout and the number of overseas networks.

---

[5]BNP Paribas, Deutsche Bank UBS were not included.

4.4.1 Chinese Banks' Global Network Extended to Six Continents with Asia-Pacific Being Their Primary Focus

At present, different types of Chinese banks vary significantly in their layout of overseas network. China's Big Five Banks have larger business scale and are able to have more extensive footprints in overseas countries. In contrast, joint-stock banks are still at an initial stage of globalization and establish overseas institutions in Asia and Southeast Asia. By the end of 2015, China's Big Five Banks have 71.4% of their branches in Asia and Europe (close to 3/4 of their total number of branches), among which 44.4% are located in Asia. BOC was still in the leading position of all Chinese banks for over 1/2 of its branches are overseas branches, which dropped 1% compared to 2014. The runner-up is ICBC with 20.9% and declined by 0.6% in 2015. CCB actively expanded its overseas network during 2015 which led to a growth rate of 1.5%.

Secondly, with "the Belt and Road" Initiatives implemented and deepened, major financial intuitions have joined and provided financial support to "the Belt and Road" from an integrated but mufti-dimensional view. BOC set up 5 new branches in Southeast Asia area in 2015 along with Maritime Silk Road, which included 3 branches in Thailand, 1 in Laos and 1 in Burma. Meanwhile, financial activities grew actively along the Silk Road connecting the Eurasian continent. During 2015, CCB established 5 branches in Europe covering UK, France, Spain, Italy and The Netherlands.

Finally, Table 4.10 demonstrated the global network of the selected Chinese and foreign banks. By analyzing the number of countries with operation network established, Chinese banks lagged behind foreign banks. Nevertheless, BOC managed to enter to top 10 and ICBC closely followed with its ranking as 11th, both have overseas branches in over 40 countries. While Chinese banks continued to increase their number of overseas branches at a steady growth rate, foreign banks' layout of global network remained stable or even declined slightly in recent years after their golden age of global expansion.

Table 4.10 Global network distribution of selected Chinese and foreign banks in 2015

Ranking	Number of countries banks' institutions covered		Ranking	Growth rate of banks' institutions covered countries (%)	
1	Citibank	93	1	CCB	23.8
2	BNP Paribas	75	2	*CITIC	20.0
3	HSBC	71	3	*CMB	16.7
4	Deutsche Bank	70	4	Bank of New York Mellon	14.3
5	Standard Chartered	67	5	BOC	11.9

(continued)

Table 4.10 (continued)

Ranking	Number of countries banks' institutions covered		Ranking	Growth rate of banks' institutions covered countries (%)	
6	JP Morgan Chase	60	6	Mizuho FG	8.6
7	Groupe Crédit Agricole	52	7	*BOCOM	7.7
8	Credit Suisse	50	8	ABC	7.1
9	UBS	50	9	ICBC	2.4
10	BOC	47	10	JP Morgan Chase	0.0
11	ICBC	43	10	BNP Paribas	0.0
12	Mitsubishi UFJ FG	40	10	ING Bank	0.0
13	Bank of New York Mellon	40	10	Nordea	0.0
14	ING Bank	40	10	Santander	0.0
15	Santander	40	10	UBS	0.0
16	Mizuho FG	38	10	UniCredit	0.0
17	Wells Fargo	36	10	Wells Fargo	0.0
18	CCB	26	10	*SPDB	0.0
19	UniCredit	17	10	*CEB	0.0
20	Nordea	16	10	*CGB	0.0
21	ABC	15	21	Deutsche Bank	−1.4
22	*BOCOM	14	22	HSBC	−2.7
23	*CMB	7	23	Groupe Crédit Agricole	−3.7
24	*CITIC	6	24	Standard Chartered	−5.6
25	*CGB	3	25	Credit Suisse	−7.4
26	*SPDB	2	26	Citibank	−7.9
26	*CEB	2	27	Mitsubishi UFJ FG	−11.1

Banks with * are not in G-SIBs
Source Zhejiang University CIFI, annual reports of selected banks

Column 3 American Banks' Global Expansion

Chinese banks started to accelerate their overseas expansion in recent 30 years and hence remained at a relatively lower level in globalization compared to foreign banks, who entered global markets earlier.

Taking American banks as an example, their global activities intensified in late 1960s and overseas expansion was substantially accelerated in 1970s. Statistics showed that in 1966, 12 major US banks had only 242 overseas institutions in total with overseas assets amounted to $12.4 billion. After 10 year of development, their total number of overseas institutions increased to 562 and total overseas assets grew to $113.6 billion by 1974, achieving an astonishing annual growth of 11.1 and 31.9% respectively. Furthermore, besides establishing overseas branches, American banks also accelerated their globalization through overseas M&A. Chase Manhattan Bank formed its global business network in 1970s by actively acquiring foreign banks and establishing joint-venture banks with business partners.

From business perspectives, American banks initially followed their domestic manufacturing companies' footprint in globalization by providing financial support to their overseas investment projects. They subsequently expanded their business scope by offering various services to local companies and other foreign clients. For instance, Citibank became a global financial group in 1974 and maintained 2500 multinational corporation clients by 1980.

These global financial groups are still going strong and are the main voice maker in global market. However, with the active participation of Chinese banks and the rise of several emerging economies, such global financial patterns are being broken and Chinese banks will have more power in the future international financial market.

4.4.2 Chinese Banks Continued to Establish New Overseas Branches While Foreign Banks Reduced Their Global Networks

When establishing global business network, banks ought to have overall strategies in a certain region or country, while specific business sectors such as loan and deposit need to be further planned with careful consideration. The assessment on overseas institutions of selected Chinese and foreign banks (including sub-branches) is demonstrated in Table 4.11. It was difficult to unify the measurement of overseas branches for foreign banks. Hence, the total number of overseas network may not be accurate. However, the proportion and growth rate is rather objective and therefore the ranking is made based on these 2 indicators in Table 4.11.

(1) **Chinese Banks Swayed Around 1.5% for Their Proportion of Overseas Branches and Only Accounted to 1/30 of Foreign Banks**

Compared to the total number of branches of foreign banks, the number of branches of Chinese banks is still small and significantly behind foreign banks. Figure 4.22 showed the proportion of overseas branches for China's Big Five Banks and selected foreign banks, while Chinese joint-stock banks were excluded due to their limited global presence. It can be noticed that China's Big Five Banks maintained their average proportion of overseas branches around 2% in recent 5 years. BOC had 5.5% of its branches in overseas countries while the other China's Big Five Banks are even lower in this indicator. In contrast, the average proportion of overseas branches for foreign banks remained above 50%. Despite the

Table 4.11   Ranking of overseas institutions for selected Chinese and foreign banks in 2015[a]

Ranking	Proportion of overseas branches (%)		Growth rate of overseas branches (%)	
1	BNP Paribas	80.6	*CEB	100.0
2	Citibank	73.9	ICBC	19.5
3	Santander	73.4	Mizuho FG	18.1
4	HSBC	71.3	ABC	13.3
5	UBS	56.5	CCB	12.5
6	Mitsubishi UFJ FG	51.7	*BOCOM	3.7
7	UniCredit	44.1	BOC	2.5
8	Credit Suisse	36.0	Santander	1.3
9	Deutsche Bank	34.5	BNP Paribas	−0.4
10	Groupe Crédit Agricole	22.3	Deutsche Bank	−0.6
11	Mizuho FG	12.4	Credit Suisse	−1.2
12	BOC	5.5	*CITIC	−2.4
13	*CITIC	2.9	Citibank	−8.9
14	ICBC	2.3	HSBC	−10.0
15	*BOCOM	1.8	UniCredit	−12.7
16	CCB	0.2		
17	ABC	0.1		

[a]We used estimation method for Standard Chartered, JPMorgan Chase, ING, Nordea and New York Mellon due to data availability issue. Hence, these banks were excluded from the ranking
Banks with * are not in G-SIBs
Source Zhejiang University CIFI, annual reports of selected banks

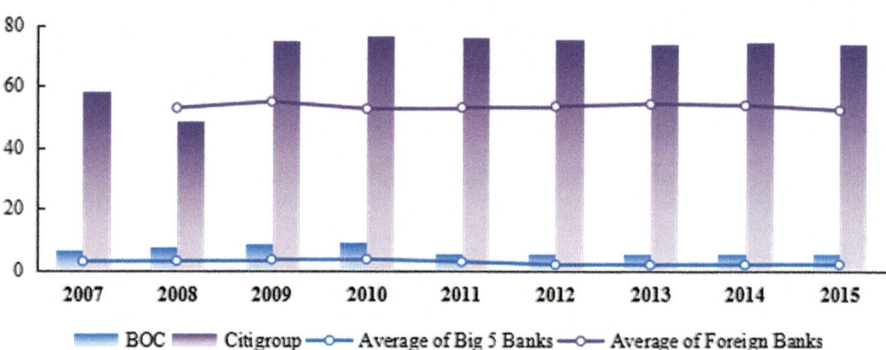

Fig. 4.22   Proportion of overseas institutions for Chinese and foreign banks (%). *Source* Zhejiang University CIFI, annual reports of selected banks

total number of its overseas branches declined in recent years, Citibank still managed to reach 73.9% in 2015 which was 13 times higher than BOC.

Individual financial institution varies in business types, operation model and strategic blueprint, which is reflected in the absolute number of their overseas branches. A bank's globalization can be better measured by the comparison in its number of branches in domestic and overseas countries. Although Chinese banks have made tremendous effort on developing its overseas business during recent years, their number of overseas branches still falls short compared to their extensive domestic branches. However, with internet technology being actively promoted and implemented, banks are urged to invest on the exploration and the development of online business model, which may supplement the inadequacy of their physical branches.

(2) **ICBC Stood Out with Its Growth Rate of Overseas Branches as 19.5% in 2015**

Compared to foreign banks, Chinese banks achieved better performance in expanding their overseas branches, even with essential fluctuation in annual growth rate. Among them, ICBC scored an eye-catching growth rate of 19.5% in the number of overseas branches by increasing from 338 to 404 in 2015. It was ranked 1st among China's Big Five Banks and 2nd in overall ranking. At the same time, BOC was relatively more stable by maintaining growth rate of its overseas branches within 3% for the past 3 years and reached 2.5% in 2015, which put BOC as 7th in the overall ranking. In general, China's Big Five Banks demonstrated great volatility in their growth rate of overseas branches and achieved 10.3% on average in 2015. The fluctuation in growth rate of joint-stock banks' overseas branches is also substantial with the focus on Hong Kong. Taking CEB as an example, its number of overseas branches grew from 1 to 2 in 2015 with a growth rate of 100% and ranked 1st. However, such rapid growth does not represent the real level of globalization and hence, joint-stock banks are not included in the below analysis (Fig. 4.23).

According to Table 4.11, several foreign banks experienced a decline in their number of overseas branches and among them, Citibank demonstrated a negative growth rate in the number of its overseas branches except for 2010 (6.7%). Though Citibank is recovering in recent years but its growth rate in 2015 reached −8.9%.

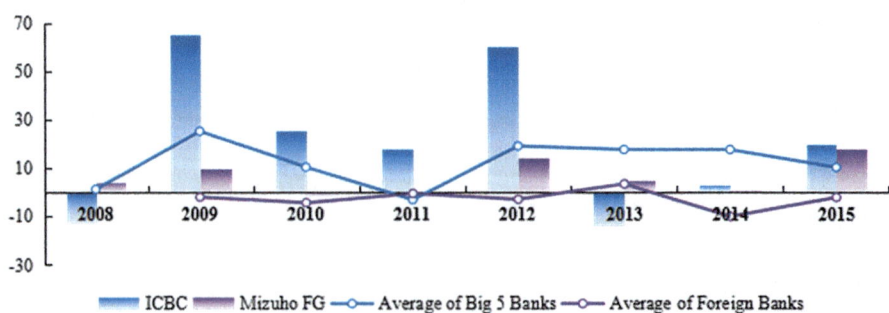

Fig. 4.23 Growth rate of overseas institutions by Chinese and foreign banks (%). *Source* Zhejiang University CIFI, annual reports of selected banks

Foreign banks' reduction in their overseas branches could be related to the impact from the global economy or banks' own strategies of adjusting their footprints in overseas business. As for Chinese banks, stepping into foreign country is the first step to go global. Facing the dynamic and evolving international market, Chinese banks must pace its overseas expansion cautiously and expand its global landscape carefully.

Chapter 5
Implications of Risks Associated with Banks' Internationalization

Financial risk refers to the exposure of future uncertainty that the financial market participants face when conducting financial activities, or the possibility of economic losses that may incur its future expected income of financial assets. According to such risk characteristics, financial risk can be further divided into market risk, liquidity risk, operational risk, legal risk, credit risk, political risk and so on (Table 5.1).

While Chinese banks actively learn from foreign banks for their expertise and experiences in global market, they also need to pay attention to the variety of risk incidents incurred and be fully committed to risk prevention and management when operating on a global scale. The journey of internationalization won't always be smooth. Chinese banks should be fully aware of various risks including market risk, M&A risk, operational risk and legal risk, in order to remain stable during the course of global expansion. In addition, although the following cases of Lehman Brothers' Bankruptcy and UBS' rogue trader scandal are not the typical "internationalization risk" cases, we still selected these two cases for our study because of their strong representativeness and profound influence, which could be regarded as good reference for Chinese banks.

5.1 Case Studies on Foreign Banks' International Risk

Since the 1990s, major risk events incurred financial institutions and enterprises, such as Barings Bank, Daiwa Bank, LTCM and the Enron. Those incidents not only had significant negative impact on the sustainability and steadiness of the global financial markets, but also caused great loss to a large number of financial institutions and some even went bankruptcy. Financial markets in China still lag behind developed countries for at least half a century, hence learning from foreign banks' experiences and lessons in their internationalization via in-depth studies of classic cases is of vital significance to Chinese banks.

© Zhejiang University Press and Springer Nature Singapore Pte Ltd. 2018
B. Shenglin et al., *In Pursuit of Presence or Prominence?* Current Chinese Economic Report Series, https://doi.org/10.1007/978-981-10-7730-2_5

Table 5.1 Common financial risks for financial institutions

Financial risk	Concept
Market risk	The risk of a change in the value of a financial position due to changes in the market value of the underlying components on which that position depends, e.g., interest rate, exchange rate, commodity prices, stock prices. These components could influence the investor directly, or indirectly by its competitors, suppliers or customers
Liquidity risk	The risk is divided into two types: market liquidity risk (i.e. asset/product risk) and funding liquidity risk (i.e. cash-flow risk). Market liquidity risk is the loss incurred when a market participant wishes to execute a trade or to liquidate a position immediately while not hitting the best price. Funding liquidity risk is the risk that a bank is not able to match the amount and timing of cash flows, forcing the financial institutions to liquidate its current asset in order to meet obligations and hence potential losses turn into actual losses. Liquidity risk occurs when the financial institutions fail to pay their debt obligations by selling current assets or converting to cash equivalents
Operational risk	The risk of potential losses results from inadequate or failed trading system, management, internal control, and technologies in financial institutions. Operational risk includes inadequate employee training, operational errors, accidents and fraud
Legal risk	The risk of failure to comply with statutory or regulatory obligations when conducting transactions, including: ① The contract is not protected by law or its financial terms are not deliberate enough; ② Laws and regulations cannot keep up with the financial innovation, so the financial innovation was unable to seek appropriate legal protection, which may lead to the loss of one or both counterparties; ③ Economic bodies will be punished when acting against the laws or regulations
Credit risk	Credit risk is also called default risk, which refers to the risk when a counterparty fails to meet its debt obligations in accordance with agreed terms. Furthermore, credit risk also includes the possibilities of losses in the value of a financial institution's debt securities caused by its credit rating lowered by credit rating agencies. Almost all financial transactions are exposed to credit risk. Besides traditional financial services, the credit risk of emerging internet financial products (such as internet banking) also becomes increasingly prominent in recent years
Political risk	A type of risk imposes on investors, corporations, and governments when political decisions, events, or conditions will significantly affect the profitability of a business actor or the expected value of a given economic action. Specifically, the political risk includes conflict among races, religions, interest groups and countries, or the change and reform in policy, system and authority

Source Zhejiang University CIFI

5.1.1 Market Risk—Citibank's Operation Crisis

Citigroup is one of the world's largest financial institutions, formed by a merger between Citicorp and Travelers Group in 1988 and went publicly listed in the same year. The history of Citigroup started from the establishment of Citibank. Its pre-decessor, City Bank of New York, was founded on June 16, 1812. After over 200 years development, Citibank established its position as one of the most well-known banks worldwide through its outstanding foreign exchange and retail business as well as its extensive global branch network. However, Citibank experienced severe operation crisis in the late 1980s and early 1990s.

5.1.1.1 Case Study

After more than 150-year development, Citibank achieved a notable business scale in 1970s. In the early 1980s of the United States, the "bubble economy" era, Citibank even experienced an explosive growth and became more committed to internationalization. Accordingly, Citibank marched to real estate (mainly residential properties) investment market in the US and South America and provided leveraged acquisition financing[1] to corporate clients. With the aim of becoming a universal bank, Citibank presented its "Five Is" business strategies, which is Individual, Institution, Investment Banking, Information, and Insurance.

However, in the early 1990s, following the burst of American economy bubbles and debt crisis in non-oil producing developing countries, US banks suffered huge loss and some even went bankruptcy. Citibank had not been immune to this phenomenon. Additionally, excessively rapid international expansion greatly accelerated its asset risks, resulting in massive non-performing loans. Citibank's provision for overseas credit loss reached $3.2 and $1 billion in 1987 and 1989 respectively. From 1990 to 1992, its total credit loss provision accumulated to $2.66, $3.87 and $4.15 billion respectively. Despite the healthy financial performance of its subsidiaries, Citibank's after-tax profit was only $318 million in 1990, with its bad debt ratio as high as 7% and the total bad debt amounted to $10 billion. In 1991, Citibank's after-tax profit suffered even more severe decline along with the downgrading of its credit rating from AA to Baa.

5.1.1.2 Lessons Learned

Even as one of the largest commercial banks worldwide and with its abundant capital, Citibank still encountered great financial risks and incurred substantial losses during its globalization expansion. The reasons behind this could be summarized as follows:

---

[1]Leveraged acquisition finance is the provision of bank loans and the issue of high yield bonds to fund acquisitions of companies or parts of companies by an existing internal management team (a management buy-out), an external management team (a management buy-in) or a third party (an acquisition).

(1) **US Financial Reform Brought Changes to Financial Market Triggering Market Risk**

Since 1930s, the US banking industry was under the business regulation and supervision based on the *Banking Act of 1933*, which required separation management and interest rate setting within commercial banks and securities firms. However, from the 1960s, financial institutions began to initiate a variety of financial innovations to circumvent these regulations. Thus in the 1980s, the US government launched a major reform on deregulation and liberalization of interest rates for its financial system. Furthermore, the Basel Accords continuously raised its requirements on banks' capital adequacy ratio. The financial liberalization along with the equity capital regulation had brought vitality as well as problems to the financial market. Interest rate liberalization intensified the competition among commercial banks, which triggered interest rate war. Meanwhile, in the capital market, the new form of financing without banks or other intermediaries, "Junk Bonds", had gradually arisen. This phenomenon of "disintermediation" continued unabated and brought the risks to financial markets.

(2) **Leverage Financing in Domestic and Overseas Markets Accelerated Market Risks**

Financial institutions in US actively promoted leverage financing business in home and foreign countries, and Citibank was no exception. However, in later stage, the majority of companies funded by leverage financing were unable to afford high interest rates and resulted in bankruptcy. Consequently, the credit risk led to extremely high bad debt ratio for Citibank.

(3) **Drastic Expansion Intensified Risk Exposure**

In order to transform to an international and universal financial institution, Citibank expanded too rapidly into unfamiliar areas in the absence of prudent planning. Thus, a large number of non-performing assets resulted in high bad debt ratio while new areas did not produce immediate return to its investments. Citibank was buried deeply and struggled in the cost-revenue balancing dilemma.

5.1.1.3 Citi's Three-year Recovery Plan

Citibank received harsh criticism from its shareholders and public due to its deteriorative operation. Faced with such difficult situation, management led by the Chairman and Chief Executive Officer, John J. Reed, quickly initiated an adjustment plan. In 1991, Citibank began to implement its plan of selling assets in order to increase Tier I capital and reduce the cost. In 1992, Reed led Citibank to implement a "three-year recovery plan" with the goals of rebuilding its capital strength and returning to credit rating of "AA". To achieve the above goals, Citibank carried out its restructuring and reform in following aspects:

Firstly, in terms of organization structure, Reed announced to abandon the hierarchical-decision system and established G-15 committee. This committee was formed by 15 principals worldwide who directly reported to Reed and held meetings on a regular basis. At the same time, Global Financial Office in Citi North America also set up 6 special working teams with service period as 6 months. The mission of these working teams was to enhance the efficiency of credit process, the marketing effectiveness of corporate financing business, and to raise sales and services quality of transaction banking business.

Secondly, in order to rebuild its capital strength, Citibank cut costs through employee layoffs and operating expenses reduction. Citibank also increased its Tier I capital level through sale of assets, such as the selling of Citi Information Resources Department and Citi Insurance Partners successively, as well as postponing dividend payments and issuance of bonds and new shares.

Thirdly, in terms of business restructuring, Citibank stood firm on its local market while carrying out its global expansion. Citibank re-focused on its core business with high profits and suspended its plan of developing universal banking. In view of the operation process, Citibank hired the Chief Financial Officer of Kodak to lead the business process reengineering.

Although Citibank put a stop to its development strategy of universal banking, the "three-year recovery plan" still generated great successes. Citibank was able to quickly adjust its capital structure and restore its capital strength. In 1994, Citibank's net income reached $3.5 billion and the total capital rose to $27.7 billion. Its Tier I capital amounted to $19.24 billion, ranked 4th in the global 100 largest banks. In 1997, Citibank's total assets amounted to $319 billion with net income of $7.6 billion. Its annual net profit reached $3.6 billion, return on equity (ROE) of 18.11%, and equity capital ratio of 12.31%. The stock price of Citibank also recovered from $8.5 up to $150 in 1997.

Although Citibank encountered a major crisis due to its strategic mistakes and volatility in the domestic and global financial markets, its management managed to quickly recognize the bank's status and adjust its strategy timely while adhering to its own business characteristics. Eventually, Citibank successfully reversed the deteriorative circumstances and recovered. This is worth learning for Chinese banks.

5.1.2 Liquidity Risk—Bankruptcy of Lehman Brothers

Since the 1980s, there were recurrent liquidity risk incidents in the international financial market. Several well-known financial institutions suffered tremendous losses or even went bankruptcy, as shown in Table 5.2.

Frequent occurrence of liquidity risk incidents had enormous negative impact on the global financial markets. One of the most typical cases is the bankruptcy of Lehman Brothers.

Table 5.2 Liquidity Risk Incidents since the 1980s

Year	Institutions	Details	Outcome
1984	Continental Illinois Bank	Suffered a bank run with $15 billion loss in deposits within 2 months	Acquired by the Federal Deposit Insurance Corporation
1991	Bank of New England	Suffered liquidity crisis for deposit payment resulted in huge losses	Bankruptcy
1998	Hainan Development Bank	Unable to pay maturing debts, accumulation of liquidity risk, resulted in a bank run	Bank closure
1998	The Long-Term Credit Bank of Japan	To meet the regulation requirement of not less than 8% of core capital, massively collected loans from companies, which caused liquidity crisis	Bankruptcy
2007	British Northern Rock Bank	Suffered a bank run	Depositors withdrew £2 billion in a few days, equivalent to 8% of all deposits in Northern Rock; its share price fell 70%
2008	British Northern Rock Bank	Affected by the US subprime mortgage crisis, Northern Rock suffered liquidity crisis and followed by a bank run	Nationalized
2008	American International Group	Affected by the US subprime mortgage crisis, American International Group suffered liquidity crisis due to its large net exposure of CDS (credit default swaps)	Nationalized: The US government provided $85 billion loans to American International Group with all of its assets as collateral, and held 80% of its equity.
2008	Bear Steans Cos.	Suffered a bank run due to the liquidity risk caused by the loss in its proprietary investment	Acquired by JPMorgan Chase at the price of $2.2 billion
2008	The Bank of East Asia	Suffered an unexpected liquidity crisis due to a bank run caused by rumors	
2008	Lehman Brothers	Being affected by the subprime crisis, suffered severe shortage of liquidity due to having excessive commercial real estate with highly leveraged financing	Bankruptcy with total debt amounted to $613 billion
2008	IndyMac Bank	A large number of the credit assets included subprime mortgage loans turned into non-performing loans, causing huge loss and severe shortage of liquidity, triggered a bank run crisis	Bankruptcy
2012	Credit Immobilier de France	Sought public auction due to liquidity issue	Failed to find suitable buyers

Source Zhejiang University CIFI, bank news

Founded in 1850, Lehman Brothers Holding Inc. (Lehman Brothers) was a diversified financial institution and investment bank providing global financial services. It was headquartered in New York City and regionally headquartered in London, Tokyo, and Hong Kong with offices in 48 cities worldwide. Relying on its reputation in its global investment banking and financial services, prodigious financial resource and strong research capability, Lehman Brothers was ranked top in the *Institutional Investors*, named the best investment bank by *Business Week* magazine, awarded as the best investment bank of 2002, elected as one of the fortune 500 companies in 2007 and ranked 132th. Lehman Brothers was also the fourth largest investment bank in the US.

As such a world-famous investment bank, Lehman Brothers suffered severe shortage of liquidity, affected by the global financial crisis arising from the US subprime crisis in 2008. Lehman Brothers eventually filed for bankruptcy protection on September 15th in the same year with total debt amounted to $619 billion.

5.1.2.1 Case Study

In November 1999, after the *Glass-Steagall Act* was abolished, Lehman Brothers was no longer limited to the traditional investment banking business such as public offering and underwriting of securities, trading and brokerage, etc. Lehman Brothers set off to change its business model and stepped into commercial banking and real estate investment.

From January 2001 to June 2003, the US government responded to the sluggish economy by lowering the federal fund rate 13 times consecutively in order to avoid recession if the Internet bubble burst. The interest rate dropped from 6.55% on January 3rd, 2001 to 1.0% on June 25th, 2003. Monetary expansion and low interest rate reduced the borrowing costs, coupled with misleadingly incentive housing policy, steering Americans swarming into real estate sector. In anticipation that the house price would continue to rise in the future, Lehman Brothers also started to engage in the subprime market.

In the next few years, Lehman Brothers not only actively developed its subprime mortgage business, but also expanded rapidly in the subprime mortgage-backed securities market. In 2006, Lehman Brothers held over $50 billion subprime securities. Since 2007, to avoid the unfolding crisis of the US subprime mortgage-backed securities market, Lehman Brothers invested in a number of commercial real estate. These included investing substantially in the Texas Energy company (TXU), acquiring Clare Corporation, jointly acquiring Archstone-Smith Trust (one of the best US real estate investment trust) at the price of $22.2 billion with Rockefeller Center. Furthermore, Lehman Brothers increased its subprime loans and heavily involved in leverage financing business, which significantly raised its liquidity risk. This inevitably led to some of its assets with low liquidity being unable to trade easily in the market during the crisis.

In 2007, the US real estate price fell drastically with continuously rising interest rate. A large number of borrowers were unable to repay their mortgage loans on time, which turned great proportion of subprime mortgage into bad debt and gave rise to the US subprime crisis. Due to the shortage of liquidity in the market and the collapse of the counter-parties' confidence, the housing mortgage market nearly lost its hedging abilities. Lehman Brothers encountered increasing difficulties in conducting hedges in the housing mortgage and commercial real estate mortgage market. The subprime crisis severely devastated its ability of assets securitization and trading of housing mortgage-backed loans. Lehman Brothers' massive housing mortgage-backed assets and commercial real estate mortgage-backed assets slumped abruptly in value and suffered huge loss due to the credit crisis.

On September 15, 2008, Lehman Brothers, a financial institution with a 158-year history, filed for bankruptcy protection in the US Bankruptcy Court in Manhattan. Its total debt amounted to $619 billion. On September 22nd, 2008, Nomura Holdings announced its acquisition of Lehman Brothers' business in Europe, Middle East, and Asia including Japan and Hong Kong of China. On September 17th, 2008, Barclays announced its acquisition of Lehman Brothers' investment banking business in America, operation headquarters in New York and two data centers in New Jersey at the price of $1.75 billion.

5.1.2.2 Lessons Learned

From the perspective of liquidity risk, the causes of Lehman Brothers' bankruptcy demonstrate in the following aspects.

(1) **Holding Excessive Commercial Real Estate and Heavily Dependent on Short-Term Financing**

From this case study, we noticed that the mismatch between short-term financing and long-term assets had got Lehman Brothers into deep liquidity trap. First of all, Lehman Brothers was over optimistic about the returns that mortgage market and traded risky derivative instruments may generate. When the overall credibility of the market was compromised by the subprime crisis, a large number of illiquid mortgage assets and commercial real estate mortgage assets of Lehman Brothers could not be efficiently hedged during the crisis. Additionally, with short-term financing not accessible, the difficulties of being temporarily unable to get rid of liquidity difficulties ultimately led Lehman Brothers to bankruptcy, even though it had sufficient assets to fund its payment.

(2) **Insufficient Capital Adequacy Ratio and Excessively High Leverage Ratio**

In its pursuit of the rapid expansion, Lehman Brothers adopted an aggressive development strategy by blindly using a large number of highly leveraged financial products. Such strategy led Lehman Brothers to bear excessively high liquidity risk. When the asset prices dropped, the company not only suffered the loss from leverage ratio amplification, but also faced the difficulties in gathering fund due to its liquidity issue. By the end of 2007, the leverage ratio of Lehman Brothers went up to 34 times. This implied that once the asset price fell with 3% loss in net value, it would lead the company to bankruptcy.

(3) **Drastic Changes in Financial Environment and Panic Caused by Subprime Crisis**

In the context of external environment, the subprime crisis created resistance for Lehman Brothers to effectively resolve its liquidity risk. Under the financial market turbulence, investors' growing anxiety and asymmetric information, investors would quickly terminate their transactions once having doubts about the company's credibility. Thus, the credit crunch arisen from subprime crisis hampered Lehman Brothers' business of asset securitization and sale of mortgage loans. Due to lack of counter-parties' willingly to trade with Lehman Brothers, its substantial mortgage assets and commercial real estate mortgage assets suffered significant impairment loss.

Additionally, without strong support or bailout from the US government and the Federal Reserve, Lehman Brothers eventually went bankruptcy after undergoing significant short-term liquidity and reputation risks.

5.1.3   Operational Risk—The UBS Rogue Trader Scandal

Since the 1980s, operational risk cases emerged continuously in the global financial markets and underwent dramatic changes of situation. Specific details as are shown in Table 5.3.

It can be seen that not only the occurrence of operational risk is frequent, but also it has substantial negative impact. Among the cases above, UBS fraud case is one of the most typical operational risk cases in recent years.

United Bank of Switzerland (UBS) is a Swiss global financial services company with its headquarters in Zurich and Basel. UBS is one of the largest banks worldwide and is also the largest private wealth management institution. By the end of 2015, UBS's total assets under management reached 2.689 trillion Swiss francs with net profit of 6.20 billion Swiss francs. It has branches operating in 56 countries with more than 60,000 employees in total. UBS was rated as the best private bank consecutively from 2004 to 2007 by *Euromoney*. It was also named as Asia's best private bank consecutively from 2002 to 2006 by *Finance Asia*. UBS ranked 27th in the global top 500 companies in 2007 and 308th in 2015 released by *Fortune* magazine. As such a prestigious bank, UBS lost $2.3 billion due to a trader's operational incident in 2011, and was fined with heavy penalty by the United Kingdom Financial Services Authority (FSA). Three major rating agencies nearly downgraded UBS' bond rating due to this incident.

5.1.3.1   Case Study

The trader named Kweku Adoboli, one of the four traders at the trading platform "Delta one", worked at the UBS's European assets department in London. Delta one trading platform as company's ETF trading department was responsible for risk hedging of clients' securities and UBS's own proprietary trading. Delta one also engaged in some speculative trading. Such profitable department was one of the most popular divisions in the entire banking industry. According to JP Morgan's

Table 5.3 Operational risk incidents since the 1980s

Year	Financial institution and traders	Case	Results
1984–1995	Daiwa Bank Toshihide Iguchi	Illegal transactions with US treasury bond as underlying assets for 11 years, resulted in a loss of $1.1 billion	Sentenced to 4 years in prison and fined $2 million by the New York District Court; Daiwa Bank was fined $340 million by the US Federal Reserve Board and retreated from the US market
1989–1994	Codelco Juan Pablo Davila	Between 1989 and 1994, participated in copper futures trading without authorization, caused at least $170 million loss for Codelco.	Convicted of fraud and tax evasion, and dismissal from the company
1986–1996	Sumitomo Corporation Yasuo Hamanaka	Participated in the copper futures trading without authorization, resulted in a loss of $1.9 billion	Sentenced to 8 years in prison on the charges of fraud and forgery
1992–1995	Barings Bank Nicolas Leeson	Unauthorized purchase of $7 billion Japanese stock index futures, the failed investment caused a loss of 860 million pounds and Barings bank with a 233-year history to fail	Sentenced to 6 and a half years in prison
1996–2002	Allied Irish Banks John Rusnak	A large number of forged trading documents, caused a loss of $691 million and the dramatic loss in the market value of Allied Irish Banks	Sentenced to 7 and a half years in prison and faced $691 million in recovery
1997	National Westminster Bank Group	Since the second half of 1994, signed option contracts which had margins and option premiums lower than the market standard with clients, and covered loss and actual transactions by false accounting, resulted in a loss of £50 million	The trader and a batch of senior executives including president were ousted
2004	National Australia Bank David Bullen and Three Other Traders	Participated in foreign exchange futures trading without authorization, causing a loss of 360 million Australian dollars	Charged by Australian Securities and Investment Commission
2006	Amaranth Advisors LLC Brian Hunter	Bet on natural gas futures, caused a loss of $6.5 billion and the fund went bankruptcy	Bankruptcy
2007–2008	Societe Generale Jerome Kerviel	Shorted European stock index future with over $72.8 billion without authorization, created false hedge positions, caused Societe Generale a loss of $7.1 billion	Sentenced to 5 years in prison and €4.9 billion compensation with three charges including "abuse of trust", "forgery and using false documents", and "invasion of information data system"
2008–2011	UBS Kweku Adoboli	Used illegal virtual cash ETF (Exchange Trade Fund) positions to extend actual trading limit, caused UBS a loss of €2 billion	Charged with fraud and false accounting
2012	JPMorgan Chase Bruno Iksil	Accumulated huge hedging exposure after a large number of derivatives transactions, leading to a liquidity crisis	Billions of US dollars in loss

Sources Zhejiang University CIFI, *The Wall Street Journal, Financial Times, Neue Zürcher Zeitung*

report, the return of such business sector was more than 100% in Societe Generale and 72% in UBS.

However, UBS suffered great loss during the subprime crisis. The bank had to make large-scale layoffs and Mike Foster, the former senior manager of Delta one, switched to Barclays bank. Consequently, Adoboli became the head of the department. During that time, every trader was under enormous pressure and aware that poor performance would lead to dismissal by the company. To obtain greater profits, Adoboli illegally used virtual cash ETF positions to bypass the company's regulatory trading restrictions and amplified the actual trading limits. In addition, the limits set by UBS investment banking trading system could be breached by using unilateral trading. For instance, assuming that the transaction limit was $11 million in the system, a trader could make a unilateral trade of $10 million, and hence remained only $1 million of transaction limit theoretically. However, if a $3 million trade was made to hedge the position from the opposite direction, the actual transaction limit was increased to $4 million.

In July 2011, Adoboli believed that the US market would continue to decline while other traders in the department had the view that the market would rebound. Under the pressure from other colleagues, Adoboli held a large amount of long positions of S&P 500 Index. However, on August 5th, S&P downgraded the US bond rating, causing the index fell sharply. The department suffered a huge loss of nearly $300 million. When Adoboli changed the long position to short position based on his perception of the market's continuous decline, the US market began to recover. This mistake made the loss of $300 million surge up to around $2 billion.

On September 15, 2011, UBS disclosed Adoboli's rogue-trading and the huge loss incurred. Adoboli was sentenced to 7 years in prison by the London Court. On the same day, UBS share price took a plunge of a 10.8% drop while the overall share price of the European banks rose 3–6%. On September 24th, Oswald Grubel, UBS Chief Executive Officer, resigned. On October 5th, Francois and Yassin, co-heads of UBS global securities trading, both resigned.

5.1.3.2   Lessons learned

The following aspects have accounted for the root causes of the UBS rogue-trading scandal:

(1) Excessive Authority of Traders and No Duties Segregation between Front and Back Offices

Before being assigned as the in-charge of the trading department, Adoboli worked at the back office. Through this position, he was able to gain familiar with the monitoring mechanism of the back office, which facilitated him to disguise his illegal transactions. Moreover, Adoboli was the head of Delta one department, which granted him the authority to both "trade and supervise" roles, which in the end prevented effective risk control. Before his arrest, transaction fund under his management account had amounted to $10 billion with illegal transactions traced back to 2008.

(2) Executives' Dereliction of Duties and Chaotic Internal Control

On August 8, 2011, the risk exposure under Adoboli's management had reached $11.85 billion. However, the intraday risk exposure limit for a trader was only $100 million and $50 million overnight in accordance with UBS' internal policy. Such abnormal status had not attracted any attention from UBS executives, which reflected that the organizational structure of UBS was inefficient and the internal management was out of control.

(3) Bonus Structure and Risk Parameter Was Improperly Proportioned

Traders' bonus accounted as high as 60% of their total income in UBS, way above the industry average level. Adoboli's annual income was up to 600 thousand pounds (equivalents of 6 million yuan). It is reasonable to link trader's performance with bonus in order to motivate them. However, when the bonus structure and the risk parameters became imbalanced, the gambler psychology would be stimulated and traders would blindly pursue bonus while neglecting risks. At the hearing in London, Adoboli pointed out that "Colleagues in Delta one, management and back office all knew about what I was doing, but they turned a blind eye to it as long as I was making money". In this case, both Adoboli and UBS executives were obsessed by the hefty bonus, so being repeatedly reckless without considering risks the bank may carry.

5.1.4   Legal Risk—Severe Penalties Imposed on BNP Paribas

French bank BNP Paribas (BNP) is a leading bank and financial services institution in Europe, rated as one of the world's biggest four banks by S&P. BNP operates in over 85 countries worldwide, playing a significant role in the three areas including corporate and investment banking, asset management and services, and retail banking.

5.1.4.1   Case Study

In the early June 2014, the US department of Justice announced that BNP violated the US foreign sanctions regulation *International Emergency Economic Powers Act*. Between 2004 and 2012, BNP broke US sanctions against trade with Cuba, Iran, Sudan, and Libya, and a settlement of a record fine of $10 billion (67 billion yuan) and ended in having its business license revoked in the US. This was a punishment without trial and the large size of the settlement for such a case triggered uproar in France. According to the US department of Justice, in recent years, BNP transferred funds of more than $500 million for an Iranian energy company, and transferred funds of $1.7 billion for Cuba. Since these transactions were settled in US dollars and must be conducted by the US clearing house, these transactions were subject to US laws.

BNP initially planned to create a new subsidiary to plead guilty, but was rejected by the US. BNP then approached to the highest-ranking French government official for help. President Hollande personally interceded with President Obama had been declined as well. In the end, BNP, the US Federal and state government reached a settlement and released a statement. According to the statement, BNP violated the US laws by transferring funds for the countries that the US imposed sanctions against. If BNP agreed to pay a record-high $8.97 billion for the settlement and plead guilty, it could keep its business license in the US but needed to terminate specific US dollar settlement business for one year. Additionally, 13 senior employees had to be dismissed as stated in the settlement.

Although $8.97 billion was less than the initial $10 billion, this heavy penalty was equivalent to one-year profit of BNP. Moreover, part of its US dollar settlement business had been suspended for one year. This also had affected its international reputation and capital adequacy.

5.1.4.2 Lessons learned

BNP's heavy penalty was a typical case of legal risks that banks may encounter when extending its overseas development. Financial institutions are more likely to experience such legal risks without adequate understanding of the laws in the host country.

(1) Being Unfamiliar with US Laws and Encountered Legal Risks

According to the international law, no countries shall be allowed to interfere in other countries' sovereignty, including sanctions against banks from other countries. However, after the "9.11 incident", in order to cut off the financial resources for international terrorism and crack down fund transactions for financing of terrorist activities, the US adopted the USA PATRIOT Act. This Act strengthens the supervision on domestic and foreign financial institutions through anti-money laundering. The definition of money laundering is very broad. The "predicate offenses" of money laundering is described as "a certain forms of illegal activities". Manufacturing, selling contraband, murder, kidnapping, robbery, extortion, fraud, bribery, embezzlement, theft, and smuggling, etc., may all constitute the predicate offenses of money laundering.

Moreover, the USA PATRIOT Act also introduced the new concept of "preliminary involvement in money laundering". When certain jurisdictions, financial institutions, or financial activities outside the US are considered as "preliminary involvement in money laundering" by the US authorities, US Finance Minister is entitled to take "special measures" in the US. USA PATRIOT Act section 317, Long-arm jurisdiction over foreign money launderers[2], explicitly stipulates that the district courts shall have jurisdiction over any foreign person, including any financial institution authorized under the laws of a foreign country, against whom the money laundering action is brought, as long as service or process upon the foreign person is made under the Federal Rules of Civil Procedure or the laws of the country in which the foreign person is found. To ensure that the economic sanctions against some foreign institutions and organizations are enforced, the USA PATRIOT Act allows US authorities to recover relevant institutions' and organizations' assets deposited in foreign banks by taking actions within the United States. Section 319 stipulates that if funds are deposited into an account at a foreign bank, and that foreign bank has an interbank account in the United States with a covered financial institution, the funds shall be deemed to have been deposited into the interbank account in the United States. Meanwhile, any restraining order, seizure warrant, or arrest warrant in rem regarding the funds may be served on the covered financial institution, and funds in the interbank account, up to the value of the funds deposited into the account at the foreign bank, may be restrained, seized, or arrested. In such a case, it shall not be necessary for the US government to prove that the funds in the US account of the foreign bank has direct associations with the seized funds deposited in the foreign bank account, or it shall not be required to have actual funds transferring between the above two accounts.

(2) **Not Learning from Previous Lessons**

In recent years, several penalty cases were reported about international financial institutions violating USA PATRIOT Act or International Emergency Economic Powers Act. For instance, in 2012, the US imposed fines of $619 million and $667 million to ING and Standard Chartered bank respectively for their trading with Iran, Myanmar, Libya and Sudan. In July 2014, HSBC's "money laundering" scandal ended up with a fine of $1.9 billion. In the early May 2014, Credit Suisse was also fined $2.6 billion, or about €2 billion for helping an American millionaire evade tax. Although the United States seems to be playing power politics by relying on its dollar's status as well as their strong economic and political strength, these relevant cases shall be paid great attention to and such risks also shall be avoided before major shift in the international landscape.

(3) **Diversification in International Currency and Introducing New Settlement Currencies Besides US Dollars**

The relevant US laws are enforced thanks to its dollar's status in world currency to some extent. However, in recent years, the global economic landscape underwent constant adjustments, along with the change in the world currency composition. In 2015, International Monetary Fund announced that RMB would officially join the

---

[2]Long-arm jurisdiction allows the state to exercise jurisdiction over an out-of-state defendant, provided that the prospective defendant has sufficient minimum contacts with the forum state.

SDR on October 1st, 2016, which marked an important milestone in RMB internationalization. In the internationalization roadmap, there have been a growing number of financial institutions who started to seek alternative currencies in their international transfer settlements.

5.1.5 Integrated Risk—RBS' Struggle

The Royal Bank of Scotland Group plc (RBS), founded in 1727, is one of the five oldest banks in the UK. It has currently headquartered in Edinburgh, Scotland with business operations throughout UK and worldwide. The establishment of RBS broke the monopoly of Bank of Scotland in Scotland by developing and expanding through M&A deals. In 1969, its merger with National Commercial Bank of Scotland made it the biggest bank in Scotland with 40% local market shares according to Nohria & Weber in 2005. In 2000, RBS successfully merged with the National Westminster Bank (NatWest), whose stock market value was three times greater than RBS. With this merger, RBS quickly climbed in the ranking and earned itself a position as one of the largest commercial banks in Europe. In 2010, RBS ranked 55th among the Global 500 by *Fortune* magazine.

Although being such a successful bank, RMB was still unable to recover after the 2008 financial crisis. Later in 2016, after the UK's EU referendum, RBS was reported to incur a huge loss with operating performance and reputation plummeting.

5.1.5.1 Case Study

The Rise of RBS

RBS had actively accelerated its international expansion since 1980s. In the 1980s, RBS acquired Citizens Financial Group in the US and successfully entered the market. At the same time, it set up a joint venture with Banco Santander Central Hispano, S.A. in order to explore the European market. Subsequently, RBS launched online banking services in the UK, who was the first bank providing full-scale internet banking service in the UK. In mid-1990s, RBS started to implement the "Plan Colombia" to fully computerize its back-office functions, which essentially reduced the operating costs.

In February 2000, RBS took over NatWest with a price of £21 billion, which is the largest banking M&A deal in the UK's history. At that time, although NatWest was three times larger than RBS, it had a recent history of poor operating performance caused by low management efficiency and high operating costs. After the takeover, RBS experienced a difficult period of integration along with series of strategic reform, such as wiping the redundant management structure, integrating business processes and unifying database system. However, this deal enabled RBS to rank as one of the top commercial banks in Europe and made their investors satisfied with the stock price soaring. This built up the foundation to its successive merger with Churchill Insurance (a UK insurance group) and purchase of the retail banking division of Mellon Financial Corporation. Led by their CEO, Fred Goodwin, RBS had more than 20 million customers and 110,000 employees with total assets of £400 billion as of 2003.

In 2005, the most glamourous year for RBS, it developed quickly with total assets reaching £777 billion, almost double compared with 2003. Also, RBS ranked 12th in the world with its 137,000 employees, and further reduced the operating costs ratio to 42%.

RBS' Struggle

Such rapid development of RBS could not be achieved without the successful acquisition of NatWest. However, dramatically, the turning point of RBS' fall was its failed takeover of ABN Amro (ABN). The NatWest deal drove RBS to develop and expand by merging, making the executives believed they could continue to accumulate the capital reserves, so their selection of M&A target became more aggressive.

In October 2007, in order to further its internationalization, RBS formed a consortium with Fortis Bank and Banco Santander and defeated Barclays in a takeover bid of ABN Amro, with a whopping price offer of €72 billion ($101 billion). Although ABN had branches in 53 countries with core advantages in investment banking, the financial analysts generally believed that its value was overestimated. While the executives of RBS still confidently believed this deal was the key step of its internationalization. Unfortunately, ABN didn't survive in 2008 financial crisis and its financial performance worsened drastically, making the bank bear huge asset losses. All these have brought great pressure to RBS.

From the outsider's point of view, this takeover was known to be one of the worst and most inopportune M&A cases. Internally, Sir Tom MacKillop, the former Chairman of RBS, expressed remorse in front of British parliamentarians. He said that the acquisition of ABN was an "awful mistake" when the financial market was in heyday. As the global financial crisis continued to spread, the "disaster" of RBS was constantly ferment. Facing the most serious economic downturn of the UK, the performance of RBS, used to rapidly develop, fell linearly and led to their CEO (Sir Fed)'s resignation.

Finally, under the double strikes of great losses in both acquisition and subprime products, the net loss of RBS amounted to over £28 billion in 2008. Once the news was announced, the stock price of RBS plunged 67%, which was the biggest one-day decline in two decades (see Fig. 5.1). Since then, RBS was on the very verge of bankruptcy and was forced to seek help from the UK government. After receiving the government bail-out and signing a binding agreement, RBS was injected £45.5 billion ($71 billion) by the government, who in return holds the 83% shares of RBS.

In spite of all these measures, RBS was still buried in various troubles. On May 2009, in such a harsh business environment, RBS still distributed nearly £5 million of stock bonus to its four executives, ignoring the controversy it may stir. This

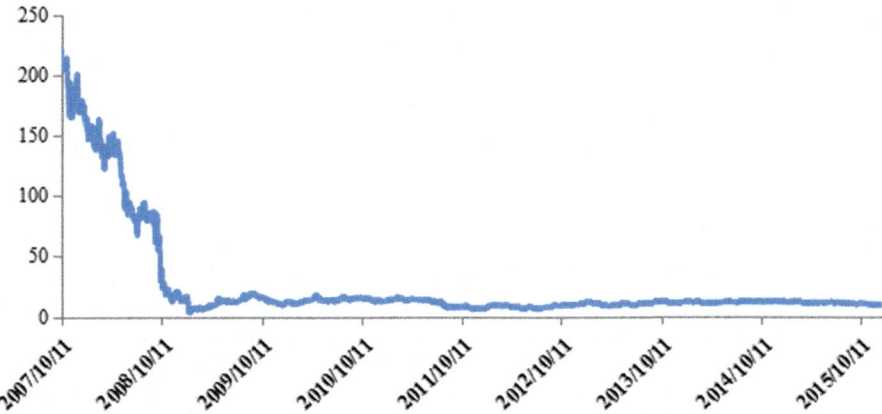

Fig. 5.1   Stock Price of RBS from 2007 to 2015. *Source* Zhejiang University CIFI, NASDAQ

behavior was severely criticized by the British public and the media. In February 2014, RBS published its 2013 annual report showing the biggest loss since 2008, and announced its plan to downsize its investment banking and overseas business. In July 2015, RBS announced to sell its shares of Citizens Financial Group and reduced its stockholdings from 40.8 to 26.8%. This was the second time that RBS sold its shareholdings of US commercial banks in 2015 and also part of the new CEO's (Ross McEwan) plan to shrink the global business. During the first half of 2016, again, RBS announced a huge net loss of £2.05 billion ($2.68 billion), which caused the collective decline in the UK banks' stock prices. Ross McEwan, the CEO, had to admit that the current deficit was the pay-back to their previous ambition of being the world's leading investment bank. Then RBS announced to continue reducing its Asian and American business and exit all the business in Middle-Eastern Europe, Middle East and Africa, so as to reduce the number of countries from 25 to 15 or below.

However, things are perhaps far from being over for RBS. The Brexit made a further impact on UK financial industry and "independence intent" from Scotland has also added more instability. To RBS, who is sucked into the center of whirlpool, the business outlook is likely to be more vulnerable.

5.1.5.2   Lessons Learned

The reasons behind RBS's journey from a prosperous start to a wane are quite complex, which can be mainly concluded as follows:

(1) **Excessive International Expansion**

Internationalization can bring opportunities as well as risks to companies. Although RBS succeeded in 2000 through its acquisition of NatWest, it was devastated by the high premium from its acquisition of ABN and ultimately suffered the negative consequences in the 2008 financial crisis from its excessive international expansion. As ABN had huge amount of subprime assets, this takeover also greatly increased asset risks of RBS. Furthermore, since RBS had expanded too fast, the quality of its assets could not be guaranteed, which also accelerated its asset risks.

(2) **Vulnerable Financial Performance**

Financial analysts commented ABN's takeover as "a typical case of wrong price, wrong payment, wrong timing and the wrong target". This deal, the largest one in banking industry, was entirely funded by debt financing instead of equity financing, as determined by the Board of RBS. This further reduced RBS's capital adequacy ratio. More severely, RBS was highly dependent on its short-term loans. About £12.3 billion of loans was one year duration out of the £22.6 billion loans borrowed to fund the takeover. These short-term loans substantially increased the liquidity risk, weakening RBS during the financial crisis.

(3) **Reputation Damaged by Executive Reward**

After the £45.5 billion injected by the UK government, RBS still issued a record £4 billion of salary and bonus in 2009 and their executives received up to £5 million, even exceeding the bonus payment in 2007 when the economy was still booming. This inappropriate reward completely unveiled management failure and received strong criticism from the public and media. This resulted in RBS's reputation being greatly savaged along with losing trust from its clients and employees.

5.2 Case Studies on Chinese Banks' International Risk

History can be used as a mirror which allows us to identify alarming signs of rise and fall. At the beginning of internationalization, Chinese banks also suffered a few failure and risks. Accordingly, studying and learning from Chinese banks' internationalization can help us to make concrete conclusions and suggestions.

In this section, we will begin with early internationalization cases of Chinese banks, and analyze the process and summarize the main reasons as well as measures to avoid the risks, hoping to provide valuable advices to Chinese banks in their future globalization journey (Table 5.4).

During a short period of ten years, various risk incidents had occurred when Chinese banks went global and led to huge losses. After paying all these expensive "tuition fees", Chinese banks should deeply reflect and summarize the reasons. In the following section, according to the risk type, we will choose three classic cases from the table above to further analyze.

Table 5.4 Risks of Chinese banks' internationalization

Year	Financial institution	Case	Risk type
2000–2002	Bank of China	Due to poor risk management, BOC New York Branch was cheated by the couple Zhou Qiang and Liu Ping of over $34 million loans in eight years and also was fined $10 million by the US Office of the Comptroller of the Currency (OCC) and China's PBOC respectively	Operational risk
2003	Bank of China	BOC New York Branch was accused of helping customers evade tax by U.S. authority. Although the bank didn't admit it, BOC still paid $5.25 million settlement to avoid paying high litigation costs	Legal risk
2007–2008	China Development Bank	CDB purchased 3.1% shares of Barclays Bank using €2.2 billion (£1.45 billion) at £7.2 per share. However, because of the financial crisis, it suffered 50% loss in one year	Market risk
2007–2009	China Minsheng Bank	After two capital injections, UCBH, the merger target, urgently published a statement and acknowledged that it had a large number of bad debts and financial fraud causing by the Subprime Mortgage Crisis. Afterwards, UCBH was shut down by the U.S. regulator. Finally, CMBC lost 824 million yuan in this investment	Market risk operational risk
2012	Industrial and Commercial Bank of China	The acquisition of Bank of East Asia in the US by ICBC caused the demonstration by All America Asian Union, as the acquisition including discrimination against minority communities. During the demonstration, ICBC didn't react quickly, resulting in adverse social impact and litigation risk	Other risk
2015	China Construction Bank	CCB New York Branch was accused of having loopholes in monitoring anti-money laundering by the Federal Reserve. While CCB agreed to complete a plan to correct the mistakes and then reached a settlement with the Fed, its reputation suffered damage	Compliance risk
2015	Bank of China	BOC Milan Branch was accused of helping local Chinese smuggle over €4.5 billion goods to China from 2006 to 2010 by Italian prosecutors. Although BOC denied, it still caused litigation risk	Legal risk
2015	Bank of China	As BOC New York Branch refused to provide customer account information to cooperate US government's investigation of selling fake Gucci products, it was fined $50,000 per day for contempt of court by New York local court	Legal risk
2016	Industrial and Commercial Bank of China	ICBC Madrid Branch was accused of money laundering by Spanish authority with six directors detained, facing litigation charges	Legal risk

Source Zhejiang University CIFI, announcement and related news of each company

5.2.1   Market Risk—CMBC's Acquisition of UCBH

In 2007, the Subprime Mortgage Crisis broke out in the U.S. and quickly spread worldwide, which caused the market value of many financial institutions shrinking dramatically. In such context, China Minsheng Bank (CMBC) attempted to seize the opportunity to expand its business overseas. In the end, it chose UCBH Holdings Inc. (UCBH), a local bank in the U.S., to be its first target to execute

CMBC's first overseas M&A since its establishment. The basic information of the two banks is as follows:

China Minsheng Bank, founded in 1996, is the first private commercial bank in China. After over ten-year development, it has established good reputation domestically and internationally with steady market shares. UCBH Holdings Inc., founded in 1998, was one of the big three overseas Chinese banks, which primarily served small and medium-size businesses run by Chinese Americans. Before the merger, the total capital of UCBH was $11.8 billion, which was 10% of CMBC's capital.

5.2.1.1 Case Study

CMBC held a Board Meeting in September 2007 and announced a three-phase acquisition plan of UCBH. The total acquisition price amounted to $96.90 million with $17.79 per share. CMBC issued 5.4 million new shares to complete the first phase of capital injections, which accounted for 4.9% of UCBH's total capital.

However, the subprime mortgage crisis was not over in 2008 and continued to influence the U.S. and European markets with "Freddie Mac and Fannie Mae". The share price of UCBH dived straight to $5.16 per share on August 2008, a 70% decrease compared to the initial acquisition price of $17.79 per share. This inevitably made a huge loss in CMBC's balance sheet. Later in December 2008, under the attraction of bottom fishing, a second round of acquisition was still taken with $30 million dollar by CMBC, increasing its ownership to 9.9%. With the continuous fermentation of the subprime crisis, UCBH's share price continued to plunge, which caused the loss on CMBC's financial book to grow higher.

On September 8th, 2009, being urged by Federal Deposit Insurance Corporation (FDIC), UCBH published an independent report. In the report, it acknowledged that as a large part of its loans were commercial real estate loans, a lot of bad loans and subprime mortgage losses had occurred with deteriorated financial situation. Meanwhile, it was unveiled that UCBH also concealed tens of millions dollars bad debts in its 2008 annual report and 2009 Q1 report.

In November 2009, UCBH was shut down by the California Department of Financial Institutions and taken over by East West Bank, another overseas Chinese bank in the US. Although CMBC pleaded to complete the injection plan, the Fed rejected. Later on November 10th, 2009, CMBC confirmed that the total loss caused by its investment in UCBH was recognized as 824 million yuan ($120.6 million).

5.2.1.2 Lessons Learned

The subprime mortgage crisis is not the only reason why CMBC failed this M&A deal, and there are various other reasons as below:

(1) Lack of Good Strategic Planning

Firstly, how CMBC chose the M&A target is open for discussion. Targeting UCBH during the subprime crisis, whose loans were concentrated on real estate, certainly lacked thorough considerations. Secondly, CMBC didn't have adequate knowledge of U.S. laws and was treated harshly by U.S. authorities during the process, which put CMBC in passive position and lack of negotiation power. At last, CMBC didn't do thorough studies on M&A related regulations in the US. US regulators have always been strict on overseas buyers and even placed various obstacles, so their rejection to CMCB's request to complete the third injection was not surprising.

(2) Ignoring Market Risk

Firstly, the value of UCBH was overly estimated. With the subprime crisis intensifying, CMBC still thought of acquiring UCBH an opportunity for bottom fishing, without realizing that the loan structure of UCBH could easily result in bad debts. Secondly, the financial risk and exchange rate risk were prominent in this case. The original plan required no more than 2.5 billion yuan to complete this acquisition with cash payment, which inevitably led to CMBC's lack of liquidity, tightened bank capital chain and triggered a financial crisis. During that period, the exchange rate between RMB and U.S. dollar dropped from 7.52: 1 in September 2007 down to 6.83: 1 in 2009, when the suspension of the deal was announced. Hence, the losses caused by exchange rate decrease could be up to 34 million yuan if taking the total acquisition price as 2.5 billion yuan.

5.2.2 Operational Risk—BOC New York Branch's Loan Fraud

BOC is one of China's big five commercial banks. As the most internationalized and diversified bank in China, BOC provides a comprehensive range of financial services including commercial banking, investment banking, insurance and aircraft leasing. It has clients across the China and other 40 countries and regions.

5.2.2.1 Case Study

Early in 2000, during one of its self-review and reform, BOC New York Branch raised suspicion in several short-term doubtful loans issued to Chinese-American couple, Zhou Qiang and Liu Ping. Zhou and Liu schemed to get BOC to pay the beneficiaries of letters of credit, which were shell companies on behalf of NBM and Yangmei that the couple owned. BOC also either extended or granted short-term loans for international trade transactions that never took place. The couple also bribed Yang Zhongqi, the former assistant manager of credit department in New York Branch, to participate in the fraud. Zhou and Liu managed to repeatedly repay old loans with new ones. During the eight years from 1992 to 2000, they loaned over $80 million from BOC New York Branch, who took a loss of $34 million. In February, 2001, Zhou Qiang, Liu Ping and other related 14 companies and individuals were sued by BOC New York Branch to the Federal District Court in Manhattan.

On January 18, 2002, BOC New York Branch was fined by the US Office of the Comptroller of the Currency (OCC) and PBOC in China over its "unsafe and unreliable misconduct". US OCC imposed a fine of $10 million and the parent company was also fined $10 million by PBOC, hence the total amount of penalties is up to $20 million.

On July 11, 2002, the jury from the Federal District Court in Manhattan reached a verdict of a compensation of $35 million to BOC New York Branch. In accordance with Racketeer Influenced and Corrupt Organizations Act (RICO), a United States federal law, this amount might increase to $125 million by three times. In September 2002, the conclusion of the judge from the Federal District Court was consistent with the jury's decision. After two years, with the settlement of the fraud case, the BOC New York Branch finally won the lawsuit. However, the bank invested massive amount of manpower, material and financial resources in these two years and may not be able to recover the $125 million compensation even with the imprisonment of Liu, Zhou and others.

5.2.2.2 Lessons Learned

This case shows the loopholes in internal KYC and credit risk management in Chinese Banks' overseas branches. The details are as follows:

(1) Vulnerable Credit Approval Procedures Leads to Operational Risk

While reviewing a loan application, banks need to collect the information of the client, its business and competitors. At the same time, proper distance must be kept in order to prevent being used by the client. In this case, the credit approval process in BOC New York Branch had quite some loopholes. Most loans this couple applied were based on written documents and the bank was lack of the high-end security equipment to detect forgery, which provided the fraud criminals an opportunity. Meanwhile, lack of field trips and post-loan check also gave rise to credit risk.

(2) **Weak Risk Management Framework Intensifies Operational Risk**

The reason why this couple succeeded in cheating BOC New York Branch was because they not only took advantages of the loopholes of the credit approval process, but also received the "assistance" from both high-level and middle-level managers in the bank including Yang Zhongqi. This fraud scam would not last for 8 years if only with the help from Yang, who was a middle-level manager of BOC New York Branch. According to the survey from OCC, from 1992 to 2000, "some former executives provided preferential treatment to their affiliated individuals, which brought significant losses to the bank". Unfortunately, for these management especially senior management connected with this case, BOC didn't file any lawsuits against them or asked them to take legal responsibilities, from which we could only assume that they might have been punished internally.

(3) **Lack of External Regulations**

This fraud lasted for eight years, but the U.S. regulators only noticed and began its investigation in 2000. This indicated that no matter how advanced the regulatory system is, loopholes still exist. Therefore, it is necessary for regulators in all countries to strengthen their supervisions. Once any fraud or illegal operation is found, the banks involved must be punished strictly.

Therefore, during their journey of going global, Chinese financial institutions should not blindly seek for scale expansion by opening branches overseas or M&A, also they must pay closer attention to the quality of its assets and have robust risk management.

5.2.2.3 Detailed Information of the Consent Order from OCC[3]

Along with the fine, the U.S. OCC issued a 39-page consent order to all the BOC Branches in the U.S. (New York Branch, Chinatown Branch, Los Angeles Branch), which included, but is not limited, credit transaction, trade settlement transaction, account opening and internal audit, and gave complete recommendations on hiring independent Chief Risk Officer, external auditor, independent due diligence companies, which provided constructive advices for other banks. The details are as follow:

(1) **Hiring a Chief Risk Officer (CRO)**

The order required not later than April 30, 2002, the BOC New York Branch, in consultation with the Bank, shall expand the duties and authority of the Risk Management Department and retain the services of an individual for the position of Chief Risk Officer (CRO), who shall manage the Department. The authority of the CRO shall include: ① Gain access to all documents, files, correspondence, and

---

[3]Source: The consent order #2002-1.

personnel of the Branches, without any restriction; ② Terminate any type of customer relationship, deny any loan request and conduct investigations into any matters independently without permissions from BOC New York Branch; ③ Recommend that the Branches or the Bank terminate the employment of any officer or employee of the Branches based upon breach of duty, wasting of assets, lack of candor, dishonesty or any other basis within the purview of the CRO or the Risk Management Department. All these may be overturned only by the General Manager of the Branch, provided that a written statement by the General Manager of the specific reasons for overturning the denial. All documents related should be sent to the OCC within 30 days from the date the General Manager overturns the denial. The responsibilities of the CRO shall include: ① Chair the periodic risk meetings of the Branch not less than monthly; ② Produce periodic reports to the Bank and OCC, not less than monthly and copy to the OCC. The supervision on the CRO shall include: ① The New York Branch's evaluation report of the CRO's performance shall be reviewed and approved in writing by the Bank; ② The New York Branch shall provide written notice to the Director of the Special Supervision of the OCC prior to disciplining or terminating the CRO.

(2) Hiring External Auditor to Restraint CRO

The Consent Order required: ① The external auditor should perform annually audit on the operations of the CRO and Risk Management Department following the Order; ② The external auditor should perform special audit on CRO's and the Risk Management Department's compliance with certain key terms of this Consent Order.

(3) Review by Independent Third Party

Not later than March 31, 2002, the New York Branch, in consultation with the Bank, shall retain an independent third party to perform random check by selecting 15% of bills of goods for last month. BOC should also hire an independent third party to conduct due diligence on every customer who has trade settlements through the Branch totaling $1 million or more during any 12 month period.

(4) Better Credit Management

The Consent Order required: ① All credit granted to Related Accounts shall be treated as one borrower for loan approval and monitoring purposes. All loan recommendations shall include an analysis of all Related Accounts of the proposed borrower. All cash collateral and pledged securities for all the Branches shall be held by the Branch extending credit. ② Prior to extending, renewing or modifying any credit of $1 million or more, aggregating credit extended to the customer and the customer's Related Accounts by all the Branches: The customer shall be required to provide audited financial statements, tax returns, as applicable, credit and deposit account statements from all other financial institutions where the customer conducts banking and a list of the customer's Major Suppliers and Major Customers. Additional Due Diligence shall be conducted on the customer as well as the customer's Major Suppliers and major customers, by an independent third party. If a guarantee is provided, or proposed to be provided, in connection with the credit, the authenticity of the guarantee shall be verified, through direct verification with the guarantor, by an independent third party. ③ Prior to extending, renewing or modifying any credit of $2,000,000 or more, aggregating all credit extended to the customer and the customer's Related Accounts by all branches of the Bank worldwide. The requirement is the same as point 2. ④ The Branches shall immediately suspend any credit for whose before information is required but not produced. Based on information provided by the independent third party, the Risk Management Department shall file SARs on all customers, Major Suppliers and Major Customers for whom the Due Diligence investigation indicates fraud or suspicious activity, and on all customers who produced guarantees that cannot be verified by the independent third party. Once a SAR is filed, the Branches/New York Branches may extend credit to the account of the customer only with the prior written approval of the CRO or the Risk Management Department.

(5) **Account Opening and Monitoring**

The Consent Order required "Not later than April 30, 2002, the Branches in US shall adopt, implement and thereafter adhere to, expanded account-opening procedures for all accounts by requiring". For all credit customers and all customers depositing $10,000 or more, a credit reporting agency reports on, as applicable, the account owners, beneficial owners, the business, and the business officers, directors, major shareholders and partners. The Branches shall not open any new account, and shall immediately close any existing account, if the information required by this Article is not received by the Branches, by the date the information is due. Documentation review is required to all credit accounts of $100,000 or more and all deposit accounts the balance of which reached or exceeded $10,000 during the last 12 months. Also, the Branches shall not open any type of account for a customer, and shall terminate all accounts of a customer, if the information available to the Branches indicates that the customer's relationship with the Branches would be detrimental to the reputation risk of the Branches or the Bank.

5.2.3 Legal Risk—ICBC Madrid Branch's Money-Laundering Claim

Industrial and Commercial Bank of China Ltd. (ICBC), founded in January 1984, is the largest commercial bank in China, providing comprehensive financial products and services to 5.32 million corporate and 496 million individual clients across 6 continents with business network in 43 countries and regions apart from China. With its focus on commercial banking, ICBC adheres to a cross-market development approach as well as an internationalized development strategy, which keeps it atop in most banking business in domestic market. In 2015, ICBC was named "the

Best Bank in Emerging Markets" by *Euromoney*, and ranked 6th among the Top 1000 World Banks by *The Banker* magazine for the third consecutive year.

ICBC opened its Madrid Branch in January 2011, which is the first Chinese financial institution set up in Spain. The Madrid Branch provides services mainly in Spain and Portugal and is regarded as one of the most important financial bridges among China, Spain and Portugal.

5.2.3.1   Case Study

On February 17th, 2016, over 100 Spanish policemen raided ICBC Madrid Branch under the support of Anti-Corruption Procuratorate and the order of Parla count. They also detained 6 directors, including general manager, deputy manager and department managers, and copied data from computers. The search lasted nearly 16 h, which was known as "Operation Shadow".

The investigator said that ICBC helped some people transfer money to China without checking their origin as required by law, amount of which was known to be as of €40 million. *El Mundo* quoted the Spanish investigator: "ICBC Madrid Branch had a complete crime network of money laundering earned through illegal activities." The Spanish document did not name the groups but said they operated both in Spain and China and were involved in smuggling and tax fraud. The document also said that the illegal transfers were limited to €50,000 at a time to reduce the risk of detection and involved a web of shell companies to mask the trail. If found guilty of money laundering, ICBC would face an unspecified fine. The case could also lead to a review of its Spanish banking license.

On February 20, 2016, Spanish High Court announced that three of the arrested directors were released after paying a bail of €100,000 at the time of arrest. However, the other three still kept detained. All of them were accused of lacking monitoring of money laundering.

Some analysts believed that this case may have the problem of using excessive law enforcement. The Spanish general election was held on December 20, 2015 and lasted for four months without result, which was the longest and hardest election in the history of Spain. Under the pressure of political crisis, what the government did may have the purpose of releasing self-pressure to show their power. Although Chinese Embassy in Spain urged Spanish authorities to free all staff, the rest of the three were detained and bail request was denied, implying political purpose from Spain.

A spokesman from ICBC said that according to the information of the head office possessed, their Madrid Branch had strictly followed local anti-money laundering law and regulations, established an anti-money laundering system and hired local executive as Compliance Chief. Also the Branch timely reported materials in compliance with requirements from local regulators and no opinions had ever been given by regulator before. Due to the complexity and sensitivity of anti-money laundering, the challenge from information asymmetry still exists. On one hand, the head office urged the Madrid office to actively cooperate with the investigation. On the other hand, it also hired lawyers in order to protect lawful rights of the Branch and its staff.

5.2.3.2   Lessons Learned

When entering the market of another country, banks may encounter lots of legal problems, caused from the differences in policy, culture and so on. By now, no final conclusion has yet been reached in this case. There are several suggestions for ICBC Madrid Branch.

(1) **Constantly Paying Attention to Local Media Reports**

Up to April 6, three executives were still held in the jail 50 days after the investigation. According to Yihong Ji, the chief of Chinese Lawyers in Spain, S.L. and the guest professor of local police academy, certain documents which the Court published in April might trigger a new storm of news reporting from local media on the ICBC "money laundering". This could cause negative influences on not only China and Chinese companies, but also Chinese businessmen and even the whole Chinese community in Spain. Therefore, ICBC should pay close attention to the local reports and fully prepare for any outcomes.

(2) **Regular Communication with Local Media and Participation in Local Social Activities**

First of all, when communicating with local media, ICBC Madrid Branch should explain their investment and employment issues which were usually closely followed by the media and Spanish citizens. The Bank should also provide detailed explanation on its positive behaviors such as local investment and directly or indirectly creating jobs.

Secondly, given the current situation that ICBC's image being influenced by the money-laundering case, the Bank should hire professional PR companies or professionals, who would facilitate ICBC in conducting proactively, careful and thorough communication and interpretation with local government and media. This will help the bank to fully anticipate response from the local media to prevent any misunderstandings.

At last, after settling this case, ICBC should actively participate in more local social activities and make contributions to the local community. It could learn from the Spanish banks and establish fund foundations, whose major role is to take the social responsibility, promote the national culture and the corporate value.

Overall, there are various risks Chinese banks would encounter when going global. These will impose inevitable challenges when implementing their internationalization strategy. However, as long as the banks can better prepare for these risks in advance, Chinese banks' internationalization path will become smooth along with their accumulation of related experiences and the establishment of global image.

Chapter 6
Future Prospects of Chinese Banks' Internationalization

With time passing by, Chinese banks have completed another year in their journey of internationalization. During this year, Chinese banks achieved outstanding performance in their overseas development, and meanwhile they encountered various challenges. In the upcoming future, the world's economic situation will remain challenging. The US election and the Federal Reserve raising interest rate have brought uncertainties to the US economic recovery. Britain's exit from the EU also made European economic prospects unclear. Emerging markets have become more volatile under various risks. At the same time, Chinese economy will continue its "new normal" state with the supply-side structural reform at its core. Under this background, Chinese banks should adhere to steady development strategy, choose suitable internationalization path, and achieve the accumulation of overseas assets and operating outcomes in an orderly and reasonable manner. By expanding global network under the lead of "the Belt and Road" Initiatives, Chinese banks should establish a robust risk control mechanism to achieve risk prevention during its international operation.

6.1 Acknowledge the Distinct Differences Between Chinese and International Markets When Proceeding with Steady Expansion Strategy

This report analyzed the performances of selected Chinese and foreign banks with focusing on their main international evaluation indicators. Overall, there is a distinct gap in the level of internationalization between Chinese banks and foreign banks.

On the one hand, the gap arose from foreign banks' early involvement in international development. Modern banking industry in foreign countries had an early start, and their internationalization boom already appeared in the last century. Banks that could still be included in the G-SIBs list after facing fierce competition

© Zhejiang University Press and Springer Nature Singapore Pte Ltd. 2018
B. Shenglin et al., *In Pursuit of Presence or Prominence?* Current Chinese
Economic Report Series, https://doi.org/10.1007/978-981-10-7730-2_6

during their expansion into international markets, must have competitive strength, rich management experience, and discourse power. In contrast, Chinese banks have begun to accelerate their pace of internationalization in the 21st century. Hence, Chinese banks being lagged behind foreign banks is expected.

On the other hand, among the selected world's top foreign banks, most banks have their overseas business scales close to their domestic business scales, and some even surpass the domestic development. Their internationalization level also implied a huge potential of Chinese banks' future international development. At present, the overseas business scale of Chinese banks was much smaller than their domestic business scale. Even the big four banks, which are included in the G-SIBs, their achievements in overseas markets such as the proportion of overseas assets, overseas revenue, overseas profits and overseas employees remained quite low. Thus, Chinese banks, particularly those aiming at stepping up and becoming comprehensive multinational financial institutions, should fully acknowledge the significance of international markets, implement higher standards, and strive for higher internationalization level. Chinese banks can only gain greater competitive strength by competing in a tougher world stage. Developing its business in a broader global market could support more ambitious strategies and generate more prominent operating outcomes. Reflecting their value in the international financial industry could bring more discourse power for Chinese banks and Chinese financial institutions, so as to have more opportunities to participate and promote the formalization and change of global economy. Above all, catching up with foreign banks is important, whereas maintaining stability is more valuable. In addition, the current internationalization of Chinese banks is different from that of foreign banks. Also, the international financial situation and the domestic economic situation are not the same. In recent years, with the rising of financial protectionism and enterprises from developing countries expanding overseas, developed countries incline to prevent the entry of foreign investors in the form of laws and regulations for the excuse of its national economy security. Such financial protectionism also becomes a hurdle for Chinese banks to go global. Thus, under the current domestic and international environment, Chinese banks must seize opportunities during policy development, adopt new development strategies, and adjust the pace of overseas expansion, in order to achieve sustainable overseas expansion.

6.2 Seize the Opportunity of "The Belt and Road" Initiatives with Supporting Scheme

"The Belt and Road" Initiatives aim at strengthening the cooperation with countries along the routes, by reviving the Silk Road and achieving win-win economy situation. The financial support is the critical part of this strategy. Among the 5 priorities[1] of "the Belt and Road", financial integration is one of the vital cooperation priorities, not only from the design of financial products to the supply of financial services, but also from the supply of market information to international settlement functions. The positive meanings of financing support have reflected in all aspects of "the Belt and Road". Specifically, in the early development stage of "the Belt and Road", the infrastructure connectivity was the priority. Financial institutions represented by developmental financial institutions mainly played a supporting role in the early development stage by providing funding. When the infrastructure was gradually improved and trades with countries along the route increased, financial institutions would be able to provide diversified financial services and financing to global investors through domestic and overseas network, multilevel financial markets, and internet finance, etc.

As the major part of Chinese finance and the leader of international development, Chinese banks also play a significant role in the implementation of the "the Belt and Road" Initiatives. In turn, this strategy has created new opportunities to accelerate the internationalization of Chinese banks. There are a large number of countries along the "the Belt and Road" with different economies, politics, and culture environments. Chinese Banks' deployment in these countries also varied. Under the support of the new strategy, the financial exchanges with the countries along the routes would be gradually deepened, the activities of Chinese banks in these countries would correspondingly increase. At present, how to seize the opportunity of "the Belt and Road", and plan reasonable business layout based on the characteristics of countries along the routes has become the priority that Chinese banks need to thoroughly consider. While increasing their investments to countries along the routes, China could also actively attract investments from these countries to China (Table 6.1).

Particularly, countries in Southeast Asia are mostly emerging markets, and the degree of their financial openness is comparatively higher with dynamic economic growth. In the future, the commercial exchanges could be focused on the support of offshore projects as well as import and export trades. Mongolia, Russia and the 5 countries in Central Asia frequently trade with China and there is close political and military cooperation due to their geopolitical influence. The existing cooperation mechanism should be enhanced and institutions establishment in each country also needs to be pushed forward. The oil and other strategic energy reserves are rich in West Asia and North Africa, and Chinese banks should strengthen their financial support of energy infrastructure projects. However, considering the complicated political situation in such regions, Chinese banks should pay closer attention to preventing political risks and develop a robust risk management and control mechanism. South Asia region has a large population and diversified culture with tremendous market potentials. Chinese banks could expand their network in South

---

[1]According to *Vision and Actions on Jointly Building Silk Road Economic Belt and 21st-Century Maritime Silk Road*, the five cooperation priorities are policy coordination, facilities connectivity, unimpeded trade, financial integration and people-to-people bond.

Table 6.1 Strategic planning of countries along the "the Belt and Road"

Region	Characteristics	Future strategy
Southeast Asia	Emerging markets, and high degree of openness	Offshore project cooperation
Mongolia, Russia, and 5 central Asian countries	Frequent economic trade cooperation, and close political and military cooperation	Improve the existing cooperation mechanism, and promote establishment of network in each other's country
West Asia and North Africa	Rich strategic resources, and complicated political situation	Strengthen the support to energy cooperation projects, and improve risk management and exit mechanism
South Asia	Large population, and diversified culture	Utilize local labor resources
Central and Eastern Europe	Connection between Asia and Europe	Fill the blank of the current financial services
CIS	Small size of economy, and rich energy resources	Strengthen the support of multilateral trade and strategic financing cooperation projects

Source Zhejiang University CIFI

Asia through mergers and acquisitions, and utilize their rich labor resources to reduce management cost. Central and Eastern Europe, as adjacent to the Western European developed countries, is the important connecting point between Asian and European economy. Chinese banks rarely step on such regions and need to establish more institutions and develop local financial services. Other CIS countries have small size of economies but with rich energy resources. Chinese banks should focus on providing financing support and implementing risk prevention mechanism through bilateral trade and oil strategic projects.

6.3 Implement Internet Finance and Adopt Innovative Business Model

Although internet finance was not originated in China, its development in China has been at the forefront of the world in recent years. The booming of internet finance was mainly due to long-time financial repression in domestic market, which provided golden opportunity for domestic financial industry to step up. Besides, there has been an emerging rise in the internationalization of Chinese internet finance.

In addition to the establishment of various types of cross-border e-commerce industry parks, internet finance companies have also carried out broad practice in the countries along the "the Belt and Road". Alibaba has developed its business in fields

Table 6.2 Strategic layout of "the Belt and Road" from Ali Group

Financial supporting type	Cooperation projects	Cooperation countries	Cooperation methods
E-commerce investment	Lazada	Indonesia	Holds 20% share
	Flipkart, Snapdeal	India	Investment of $500 million
Internet payment	Paytm	India	Two rounds of investments, and holds 40% share
	Ascend Money	Thailand	Holds 20% share
	VTB Bank	Russia	Cooperation, and promotion of Alipay
	K Bank	Korea	Holds 2% share
Big data finance	Data Center	UAE, Singapore	Sets up regional data service center

Source Zhejiang University CIFI

like e-commerce investment, internet payment, and big data finance (see Table 6.2). Ant Financial of Alibaba Group has bought shares of commercial platforms like Lazada in Indonesia, Flipkart and Snapdeal in India. It has also signed a cooperation agreement with Krung Thai Bank to provide e-commerce channels for small and medium enterprises in Thailand. Ant Financial has conducted a two-round stock purchase of Indian largest mobile payment platform Paytm and gained its 40% shares. It also obtained the first payment banking license issued by the Reserve Bank of India, which was regarded as a milestone in Chinese financial industry signifying Chinese internet finance industry going global. Other internet finance companies such as Baidu and Tencent have also entered into Southeast Asia, West Asia markets with their leading payment business actively cultivating overseas customers.

Meanwhile, traditional financial markets in other developing countries are also experiencing financial repression with poor management ability. If taking internet finance as a breakthrough, Chinese financial institutions can rely on their technology as a winning technique rather than solely on management. In future, emerging financial companies represented by internet finance could take full advantage of its characteristic in inclusive finance. They could adopt the strategy of "encircling cities from the rural areas" in order to attract small and micro enterprises and general public in developing countries, by providing customized and professional financial services to meet their investment needs.

Additionally, in 2014, there were two internet banks in the first pilot batch of approved private banks—Mybank and WeBank. Although these two banks were still at their preliminary development with various types of business being in the exploratory stage and it is too early for them to consider going global, these internet banks did bring a reform to traditional banking industry. Internet finance has made people recognize the glamour and potentials in internet thinking, and it may become a powerful means for Chinese banks to go global.

6.4   Establish a Robust Risk Control Mechanism and Prevent Various Types of Risks

Chinese banks have suffered a variety of risk incidents during their international operation. For the future overseas development, Chinese banks should strengthen their global vision and thinking in order to prevent risks by implementing strategic planning, compliance management, and environment studies, etc.

6.4.1   Enhance Strategic Planning to Prevent Strategic Risk

Clear and rational strategic planning forms the basis of the global blueprint. Whether it is the selection of branch location, timing of making market-entry, cross-border negotiation, expansion target of international business, or development of new technologies, each bank needs a clear and prudent development strategy from all aspects. International development involves various aspects, and insufficient strategic planning could lead to a lack of self-assessment. Chinese banks would easily confront strategic risks caused by reckless expansion driven by their "enthusiasm" in internationalization.

In the 1990s, without prudent planning, Citibank's rapid and reckless expansion put itself in a dilemma caused by accumulated non-performing assets and low investment return. Consequently, Citibank suspended its strategy of "universal bank", and adopted a three-year renovation plan to adjust its asset structure and restore capital strength. From the case of Citibank, we could see that a careful strategic planning which matches the strength of the bank will not only assist banks to adhere to their own characteristics, but also avoid various strategic risks.

Among all Chinese banks, large commercial banks have greater advantage of financial strength, and have accumulated overseas experience in exploring international markets as well. They gradually form a comparatively clear "going global" strategy, which enabled them to seize opportunities to accelerate the pace of their international expansion. While joint-stock banks could choose a more prudent strategy by setting up representative offices in places that meet conditions, and then fasten the pace of branch establishment and mergers and acquisitions when the time is right. As for city and rural banks, since they temporarily are not equipped with strength to conduct global development and their demands for internationalization are relatively low, they should firstly focus on the domestic market, enhance their internal management, solidify their advantages, and prepare a foundation for future development.

6.4.2   Improve Risk Control Management System to Reduce Operational Risk

Greater power brings greater responsibilities. When Chinese banks demonstrate their strength on the world stage, there are stringent requirements from different countries, regions, organizations, and individuals. Thus, in order to implement prudent management of overseas branches, improve customer services and branding, Chinese banks should set higher standards on its internal control and compliance management and establish a risk prevention and control system in view of global environment.

Given the nature of operational risk, the remote communication between head office and its overseas branches could cause a rise in such risk. Baring Bank had to file for bankruptcy just because one trader in their Singapore Branch triggered operating risks. It not only caused Baring Bank's fall but also made a serious impact on the international financial market. Lack of independent management of front and back office and imbalanced bonus structure were two main factors triggering such fatal operating risk to Baring Bank. However, how could it be possible that such anomaly went unnoticed unless their internal management was in chaos and out of control? Thus, a structured and efficient internal control and compliance department become important components of risk prevention and control system. Regular and comprehensive risk monitoring and control are significant for the reduction of operating risks.

Chinese banks also need to attach great importance to developing their risk prevention and control department during their overseas expansion. Chinese banks should conduct dynamic supervision and management on business data and staff to timely detect and handle various types of operating risks, so that negative consequences and impacts could be effectively avoided.

6.4.3   Be Familiar with Business Environment of Host Countries to Minimize Country Risk

Different political, legal, and cultural environment have brought great challenges to Chinese banks' internationalization. Before entering the host country, better understanding of the local cultural backgrounds and being familiar with the legal environment is essential to ensure the security of branches, reduce financial disputes and litigation, and avoid conflicts with local residents.

During the financial crisis, government interventions have increased evidently, which could easily cause negative impacts on the overseas business of Chinese banks and lead to political risks. With the prevalence of litigation in the US, 18.4% of American listed companies had been prosecuted. Foreign companies who are unfamiliar with American regulation and legal environment are more easily to encounter legal risks. Furthermore, conflicts among different cultures would also form resistances in the overseas development for Chinese banks.

Therefore, Chinese banks ought to learn the play rules in foreign countries, strengthen their communication with overseas market, and diligently meet the obligation of information disclosure. In order to ensure that investors could access accurate company information anytime and anywhere, Chinese banks should attach great importance to their relationship management with investors, build professional team to manage investors, and develop comprehensive information database including relevant national policies, history of development, strategic planning, financial reports, introduction of products and industry, and overview of investors.

In conclusion, there is still a long road ahead for Chinese banks to go global. They must fully recognize the disparity and learn from foreign banks to avoid detours. While grasping opportunities from new policy and innovated technologies, Chinese banks must design their own path of internationalization with steady expansion in overseas countries. Only with such strategies, shall Chinese banks be able to strengthen their positioning in overseas countries in long term.

Acknowledgement

After one year's efforts, the second outcome of our Series of Reports on Chinese Banks' Internationalization "*In Pursuit of Presence or Prominence?—The Prospect of Chinese Banks' Global Expansion and Their Benchmarks*" has finally met readers. In 2015, both the situation of world's economy and the economic environment in China have undergone new changes. In the context of breakthrough progress in RMB internationalization and "the Belt and Road" Initiatives, Chinese banks are still making progress towards "going global". In light of this, Zhejiang University CIFI, Zhejiang University AFR, and IMI formed a joint team and completed this report.

The successful completion of this report is thanks to the tireless efforts of all members and support from our experts. Numerous experts from universities and financial industries have provided professional instructions and constructive suggestions.

Meanwhile, when developing BII system, more than 100 experts and scholars provided detailed guidance to our team, including Yang Liuyong (Vice Dean, School of Economics, Zhejiang University), Wang Wei'an (Director, Institute of Finance Research, Zhejiang University), Huang Yanjun (Deputy Director, Institute of Finance Research, Zhejiang University), Ma Lianghua (Deputy Director, Industrial Economy Institute, Zhejiang University), Xu Jia (Institute of Finance Research, Zhejiang University), Tang Jiping (Institute of Finance Research, Zhejiang University), Yang Biao (Vice-President, E-Capital Transfer), Wang Wenlie (General Manager, Finance Company, SMG), Sun Lisheng (Director, China Banking Regulatory Commission Zhejiang Office), Fu Huaming (PBC Ningbo Central Sub-branch), Zhang Jingjing (China Banking Regulatory Commission Ningbo Office), Chen Ru (China CITIC Bank Hangzhou Branch), Gao Jiaheng (ICBC Zhejiang Branch), etc.

In addition, we'd like to mention below entities and individuals who have made tremendous contributions to this report. China Everbright Bank provided data support. Wang Aihua [Executive Director, Shanghai branch, J.P. Morgan (China)], Wu Wenlu [Vice-general Manager, Financial Institutions Department, HSBC (China)], Mo Ziwei (Partner, SBCVC), etc. also provided data support to the report. Ma Lina (Zhejiang University), Chen Huihui (Zhejiang University) assisted the

© Zhejiang University Press and Springer Nature Singapore Pte Ltd. 2018   147
B. Shenglin et al., *In Pursuit of Presence or Prominence?* Current Chinese
Economic Report Series, https://doi.org/10.1007/978-981-10-7730-2

compilation of information. Zhejiang University AIF office of general affairs was responsible for administration coordination.

Along with releasing this report for publication, on behalf of all the members of the team, we'd like to express our sincere gratitude to the experts, entities and individuals who have provided supports to our research and report compilation.

Appendix A
Banks Internationalization Index (BII)

Financial institutions as a unique kind of enterprise, the internationalization refers to the process of active expansion of overseas branches and establishment of a broad international network aiming at commercial profit growth. In Chinese finance practice, banks play a significant role by becoming the key representatives and leaders in the internationalization of Chinese financial institutions. With the promotion of internationalization, where Chinese economy entered into the new normal of "implementing a more proactive opening strategy" and Chinese currency, RMB has been added to SDR currency basket. We analyzed the Banks Internationalization Index (BII) in this report, by assessing their achievements on internationalization, comparing between Chinese and foreign banks in their globalization process, exploring Chinese banks' internationalization path, and analyzing the risks. We hope this report could bring a more intuitive understanding on the degree of Chinese banks' internationalization and reflect the opening and the development of the Chinese financial markets from the other side.

Definition of BII

The internationalization of financial institutions reflects not only on the expansion of their overseas business and the establishment of overseas branches, but also their power of discourse and the pricing in the international financial market. Accordingly, the development of internationalization contains enhancements in two aspects, "hard power" and "soft power". "Hard power" is measured by specific numbers such as the number of overseas branches, amount of overseas assets and overseas operating profit which shows a bank's basic level in globalization. However, "Soft power" could not be measured by quantitative methods, and it indicates a higher level of international development. As "soft power" is difficult to measure, we used "hard power" as the subject of study. In this report, banks' internationalization refers to the process that commercial banks proactively develop their international business, by expanding overseas branches, participating in

© Zhejiang University Press and Springer Nature Singapore Pte Ltd. 2018
B. Shenglin et al., *In Pursuit of Presence or Prominence?* Current Chinese
Economic Report Series, https://doi.org/10.1007/978-981-10-7730-2

overseas M&A, forming extensive international networks, and developing offshore deposits, loans and international settlement business.

Based on the Chinese Bank Internationalization Index (CBII) initiated in 2015, *In Pursuit of Presence or Prominence? —The Prospect of Chinese Banks' Global Expansion and Their Benchmarks* selected two categories of indicators to build the Bank Internationalization Index (BII) from multiple aspects including overseas branches, assets, operating performance, etc. In addition to those representative Chinese banks, this report also rated 16 selected Global Systemically Important Banks (G-SIBs) with relatively comprehensive data. Therefore, we were able to assess the progress of Chinese banks' internationalization, to compare the divergence against foreign banks, explore the internationalization path, and analyze the potential risks, and furthermore provide valuable experiences for Chinese banks' internationalization.

Specifically, BII focused on the overseas development of Chinese banks (including Hong Kong, Macao and Taiwan) rather than foreign development, considering that the market rules and openness in Hong Kong, Macao and Taiwan are more similar to the international market. Chinese banks' exploration and business expansion in these areas can be regarded as their first step to connect with the international market. Meanwhile, BII of foreign banks will be affected by data limitation in the estimation process, and the overseas area of several banks will use approximations.

Construction of BII

Our construction of BII is based on orderly, scientific and dynamically adjustable principles. In order to measure the degree of banks' internationalization and ensure objectivity and reliability, our data selection and model building were under the guidance of more than 100 experts.

BII Construction Principles

Our first principle is to combine comprehensiveness and systematization when building BII system. On the one hand, when choosing the BII indicators, our focus was not only on methods and routes of entering foreign markets, but also on the development and operation of their overseas business. The purpose is to reflect both the breadth of coverage and the depth of their development in certain regions. This ought to reflect banks' overseas development status truly, reliably and comprehensively. On the other hand, besides considering the concept and content of each single indicator, the systematic correlation among different indicators was also our focus point, making the entire index system multiple and unified, and genuinely reflecting the internationalization from different perspectives and levels.

Our second principle is to adhere to scientificity and operability. Our design of BII is based on management theories on traditional international finance, corporate finance, and commercial banking business, following with combination with the overseas development progress and characteristics through detailed case study on both Chinese and foreign banks. So BII not only demonstrates the common rules in banks' internationalization, but also expresses the differences in different banks' process in overseas developments. It is important to note that both indicator selections and weights decisions are determined and rated by more than 100 experts. In order to better understand the current situation of both Chinese and foreign banks in their global development, it is necessary to ensure that the data is available and operable. For certain data that cannot be directly obtained, estimation was used by leveraging existing data and information to improve the data reliability of BII.

Our third principle is stability and flexibility. In order to ensure accurate interpretation and strong sustainability of BII calculating results, it is important to stabilize the selection of indicators and avoid frequent changes. However, stability does not mean rigidity. As internationalization is a long-term strategy for financial institutions, its characteristics will vary at different stages. Hence, we combined BII factors and weights with the practice of each bank's globalization and made dynamic changes so as to ensure accuracy and objectivity of BII index system.

BII Index System

Based on the basic definition and construction principles of BII, the degree of banks' internationalization is reflected by various indicators as Table A.1, including overseas branches, assets and sales.

Table A.1 BII index system

	Name of indicators	Formula
Tier 1	Overseas assets to total assets ratio	Overseas assets/Total assets
	Overseas revenue to total revenue ratio	Overseas revenue/Total revenue
	Overseas deposits to total deposits ratio	Overseas deposits/Total deposits
	Overseas loans to total loans ratio	Overseas loans/Total loans
	Overseas profit to total profit ratio	Overseas profit/Total profit
Tier 2	Number of countries with operation networks to number of world's major countries ratio	Number of countries where branch or subsidiaries are established/Number of world's major countries
	Overseas branches to total branches ratio	Number of overseas branches/Number of total branches
	Overseas employees to total employees ratio	Number of overseas employees/Number of total employees

The detailed explanations of each indicator are as follows.

(1) Overseas assets to total assets ratio: Compare between overseas and total assets to measure the outcome of banks' global business as well as the basis for future development. Meanwhile, assets represent the scale of a bank's size. This ratio can directly reflect the difference between banks' sizes in their international business.

(2) Overseas revenue to total revenue ratio: This ratio reflects the basic situation of bank's operation and expansion of overseas business.

(3) Overseas deposits to total deposits ratio: Deposits can show the clients' recognition of banks, so this ratio indicates the recognized degree in foreign markets. Meanwhile, the client categories should also be factored in. For Chinese banks, the number of overseas clients can better demonstrate their degree of internationalization than overseas Chinese clients.

(4) Overseas loans to total loans ratio: From Chinese banks' perspective, the interest income from loans is still the main source of their income. Therefore, the amount of loans and its proportion illustrates the developing status of their core business in overseas markets.

(5) Overseas profit to total profit ratio: This ratio is important to reflect a bank's profitability in overseas countries. Considering the data availability, pretax profit was selected.

(6) The number of countries with operation networks to the number of the world's major countries ratio: larger number of countries and regions where overseas branches or subsidiaries are established, which illustrate the higher degree of internationalization. This indicator mainly reflects the breadth of banks' distribution through overseas network. To maintain consistency with other relative indicators, the number of major countries in the world (replaced by the number of UN country members) is used as the benchmark.

(7) Overseas branches to total branches ratio: By comparing with the previous ratio measuring by countries, this indicator shows the depth of banks' establishment of overseas branches. That is, the higher the ratio is, the higher the degree of internationalization is.

(8) Overseas employees to total employees ratio: This ratio is an important indicator to reflect the internationalization. It should be used in combination with other indicators as certain banking business does not require large amounts of human resources.

In addition to BII computation for Chinese banks, this report measures the degree of G-SIBs banks' internationalization, according to the list published by the Financial Stability Board in 2015.

BII Measurement Model

This report used the Analytic Hierarchy Process "AHP" method, under the foundation of ratings from experts, we determine the weights of each indicator and construct the index system, in order to construct the BII index scientifically and objectively to the maximum level.

All the indicator constituting BII are ratio variables, the detailed measurement model is as follows:

$$BII_t = \sum_{i=1}^{n} X_{it}\omega_i \times 100 \tag{A.1}$$

where,

BII_t is the Banks Internationalization Index at time t,
X_{it} is the number of variable i at time t,
ω_i is the weight of variable i

In addition, to better demonstrate the overall degree of banks' internationalization, this report used the following method to calculate the Industry Consolidated BII:

$$BII_t = \sum_{j=1}^{n} Y_{jt}\omega_j \times 100 \tag{A.2}$$

The Industry Consolidated BII:

$$Y_{jt} = \frac{\sum_{m=1}^{s} P_{j,t,m}}{\sum_{m=1}^{s} T_{j,t,m}} \tag{A.3}$$

where,

BII_t is the overall BII of the industry at time t,
Y_{jt} is the consolidated number of industry consolidated j at time t,
ω_j is the weight of industry consolidated j,
$P_{j,t,m}$ is the overseas data of bank m in industry j at time t,
$T_{j,t,m}$ is the total data of bank m in industry j at time t

Meanings of BII

BII should be interpreted as follows: If one bank's overseas business is its entire business, that is, all of its business activities are carried out aboard and only aim at international market for its business development, then its BII index should be 100. Otherwise, if its business does not involve foreign markets entirely, i.e. all the business is conducted in its home country, its BII should be 0. Hence, the higher the BII is, the higher degree of a bank's internationalization is, indicating that the bank participates in the international market more actively.

It is natural that when a bank possesses the need of going global, its international development will require its business operation to inevitably migrate from domestic market to the international market. Generally speaking, as most banks will not completely give up their domestic market and only rely on the international market, there will be no banks whose BII is as high as 100. Meanwhile, since Chinese financial market has been opened only for a short period of time, the degree of internationalization of Chinese banks is still low, as demonstrated in their BII result, however which indicates huge development opportunities in future.

Data Processing for BII

The subjects of this report mainly focused on large Chinese commercial banks and joint-stock commercial banks as well as a few G-SIBs banks. The purpose of selecting large Chinese commercial banks and joint-stock commercial banks is to reveal their internationalization roadmap and their current status, in order to provide a good reference for their future development in globalization. Meanwhile, we select a few G-SIBs to understand the frontier of internationalization better and provide some experience to the international expansion for Chinese banks.

Data in this report was obtained from official annual reports published by relevant banks. For the Chinese banks listed in both A Share and H Share markets, their annual reports for Shanghai Stock Exchange have been used as main data source. Data on foreign banks is accumulated from documents published on the SEC website (10-k and 20-F) and official websites of the banks.

Overseas data for majority of large commercial banks is mostly available from 2007, however, the availability of data of joint-equity commercial banks is much lower. Due to the fact that foreign banks have a long history of business operation, the time length of their available data is much longer. Meanwhile, with adjustments made to their annual reports due to designed BII measurement rules, the availability of their overseas data may be worsened. For example, some banks' annual reports include overseas data in report for other regions and it is not likely to separate the data precisely. In such case of missing data, we use two methods for data processing. First, for the indicators whose data missing period is only 1 or 2 years and demonstrates a stable growth pattern, we estimated the missing data based on proper growth rate, as well as taking the growth rate and various factors into consideration. Although the difference exists, the discrepancy should be relatively small and will not bring a substantial impact on the result of BII. In addition, with the further development of Chinese banks' internationalization, the source and quality of overseas data will be improved, and therefore we decided that these indicators should be retained. Second, for the indicators whose data missing period is too longer to be estimated rationally, we will not include it to BII index system.

It is noteworthy that our BII system is open and dynamic. With the accelerating pace in Chinese banks' going global and the approaches becoming more diversified, the index system of Chinese banks' BII will be continuously improved. On one hand, the transparency will be greatly enhanced as more Chinese banks will disclose overseas data publicly. On the other hand, new indicators will be introduced in BII index system. During our report drafting, we have adjusted and improved BII index system according to the current market situation, which accordingly increased the accuracy and rationality. By doing so, this report would be able to offer more valuable decision references for Chinese banks.

Appendix B
Introduction of 16 Selected Foreign Banks

As introduced in Chap. 3, in order to fully understand the internationalization level of foreign banks, this report has conducted a BII calculation on 16 G-SIBs with relatively completed data, and the basic information of these 16 foreign banks is as follows.

[1] HSBC

As one of the world's largest financial institutions, HSBC provides services to more than 38 million clients through its four global businesses sectors including retail banking and wealth management, commercial banking, global banking and capital markets, and global private banking. The business network of the HSBC Group extends to Europe, Asia, the Middle East, Africa, North America and Latin America, covering 71 countries and regions around the world.

The HSBC Group was originated from Hong Kong and Shanghai Bank a long time ago. In its early stages, HSBC started to establish overseas branches around the world to expand its business scale. Since the 1950s, it began to open or acquire subsidiaries overseas. In 1998, HSBC Holdings used four English letters, HSBC, and the hexagonal mark as the global branding of the HSBC Group.

HSBC Group offers a number of businesses from individual wealth management to corporate service, mainly including retail banking, commercial banking, corporate banking, investment banking and private banking, etc. For its retail banking sector, HSBC provides extensive financial services to billions of individual clients at a global scale, such as current and savings accounts, mortgages, insurance, credit cards, personal loans, pensions and investments, etc. In corporate banking, HSBC offers financial services for small and medium-sized enterprises and intermediary corporate markets. Its clients include sole proprietorship and partnership, corporate enterprise, listed companies, associations and other organizations. In addition, the HSBC Group also provides customized financial services for corporate and financial institutions, with business scope including global capital markets, global investment banking, corporate banking and financial institutions and global transaction banks. HSBC also has established business operations in private banking, HSBC Private Banking Services serve affluent individuals and their families, and there has been substantial growth in its client assets and loan transactions in recent years.

HSBC Group's HSBC Holdings Ltd. has been listed in stock exchanges in London, Hong Kong, New York, Paris and Bermuda. It has approximately 203,000 shareholders, covering 132 countries and regions worldwide. It is regarded as one of the largest financial institutions in the world.

[2] JPMorgan Chase

JPMorgan Chase is one of the oldest financial institutions in the United States with more than 200 years of history. By the end of 2015, its assets reached $2.35 trillion. The JPMorgan Chase Group has approximately 240 thousand employees worldwide. Its business network covers 60 countries in the world, providing financial services to large companies, governments and institutions from more than 100 countries and regions. Its business includes investment banking, treasury services, small business and commercial banking, financial transaction processing, asset management, private equity and other fields.

The present JPMorgan Chase was formed by the merger between Chase Manhattan Corporation and J.P. Morgan in 2000. In 2004 and 2008, it acquired the First National Bank of Chicago, the Washington Mutual Bank and the famous American investment bank, Bell Sten. Its merger with the First National Bank of Chicago was a significant milestone in its business development. The overall assets of the new Morgan Chase Bank following the merger reached $1.12 trillion, surpassing the Bank of America Corp and just one step away from Citibank who had $1.19 trillion in assets. Its business expanded from New York to the whole Midwest in the US, becoming the second real cross regional bank after Citigroup. Since then, JPMorgan Chase fastened its business expansion globally, making strategic investments in China, India, Russia, South Africa, Latin America, Australia and other regions. It also established a large number of subsidiaries and branches in Europe and Asia.

Currently, JP Morgan's business is focused on two major areas: providing global wholesale banking to individuals, organizations and enterprises, as well as providing retail banking for about 30 million clients. Its financial services mainly cover stock issuance, mergers and acquisitions advisory, bonds, private banking, asset management, risk management, private equity, capital management, etc. In recent years, JPMorgan Chase has continued to explore new areas of investment, making long-term investment in fields such as real estate, finance, health care, oil and gas development, infrastructure construction and other industries. Among them, the real estate and banking sector have the largest investments. Moreover, JP Morgan has been increasing its capital investment in emerging markets year by year.

[3] BNP Paribas

BNP Paribas (shortened as BNP), headquartered in Paris, France, is the largest bank in France. The group's business extends to more than 75 countries, holding a substantial position in corporate and investment banking, asset management and services, and retail banking.

BNP adheres to the principle of constantly improving its profitability and creating value for shareholders, so as to keep the bank growing and become a leading European bank. In "the 2016 Top 500 Banking Brands" released by *The Banker* magazine, BNP is ranked 12th with its brand value as $15.5 billion. Meanwhile, according to the "Fortune Global 500", BNP Paribas was ranked as 39th.

BNP Paribas was officially established through the merger between two major commercial banks in France, the National Bank of Paris and the Bank of Paris, in May 2000. The bank has developed very extensive international network, including 7 important financial centers and 2 subsidiaries in Hong Kong as the BNP Paribas Peregrine and BNP Paribas Private Bank.

BNP focuses on six core business areas, which are retail banking in France, retail banking worldwide, special financing services, corporate and investment banking, private banking, asset management, securities services, insurance and real estate, and the capital market business in Paris. Through its business hub in Hong Kong while connecting Northeast Asia, BNP is essentially engaged in two businesses as corporate and investment banking, and asset management.

[4] Citigroup

Citigroup is the leading financial institution in the world. It has approximately 3000 branches in over 160 countries with its headquarters located in New York, USA. According to the rankings published by *The Banker* magazine, Citigroup ranked 6th worldwide.

The history of Citigroup can be traced back to the City Bank of New York which was founded in the USA in 1812 and became the pioneer of trade finance. Other major predecessors of Citigroup included the securities brokerage company founded by Charles D. Barney in 1873 in Philadelphia, and the securities company founded by Edward B. Smith in 1892 in Philadelphia. In 1955, New York Citibank and New York First National Bank merged and changed to the First National City Bank of New York. In 1962, the name was officially changed to First Citibank and in March 1st, 1976, its name changed to Citigroup.

Nowadays, Citigroup's subsidiaries include Citibank, CitiTravel, etc., providing a comprehensive range of financial products and services for individuals, companies, government and institutional clients, which include retail banking and loans, corporate banking and investment banking, securities brokerage, transaction services, and wealth management, etc.

Citigroup has a long history of globalization. As early as 1897, Citibank set up a Foreign Business Department and began foreign currency trading business. It was the first bank in the US setting up such overseas business unit. And in the early 20th century, Citigroup extended its business to Asia, Europe and other regions. Its history in China can be traced back to May 1902, as the first American bank in China.

[5] Deutsche Bank

Deutsche Bank is one of largest banks in Germany and one of the world's leading financial institutions. It is based in Frankfurt besides the Rhine River. It is a privately owned company whose shares are traded on all German exchanges. According to the ranking of banks worldwide published by *The Banker* magazine in 2016, Deutsche Bank ranked 18th. At the same time, It ranked 166th in the "Fortune Global 500" issued by *Fortune* magazine in 2016.

Deutsche Bank was founded in 1870 in Berlin, Germany and later set up branches in Hamburg and Bremen. In 1872, its Shanghai and Yokohama branches were opened and the London branch was set up in 1873. In 1876, Deutsche Bank acquired the Deutsche Union-Bank and the Berliner Bankverein, becoming the largest bank in Germany. During its early establishment, Deutsche Bank actively participated by providing financing for large projects around the world and played an important role in the industrialization of Germany and overseas companies.

Deutsche Bank is a universal bank that engages in investment banking and commercial banks at a global platform. Its clients include individuals, companies, governments and public institutions. Deutsche Bank offers a wide range of modern financial services along with its domestic and overseas subsidiaries, including deposits, loans, corporate finance, syndication loans, securities trading, foreign exchange and financial derivatives, etc. Deutsche Bank also offers settlement business, the issuance of securities, handling letters of credit, guarantees, tender and performance guarantees and arrangements for financing. Trade finance has become its core business, in which Deutsche Bank provides medium-term or long-term credit services independently or by cooperating with other banking groups and specialized financial institutions. In recent years, project financing, cross-border leasing and other financial instruments have effectively supplement to its traditional trade financing services. Its securities issuance business is also flourishing and Deutsche Bank has become one of the world's main securities issuing banks, participating in many important bonds and stock offerings in Germany and the global market.

As a large international bank, Deutsche Bank maintains extensive global branches and subsidiaries network, with branches operating in Luxemburg, Madrid, Tokyo, Paris, Brussels, New York, Hong Kong of China, etc.

[6] Credit Suisse

Credit Suisse Group, also known as the Swiss Credit Bank, is a financial institution and headquartered in Zurich, Switzerland. Credit Suisse is one of the world's largest financial groups. By the end of 2015, its total assets reached 820.8 billion francs and ranked 292nd in the "Fortune Global 500" published in 2016.

In 1856, Swiss Credit Suisse Institution was founded by Alfred Escher as the name of Credit Suisse. In 1990 and 1993, it acquired the 4th largest bank in Switzerland, Leu Bank, and the fifth largest bank in Switzerland, the People's Bank of Switzerland, respectively. Since then, Credit Suisse has gradually developed from a domestic bank mainly financing for infrastructure and industrial development in Switzerland to an international financial institution operating in more than 50 countries around the world.

Credit Suisse operates wholesale and retail banking in its native land, and its international service is specialized in wholesale banking. In its wide range of services offering, Credit Suisse actively attracts clients aiming at promoting business growth by leveraging its advanced technology, strong capital and the character which is neutral country.

Credit Suisse has a long history in China. As early as 1955, Credit Suisse established account relationship with the Bank of China. Also, an agency relationship was formed in 1957. In 1985, Credit Suisse set up a representative office in Beijing, becoming the first Swiss bank stepping into China market. Winterthur Swiss Insurance of Credit Group successfully acquired shares of the Chinese Taikang Life Insurance Company in 2000, becoming one of the earliest foreign financial institutions involving in the life insurance business in China.

[7] Mitsubishi UFJ FG

Mitsubishi UFJ FG (MUFG) is currently the largest financial institution in Japan. By the end of 2015, the group's assets were worth approximately 280 trillion Japanese yen. It owns the most extensive and balanced branch network in Japan. Its affiliated enterprises include MITSUBISHIL-Tokyo UFJ Bank, Taisho Bank, MITSUBISHI UFJ Trust & Banking, etc. MUFG ranked 10th among worldwide banks according to *The Banker* magazine in 2016.

Mitsubishi UFJ FG was formed through a merger between Mitsubishi Tokyo Financial Group (MTFG) and UFJ Holdings (UFJ) in 2015. In view of the merger with UFJ Holdings, Mitsubishi Tokyo Financial Group competed fiercely and finally defeated another big bank in Japan, Sumitomo Mitsui Bank. On October 1, 2005, Mitsubishi Tokyo Financial Holding signed a merger agreement with UFJ Group and announced the formation of the Mitsubishi UFJ Financial Group, shorted for MUFG.

In terms of development of overseas business, MTFG had 86 branches all over the world while UFJ had 26 branches which indicates a relatively higher degree of globalization. Among which, both MTFG and UFJ Holding have opened branches in Beijing, Shanghai, Shenzhen, Dalian and Tianjin, and most branches have obtained RMB business license. These two banks have focused on wholesale banking in China and clients are mainly Japanese companies. Their business scope covers deposits and loans, RMB and foreign exchange, import and export trade and financial derivative products, credit investigation and consulting service, etc.

[8] Bank of New York Mellon

The Bank of New York Mellon (BNY Mellon) is one of the world's largest asset management corporations, in which its managed assets and clients are at the foremost position worldwide. In 2016, it ranked 179th in the "Fortune US 500" with its operating revenue amounting to $15.5 billion.

BNY Mellon was founded by Mellon Financial Corporation and the Bank of New York Company. Inc. in 2007. The Bank of New York was founded in 1784 by Alexander Hamilton and was the oldest bank in the United States. The businesses of the Bank of New York included securities services, global settlement, asset management and private banking, corporate banking, retail banking and financial market services. BNY Mellon has over 100 branches in 40 countries and over 23,000 overseas employees.

BNY Mellon mainly engages in asset management and securities services, facilitating its clients management and circulating their financial assets. Through various asset management and securities services solutions, it helps compliance build up assets, enhance performance, improve operational efficiency, and reduce risks. BNY Mellon also provides matured financial solutions for individual clients, including investment and wealth management, private banking and shareholder services.

The service focus of its major entities, Mellon Financial Corporation and the Bank of New York, are different. The Bank of New York provides a full range of services to help institutions and individuals to transfer and manage their financial assets in more than 100 global markets. Its core businesses include securities services, treasury management, investment management and banking services for individuals and regional banks. Its global client base contains a number of leading financial institutions, companies, governments, charitable foundations, and foundations. Meanwhile, Mellon Financial Corporation provides wealth management and global investment management services for individuals and financial institutions, global investment services for enterprises and agencies, as well as all variety of banking services for individuals as well as small and medium-sized enterprises through its subsidiaries.

[9] Groupe Credit Agricole

Groupe Credit Agricole is a semi-official bank of France and was founded in 1920 with its headquarters in Paris. It has a three-tier organizational structure which is unified in financial, commercial and legal operations and decentralized in decision making. In *The Banker* magazine's 2016 World Bank Ranking, Groupe Credit Agricole ranked 13th. Also, it ranked 77th in the "Fortune Global 500" in 2016, with its annual turnover of $84 billion.

Groupe Credit Agricole was formerly known as the agricultural credit local treasury, which was formed in 1885 and provided mutual aid to French farmers to solve their short-term capital shortage issues. In 1920, the French government established the National Agricultural Credit Administration which was then renamed as National Agricultural Credit Bank in 1926. On December 16, 2002, Groupe Credit Agricole acquired 82.2% share of the sixth largest bank in France, Credit Lyonnais with a price of 16 billion euros. After this acquisition, Groupe Credit Agricole held a 17.8% stake in Credit Lyonnais. On January 27, 2009, Credit Agricole and Societe Generale merged their asset management departments.

National Agricultural Credit Bank is the central banking institution of Groupe Credit Agricole. It is the core in the group management and supervision, having branches in 40 countries. The French Agricultural Credit Bank participates in the formulation of national agricultural credit policies and its main businesses include long-term and short-term production loans to individual farmers, loans to local public utilities, loans to agricultural cooperatives and family housing loans, etc. In addition, the bank provides special loans, in order to encourage young farmers and overseas immigrants to establish farms, and the development of farming industry is to achieve modernization of agriculture as well as disaster relief. In addition, the bank also provides basic commercial banking and a wide range of financial services and insurance products through its subsidiaries.

[10] **ING Group**

ING Group is one of largest integrated financial services groups in the world, with branches extended in over 40 countries and regions. According to *Fortune* magazine, ING Group ranked 117th in the "Fortune Global 500" and 89th based on its net profit. In terms of providing comprehensive financial services in banking and insurance, it ranked the third position.

The predecessors of ING Group include De Nederlanden van, De Nationale Levensverzekering Bank (National Life Insurance Bank), Nederlandsche Middenstands Bank (NMB). The insurance company De Nationale Levensverzekering Bank and De Nederlanden van (the fire insurance company) 1845 merged to form the combined insurance company the Nationale-Nederlanden in 1963. Furthermore, a merger in 1989 with the NMB Bank led to the creation of NMB Postbank Groep. In 1991, the banking business of NMB Postbank Groep and the insurance business of Nationale-Nederlanden were merged to form ING Group.

Under the Board of Directors, the ING Group has set up 4 management and operation divisions: Group Headquarters, Global Financial Services, Corporate and Capital Market, and Asset Management. The Group Headquarters are in charge of all insurance and banking operations in domestic market. All insurance, retail and corporate banking operation in overseas are being taken care of by the Global Financial Service Division. Among which, its insurance business is divided into three major regions: Europe and Latin America, North America, and Australasia. Its banking business is under unified management by the headquarters. Corporate and Capital Market Division cover all international currency exchange and capital management, including the international banking network, financial products, trade, sales, investment banking, corporate banking, and risk management. The Asset Management Division handles the assets and accounts management of corporate investors, as well as global banking services to individual clients, and asset management service for its own insurance fund. This division also manages investment funds, real estate and trust businesses on behalf of all subsidiaries of the ING Group.

The internationalization process of ING Group started early since the 20th Century. In 1995, ING Group announced a merger with Barings Bank. In 2000, ING Group announced its merger with Aetna aiming at improving its financial service system in the Americas and Asia. In 2005, ING Group acquired shares of the Bank of Beijing and by of the end of 2015, its shareholding ratio had reached 13.64%. ING Group acquired Oyak Bank of Turkey, the ninth largest commercial bank in Turkey, in 2007.

[11] Mizuho Financial Group

Mizuho Financial Group (MHFG) is the second largest financial institution in Japan after Mitsubishi UFJ Financial Group. It was established in 2003 and headquartered in Tokyo. Its subsidiaries include Mizuho Bank, Mizuho Securities and other financial institutions. It ranked 399th in the "Fortune Global 500" in 2016.

After the burst of Japan's 'bubble economy' in 1990s, the Japanese government introduced a series of financial reform measures in order to relax the financial control and promote the restructuring of financial institutions. The establishment of MHFG was an important milestone of this reform. On September 29th, 2000, it was founded by the merger of Dai-Ichi Kangyo Bank, Fuji Bank, and the Industrial Bank of Japan.

MHFG owns four major financial institutions: Mizuho Bank, Mizuho Corporate Bank, Mizuho Trust & Banking and Mizuho Securities. Mizuho Bank and Mizuho Corporate Bank are the two core banking divisions of MHFG, the former one of which concentrates on retail banking and mainly provides comprehensive, high value-added financial services to clients and business partners. The latter one is mainly engaged in the corporate banking businesses with its goal of becoming a professional bank and making significant influence among domestic and overseas financing markets. Mizuho Trust & Banking used to offer only long-term financial services but now it also operates retail banking and real estate business, such as land trust, sales intermediary, real estate assessment, sale service for residential estate. In addition to the traditional securities business, Mizuho Securities also explores by setting new subsidiaries in domestic investment market, investment fund management, bad asset management and energy services.

MHFG has formed its modern management framework through integration according to its development roadmap. Characteristics of such framework include: (1) business lines are managed via business unit; (2) building a management system by executives; (3) establishing an external director system; (4) profit management, profit consolidation, and risk capital allocation are proceeded at the business unit level.

[12] Nordea Bank

The Nordea Bank AB (Nordea) is a financial services group in Northern Europe with headquarters located in Stockholm, the capital of Sweden. By the end of 2015, its total assets amounted to approximately €647 billion. Nordea has set up a large number of branches, subsidiaries and representative offices in 16 countries. It also has global commercial banking branches in Frankfurt, Germany, London, Singapore and New York. Its global banking division has headquarter as well as branches in Brussels, Cannes, Luxemburg, and Zurich.

The bank is the result of the successive mergers and acquisitions of the Finnish, Danish, Norwegian and Swedish banks of Merita Bank, Unibank, Christiania Bankog Kreditkasse and Nordbanken that took place in the 1990s. Its shareholding percentage in these Nordia banks is 40% in Merita, 25% in Unibank, 20% in Nordbanken and 15% in Christiana. In addition, Nordea also opened its branch in

Latvia in 2006. The main market of Nordea is Northern Europe and the Baltic region. Its largest controlling shareholder is the Finnish insurance company, Sampo, who holds approximately 20% in shares. Nordea is respectively listed in the stock exchanges in Stockholm, Helsinki and the Copenhagen.

Nordea mainly operates in 3 business areas: retail banking, corporate banking, asset management and life insurance. It has a large number of individual clients and commercial banking users all over the world. It has gained its leading position in its internet banking with its number of online users and the amount of money circulation per year being in the forefront of the world. According to the 2016 "Fortune Global 500", it ranked 132nd with annual sales of $20.8 billion.

[13] Banco Santander

Santander Group, also known as Banco Santander, was founded in middle of Spain in 1857 headquartering in Santander, Spain. It ranked 14th in 2016 according to *The Banker* magazine and 75th in 2016 "Fortune Global 500" with its annual turnover of $84.9 billion.

Santander mainly focuses on retail banking. The group has an extensive bank network in Europe and Latin America. Its business operation in Europe is extended to Norway, Portugal, Spain and the United Kingdom, while it also operates in Latin American including Argentina, Brazil, Chile, Mexico, Puerto Rico, Uruguay and Venezuela. In its homeland, Spain, Banco Santander and Banco Bilbao Vizcaya Argentaria are committed to serve affluent individual and corporate clients, which holds approximately 40% of market shares in Spain.

Santander has achieved high degree of internationalization and it is one of the few financial institutions started with global business strategies from an early stage. In 2004, Santander announced the acquisition of Abbey National Plc, which was the 6th largest bank in UK and the acquisition price reached £8.9 billion. In 2007, Santander announced that in conjunction with the Royal Bank of Scotland and Fortis, it would make an offer for ABN Amro with the price of $101 billion. As part of the deal, Santander acquired ABN Amro's subsidiary in Italy and Brazil. In 2008, the group announced to acquire 75.65% of Sovereign Bancorp, which was the biggest savings bank in the US. The acquisition of Sovereign gave Santander its first retail business in the mainland United States, including the 750 branches.

[14] Standard Chartered

Standard Chartered is headquartered in London, UK and its business is focused on the emerging markets such as Asia, the Indian subcontinent, Africa, Middle East and Latin America. In comparison, its client base in the UK is much smaller. Standard Chartered possesses a leading position in the banking industry in developing countries, after operating in most dynamic markets for more than 150 years. It has more than 84,000 employees and branches in more than 60 countries, providing financial services to individual and corporate clients in Asia, Africa and the Middle East. Standard Chartered aims at facilitating these clients in investment, trade, wealth management and enhancement. These overseas markets also bring in more than 90% of the group's operating revenues and profits.

Standard Chartered Bank is formed by the merger of two British overseas banks, the Standard Bank of British South Africa and the Chartered Bank of India, Australia and China. Moreover, Standard Chartered is one of pioneer banks to expand overseas. In the early 20th Century, Standard Chartered Bank became the first foreign bank allowed to conduct business in New York. Standard Chartered Bank opened first branch in Port Elizabeth, South Africa in 1863 and quickly grew to 600 branches throughout Africa in mid-20th century. After its listing in stock market, its branch network spread in Europe, Argentina, Canada, Panama, Nepal and the United states. Standard Chartered acquired 3 American banks in 1986 including the Union Bank of California, which facilitated Standard Chartered to gain access to Brazil and Venezuela. Standard Chartered successively opened more branches in these two countries and continuously enhanced its global influence.

Standard Chartered is currently listed on the London Stock Exchange (code STAN) and the Hong Kong Stock Exchange (code 2888). Its main businesses include retail banking services (such as mortgage, investment services, credit cards and individual loans, etc.), and commercial banking services (cash management, trade finance, fund management and trust services). Compared to other banks, it has more prominent client target, SME clients. The bank established 5Cs principles for the approval of loan financing for small and medium enterprises together with scoring system. Based on its experiences in SME client business in various countries, Standard Chartered is able to conduct quantitative analysis based on the data provided by the enterprises and observe the cash flow and financial statements of the clients, so as to make a more objective conclusion.

[15] UBS Group

United Bank of Switzerland (UBS) is co-headquartered in Zurich and Basel, with its branches distributed in more than 50 countries and regions and more than 60,000 staffs. UBS is the largest commercial bank in Switzerland as well as the 2nd largest bank of wealth management in the world. UBS ranked 20th in the 2016 *Forbe*'s Top World banks and 257th in "Fortune Global 500" list with its annual turnover amounted to $38.5 billion.

UBS emerged in 1912 when the Bank in Winterthur fused with the Toggenburger Bank. In 1919, UBS acquired Aargauische Kreditanstalt. In the spring of 1928, it acquired the Suiters Bank which was founded in 1893. In 1938, it merged with Berne Commercial Bank which was founded in 1863. Its affiliated bank, the Berg Savings Bank, acquired St. Gallen Mortgage Bank in 1938. In 1945, it merged with the Union Bank again. In 1998, UBS was integrated by UBS and the Swiss Bank Corporation is formed.

UBS is a universal bank providing wide range of banking services for domestic and foreign clients, including working capital loans, construction loans, specialized financing, securities lending and guarantees, investment advisory and trust, issuance and distribution of shares, etc. These businesses can be divided into 3 divisions as wealth management, investment banking and securities and asset management. In terms of wealth management division, UBS has more than 140 years of experience and a global operation network, which enables it to provide tailor-made services for high-end clients. In addition, this businesses covers asset management, heritage planning, corporate finance advisory and art investment. In terms of investment banking and securities, UBS demonstrates outstanding performance in stocks, stock-linked and stock derivatives business in primary and secondary market. Its asset management offers a variety of traditional and alternative investment management solutions for financial intermediaries and institutional investors around the world.

[16] UniCredit Group

UniCredit Group is headquartered in Milan and is one of the largest banking groups in Europe with 869 billion euros in assets across 17 countries. It aimed at Italy, Austria and Southern Germany as its main markets as well as a large number of business operations in Central and Eastern Europe. UniCredit ranked 300th in the 2016 "Fortune Global 500" with an annual turnover of $34.6 billion.

UniCredit Group was the outcome of the 1998 merger of several Italian banks, among which the majority ones were UniCredito and Credito Italiano. In 1999, UniCredito Italiano, as it was then known, began its expansion in Eastern Europe with the acquisition of Polish company Bank Pekao. By April 2000, UniCredit completed the mergers and acquisitions of Croatian Bank and Plitska Bank. In May of the same year, it acquired Slovakian bank Pol'nobanka, and acquired Bulbank in July.

UniCredit owns over 10 direct investments, joint ventures and share-holding companies overseas, mainly distributed in Spain, Slovakia, Romania and Bulgaria. Its business is concentrated in the richest regions in Europe, such as Italy, Austria and Southern Germany. The businesses of UniCredit Group include individual investment, commercial banking, global banking, telecommunication service, credit card services, deposit and loan business, etc. In addition, they also established the clean energy development companies in South America, North America and other regions.

Printed by Printforce, the Netherlands